UTAH STATE PARKS

A Complete Recreation Guide

UTAH
STATE PARKS

A Complete Recreation Guide

JAN BANNAN

THE
MOUNTAINEERS

Published by The Mountaineers
1011 SW Klickitat Way
Seattle, Washington 98134
U.S.A.

9 8 7 6 5
5 4 3 2 1

Published simultaneously in Canada by Douglas & McIntyre, Ltd., 1615 Venables Street, Vancouver, B.C. V5L 2H1

Published simultaneously in Great Britain by Cordee, 3a DeMontfort Street, Leicester, England, LE1 7HD

Manufactured in the United States of America

Edited by Heath Lynn Silberfeld
Maps by Jerry Painter
All photographs by Jan Bannan
Cover design by Watson Graphics
Layout by Virginia Hand
Book design and typesetting by The Mountaineers Books

Cover photographs, clockwise from upper left: "Little Bryce" pinnacles at Fremont Indian State Park; a meander of the San Juan River at Goosenecks State Park; petrified wood pieces at Escalante State Park; boating at Huntington State Park

Frontispiece: Moon and sand pipe at Kodachrome Basin State Park

Library of Congress Cataloging-in-Publication Data
Bannan, Jan Gumprecht.
     Utah state parks : a complete recreational guide / Jan Bannan.
          p.   cm.
     ISBN 0-89886-421-6
     1. Parks--Utah--Guidebooks. 2. Utah--Guidebooks. 3. Recreation--Utah--Guidebooks. I. Title.
     F824.3B36   1995
     333.78'3'309792--dc20   94-43709
                                                              CIP

Printed on recycled paper

CONTENTS

COLOR COUNTRY   169

APPENDIX   202

INDEX   205

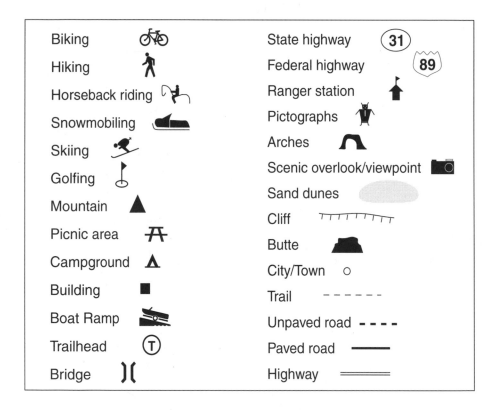

Biking		State highway	31
Hiking		Federal highway	89
Horseback riding		Ranger station	
Snowmobiling		Pictographs	
Skiing		Arches	
Golfing		Scenic overlook/viewpoint	
Mountain		Sand dunes	
Picnic area		Cliff	
Campground		Butte	
Building		City/Town	o
Boat Ramp		Trail	– – – – –
Trailhead	T	Unpaved road	- - - -
Bridge	)(	Paved road	———
		Highway	═══

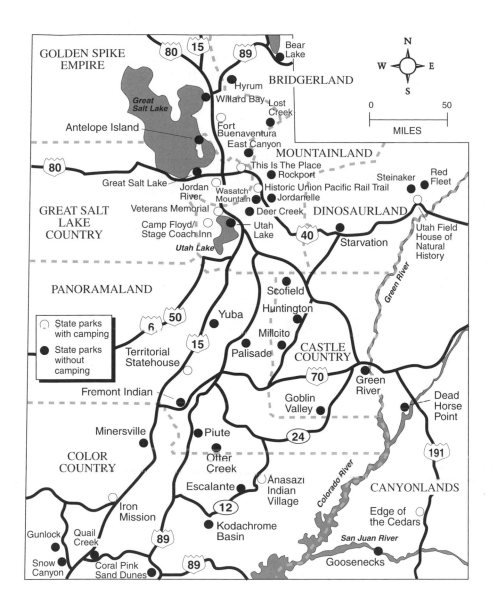

GOLDEN SPIKE
EMPIRE

Great
Salt Lake

Antelope Island

Great Salt Lake

GREAT SALT
LAKE
COUNTRY

PANORAMALAND

State parks
with camping

State parks
without
camping

Territorial
Statehouse

Fremont Indian

Minersville

COLOR
COUNTRY

Iron
Mission

Gunlock

Quail
Creek

Snow
Canyon

Coral Pink
Sand Dunes

BRIDGERLAND

Bear
Lake

Hyrum

Willard Bay

Lost
Creek

Fort
Buenaventura

East Canyon

MOUNTAINLAND

This Is The Place

Rockport

Jordan
River

Wasatch
Mountain

Historic Union Pacific Rail Trail

Jordanelle

Steinaker

Red
Fleet

Veterans Memorial

Deer Creek

DINOSAURLAND

Camp Floyd/
Stage Coach Inn

Utah
Lake

Utah Lake

Starvation

Green River

Utah Field
House of
Natural
History

Scofield

Huntington

Yuba

Millcito

Palisade

CASTLE
COUNTRY

Goblin
Valley

Green
River

Dead
Horse
Point

Piute

Otter
Creek

Escalante

Anasazi
Indian
Village

Colorado River

CANYONLANDS

Kodachrome
Basin

Edge of
the Cedars

San Juan River

Goosenecks

N

W   E

S

0   50

MILES

7

ACKNOWLEDGMENTS

In writing this book I have been helped by many individuals who are on the staff of the Utah Division of Parks and Recreation. Mary Tullius, Public Affairs, has been extremely helpful in responding to my needs to fill in gaps in information. The park managers of two new parks—Jordanelle State Park and Historic Union Pacific Rail Trail State Park—Steve Carpenter and Larry Stump, went out of their way to supply me with loads of material and maps. Tim Smith, now at Antelope Island, gave me a grand tour of Coral Pink Sand Dunes and its special life forms. Russ Martin, at Fort Buenaventura, took time to walk me through history. Brian House, at Willard Bay, answered my questions. Laurence Twitchell, at Minersville, pulled together various pieces of information for me. Curtiss Sinclear, at Steinaker, set me on the right path to find Moonshine Arch. Gordon Topham, Joe Heard, Gary Parker, Ben White, Roland Bringhurst, and Tom Shakespeare were all helpful. I thank all the kind people who read my manuscript for accuracy about the parks, as well as anyone else I have missed unintentionally.

Thanks go to the staff at The Mountaineers Books: Margaret Foster for her good advice; Christine Clifton-Thornton for putting so much together; and Graphics Project Coordinator Alice Merrill for seeing that maps and photos are on target.

I thank DeLorme Mapping Company for their helpful gift of the *Utah Atlas & Gazetteer*, with its topo maps of the entire state. And this Oregonian would have had difficulty in the dazzling summer sun of Utah without the special hat provided by Columbia Sportswear Company.

INTRODUCTION

For many years I've traveled to Utah to admire and hike in its colorful landscapes. To go from the greens and blues of my home in Oregon to the dazzling pastel colors of canyon country seemed to put me back in balance, to stir me from sameness. Utah's summers soaked into my body to warm me in a way that was impossible on the coast of Oregon. The Utah sun is so bright, shining through the dry air, that my eyes had to adjust to the intensity that cannot happen in the moist climate and low elevation of coastal Oregon.

So when I got a chance to return to do a book on Utah state parks, I naturally jumped at the opportunity to spend more time exploring Utah, to see more of its terrain. When I returned to Oregon, which does still please and balance that other side of me, my knowledge of Utah kept me writing through the rains of winter. The more I learn about Utah, the more I want to know. I will return again to Utah and its parks.

Some things I must learn from reports. I haven't tried its "greatest snow on Earth," but I've seen the mountains and the resorts so I'm sure it's true. I

Interesting geological formations along Logan Canyon Scenic Byway (near Bear Lake State Park)

got a hint at what could happen while traveling the La Sal Mountain Loop Road, near Moab, in August when a rainstorm and cold air swirled about the peaks while sun illuminated the red rock landscape adjacent to Canyonlands. I could imagine Utah's mountains in winter.

Utah state parkland covers roughly 100,000 acres. Though late in initial development, compared to some other Western states, Utah state parks are now improving and expanding rapidly and their future looks very good.

Let me toss you a few of the parks' highlights. Then try to resist a visit.

- a dinosaur garden
- coral pink sand dunes
- a landscape of sandstone goblins
- a wild island in a salt lake
- an awesome view of river meanders
- a walk through a petrified rock landscape
- Fremont rock art
- a Mormon pioneer village
- Anasazi ruins
- sand pipes in a Kodachrome desert
- an arch in a lava and red rock canyon
- mountain lakes with great fishing
- a rail trail through mountain-framed meadows

GEOLOGY

If one plans to wander about in the dramatic natural terrain of Utah, it is helpful to have a feel for the powerful geological forces that have been at work in this state.

Combine a high desert climate with the geological history and one finds that only 3 percent of Utah is agricultural land; the other 97 percent is bare rock or unproductive soil. William L. Stokes calls it the "Bedrock State." That fact has certainly influenced settlement. Tourists have different goals and find that much of that bare rock has been laid down, heaved up, or moved about in pretty impressive ways.

Stokes writes that "Geology is the study of the Earth, and rocks are its basic documents." For some fifty years he was a steady contributor to the mapping and interpretation of Utah geology, where all thirteen of the geological time periods are represented in its rock documents. For comparison, the Grand Canyon exposes only seven periods.

The fact that there is so much rock and so little rain has made Utah's rivers great carvers of the landscapes. What rain there is quickly runs into streams, amplifying the power of the rivers, causing flash floods, leaving a thirsty land, and causing mighty erosive action.

To visualize the shape of the state, it is best divided into four major physiographic regions, though these stretch past the boundaries of the state.

The Colorado Plateau. A large portion of southeastern Utah is covered by the Colorado Plateau. Roughly centered at Four Corners—where Utah,

Colorado, Arizona, and New Mexico meet—it is world famous for its many and diverse scenic attractions. It is a desert landscape of plateaus, mesas, deep canyons, sloping formations, imposing linear cliffs, mountain ranges, and barren badlands.

The Colorado Plateau covers 130,000 square miles. Over 300 million years ago, the area was a huge basin filled with a vast sea. Highlands around it shed sediments into the waters. Salts began to crystallize out of the brine in the hot rays of the Pennsylvanian Period as the ocean shrank, producing the Paradox Formation.

About 150 million years ago, shallow seas again covered the area that would become the Colorado Plateau. More deposition of sediments occurred, some colored by iron and manganese deposits. For millions of years, huge quantities of sand advanced and retreated, creating a vast desert of sand often driven by wind. Visualize a time-lapse camera capturing the waters of ocean and streams washing over these dunes periodically, carrying marine sediments that became sandwiched between sand layers. As the film advances, ever so slowly, the emulsion is exposed as these layers harden into rock.

Over 10 million years ago, the Colorado Plateau was gradually uplifted over millions of years until parts of it, like Boulder and Thousand Lake mountains, were 2 miles above sea level. Sediments long buried were exposed. Pressures on this plateau were so great that the uplifted land broke into huge chunks along fault lines—breaks in the continuity of a body of rock. Joints, or weak areas of fracture, within individual rocks and groups of rocks were created under these pressures. In some places the old salts were forced upward, cracked rocks, and formed domes that were later dissolved out by ground water, causing structures to collapse.

This uplift caused a change in climate with increased precipitation, but with no vegetation the rain made gullies and rivulets that had great erosive power. The marine deposits were the most unstable, and the harder sandstone was more resistant. Rivers grew in volume and strength. The Colorado and its tributaries did some masterful carving, rasping through 300 million years of rocks and tearing into the ancient history of Earth.

Visit the sixteen national parks, national monuments, recreation areas, and state parks of this colorful province and you'll see solidified sand dunes that remain as spectacular formations. Throughout the Colorado Plateau, fins, arches, natural bridges, reefs, and unimaginable shapes are left in the wake of the continued action of wind, temperature, and water (whether as snow, rain, ice, or standing water).

The mountains of the Colorado Plateau—the La Sal, Abajo, and Henry ranges—are volcanoes that didn't erupt. Molten lava pushed upward but did not break the top surface. Time and erosion removed the last remnant of sedimentary rock to expose the igneous cores.

Some of the sections of the Colorado Plateau are the Uinta Basin, Books Cliffs, San Rafael Swell, Monument Valley, Escalante Benches, Green River Desert, and the Grand Staircase.

The Basin and Range Province. A large portion of northwest Utah is

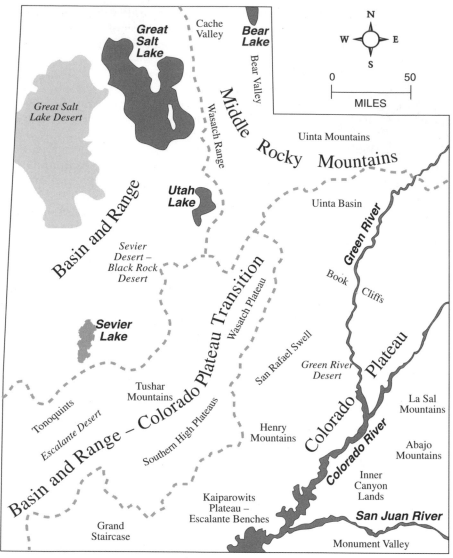

Utah's four major physiographic regions

basin and range country. It consists of thirty-five north–south-trending ranges and an equal number of alluvial valleys that are part of the Great Basin. This basin is defined as an area of internal drainage between the Wasatch Range and the Sierra Nevada. It is somewhat like a concave vessel with a lot of ridges where waters cannot escape to the sea. The Basin and Range Province of Utah extends east to the Wasatch Front, includes the Great Salt Lake and its desert surroundings, and curves around to the south of Sevier Lake and angles west.

It is interesting that while eastern Utah lay under an ocean, western Utah was elevated and being eroded. When the subcrustal material sagged and bent, the Great Basin literally collapsed along hundreds of normal faults, most of which trended in northerly directions. The structural blocks were subsequently modified by erosion into this distinctive basin and range topography.

During the Pleistocene Epoch, which lasted some 1.6 million years and ended 11,000 years ago, huge depressions in the Great Basin were filled with pluvial lakes. These are typified by Lake Bonneville, which covered most of the area of Utah that is the Basin and Range Province of today. Many geologists have been fascinated by the history of this body of water, doing research on evidence left after Bonneville's reign. Terraces were cut along the Wasatch Front by the lake's high waters. At least two especially high water periods occurred at about 14,000 and 17,000 years ago, according to some studies. It was the largest freshwater sea in those times. The Great Salt Lake and Utah Lake are remains of this great lake.

The Middle Rocky Mountain Province. The Wasatch Range and the Uinta Mountains are two very dissimilar ranges that represent the Middle Rocky Mountain Province. The Wasatch Range rises sharply at the eastern edge of the Great Basin and trends north–south, with a maximum elevation at Mount Nebo (11,877 feet). This range—narrow and sharp-crested—is essentially a tilted fault block, and is an unusual assemblage of sedimentary, igneous, and metamorphic rocks.

The Wasatch Range was uplifted along the Wasatch Fault so that crosssections of a number of west-trending structures are exposed. The western edge of the range coincides with the Wasatch Fault and is remarkable in having few foothills.

In the northeastern corner of Utah, the Uintas have an unusual east-to-west orientation. Kings Peak (13,528 feet) is the highest point in the Uinta Mountains. This range is broad and gently arched, a folded anticline. In contrast to the Wasatch Range, the Uinta Mountains do have foothills and a noticeable bench of softer sediments.

This province includes the Bear River Plateau–Bear Lake, Cache Valley, and Bear Valley sections. Much of the fertile soil of the valleys comes downhill from canyon streams.

The Wasatch and Uinta ranges intersect near Park City, making for some extremely complex geology at this "crossroads." This area has yielded millions of dollars' worth of precious metals.

The Basin and Range/Colorado Plateau Transition Province. Because so much disagreement exists about where the boundary should be between the Great Basin and the Colorado Plateau, geologist William Stokes treats this questionable region as a separate province.

This transition area is a broad belt where geologic features of typical plateau and basin and range overlap and merge in a matter of gradations. It covers a band from the southwest corner of Utah to the center of the state. Its drainage is almost entirely into the Great Basin.

Most of the alignments in this province are north–south and parallel to those of the Great Basin. These are evident in the High Plateaus and in the typical Colorado Plateau units with their visual chronology of deposition.

The most distinctive features of the Transition Province are the eight High Plateaus, ranging between 8,000 and 11,000 feet in elevation. These plateaus include the Wasatch Plateau, which is capped entirely by sedimentary rocks with a steep eastern front that is an erosional continuation of the Book Cliffs.

Other High Plateaus include Fish Lake, Awapa, Aquarius, Table Cliffs, Markagunt (Cedar Breaks is on the southwest corner of this plateau), Sevier, and Paunsaugunt (Bryce Canyon is carved from outcrops of lime sediments at the edge of this plateau).

The Tushar Mountains are eroded remnants of ancient volcanoes that still reach an elevation of 12,173 feet at Mount Delano. Mineral deposits of gold, silver, lead, zinc, uranium, aluminum, and potassium were formed during the volcanic episodes. The Sevier River has cut into this eroded volcanic pile and exposed component units.

The Tonoquints (the name of a tribe of Paiute Indians) volcanic section in the southwestern part of the Great Basin contains the Escalante Desert, a mixture of diverse geologic features, the Pine Valley Mountains, and the ore deposits of Iron Mountain.

DINOSAURS AND FOSSILS

If the success of the book and movie *Jurassic Park* and the number of children's books on the subject are any indication, dinosaurs trigger interest in a lot of people. For a look at real bones, fossils, and life-size replicas of dinosaurs, Utah is a great place to tour. Some have called the state "a King Tut's tomb of fossils."

Abundant vertebrate fossils were found in the Uinta Basin as early as 1870. One of the earliest paleontologists of that time was O. C. Marsh, from Yale University, who first identified mammals from the Eocene epoch.

Great finds were made near Split Mountain in 1909 when Earl Douglass came collecting for the Carnegie Museum of Pittsburgh. He wrote in his diary, "At last in the top of the ledge . . . I saw eight of the tail bones of a *Brontosaurus* in exact position. It was a beautiful sight." This was the beginning of the excavation of a wealth of dinosaur bones and fossils from the Morrison Formation that led to the designation of Dinosaur National Monument, in 1915, at Douglass's site.

The Morrison Formation is a strata of rock that was deposited at the height of the time when dinosaurs roamed the Earth. The Dinosaur National Monument site is a place where their bones and fossils were preserved in the sands of an ancient river that was later buried under layers of sediments. Mountain building followed, and then erosion and weathering exposed the dinosaur remains that survived in great numbers in the dry climate.

Dinosaur bones were still to be found after Douglass moved on. Today a bone-bearing layer of his quarry is enclosed as one wall of the visitor center at Dinosaur National Monument. Until recently paleontologists continued

Sign about dinosaur crossing at Red Fleet State Park

to expose fossils in this quarry wall, and many fossils remain there on exhibit. New technology now indicates that the area around the fossils contains important information about the dinosaur environment. Many of the bones are of plant-eating dinosaurs. *Stegosaurus*, with bony plates along the ridge of its spine, is a common dinosaur at the quarry, as are several types of sauropods (the largest of the dinosaurs) and the tiny *Nanosaurus* (the size of a chicken).

Another special fossil site in Utah is the Cleveland-Lloyd Quarry, a Bureau of Land Management (BLM) facility where thousands of bones and many complete skeletons have been removed for research purposes. Located near the town of Cleveland, this quarry is in a remote and rustic area, though the quarry is indoors. There is a visitor center with a mounted *Allosaurus* (a common meat-eating dinosaur found here). A nature trail leads to other bone sites. This area was once a bog where plant-eating dinosaurs were trapped and buried. The *Stokesosaurus*, a sauropod, was discovered here and named for Utah geologist William Lee Stokes.

An exciting new dinosaur discovery was made in eastern Utah in 1992. The reputation of *Tyrannosaurus rex* as the biggest and meanest of the dinosaurs may be replaced by that of this new find that so far is called *Utahraptor*, a 20-foot-long, 1,500-pound killer. "It was literally armed to the teeth," says James Kirkland, a paleontologist with the Dinamation International Society, who first identified the new dinosaur. No one had a chance to see this terrorist in action, but the equipment that nature provided it with must certainly have been used. The end of one toe on each hind foot had a 12-inch-long, sickle-shaped killing claw. One kick could be fatal. And rather than the small forelimbs of the tyrannosaurs, the *Utahraptors* had large, powerful arms with 10-inch claws on their hands. Add to this the probability that they hunted in packs and they become even more formidable opponents.

Utahraptor was a dromaeosaur, in the same family of efficient killing machines that included the velociraptors brought to our attention in *Jurassic Park*. The *Utahraptor* is the oldest yet found (125 million years ago, from the early Cretaceous Period) and largest of this family (they all have speed and killing claws, though smaller ones). Curiously, and ironically, tyrannosaurs arrived 50 million years later than Utahraptors, so there were no encounters. Though the tyrannosaurs were bigger and heavier, they lacked the speed and long claws of the Utahraptors.

This recent Utah species is closely related to specimens found on the Isle of Wight, off the coast of England, which is interesting since the Utahraptors existed at a time when animals could travel, because of connecting lands, from Utah to England and not get their feet wet.

Scientists seem as interested in dinosaurs as children are, considering the research aimed at dinosaurs and the fact that they have been extinct for 65 million years. Recent evidence suggests that dinosaurs were warm-blooded, contrary to original thoughts on the matter.

Miners in the Price area have found many dinosaur footprints in coal deposits. Also, their footprints can be found near Moab and at Red Fleet State Park.

Utah has more than just dinosaur fossils and bones and many areas where amateur paleontologists can look for them. Fossilized trilobites are common in western desert regions of the Great Basin. Petrified wood is found often on the Colorado Plateau and is easily seen at Escalante State Park. For more information on where to look for fossils, see State Paleontologist in the Appendix.

EARLY INDIAN CULTURES

As early as 11,000 B.C., perhaps even earlier, the first colonizers of America—called Paleo-Indians—were hunter/gatherers in the area of present-day Utah at a time when mammoth and giant bison provided meat. Archaeologists have pieced together fragments of their lifestyle from stone-tipped spears found in caves along the vanished shores of Lake Bonneville.

Climate changed and Ice Age mammals became extinct as great deserts formed in the Southwest. To survive, humans adapted to these new surroundings. Sometime shortly before or after A.D. 1, corn and other crops were introduced from Mexico. To tend their crops, they could stay in one place, build more permanent dwellings, make pottery, and weave baskets.

The artifacts from this time are so different from those of other times that new names were applied to these peoples. For the most part, the Anasazi Indians lived on the Colorado Plateau south of the Colorado River, while the Fremont Indians settled in the Great Basin and Uinta Basin, north of the Colorado and east of the Virgin River.

The earliest Anasazi were called Basketmakers and lived in pithouses that were partly underground. Even in those days when travel was very slow, there was frequent contact with other peoples and an exchange of ideas.

The time from A.D. 700 to A.D. 1300 in the Four Corners region is called the Pueblo Period. The beginning of this period saw the replacement of the *atlatl* (a device for throwing a notched hunting spear) with the bow and arrow. Somewhere around A.D. 900, the Anasazi began building multistoried stone structures with underground *kivas*. During the latter part of the Pueblo Period, their impressive cliff dwellings were fitted into sandstone canyons that required agile occupants.

The Fremont culture was first identified from sites found along the Fremont River near Capitol Reef. Their habitation spans the time roughly from A.D. 500 to A.D. 1300. Though less is known about the Fremont Indians, enough artifacts have been found to distinguish them from the Anasazi. They lived more in pithouses, with less impressive structures, and relied more on hunting than farming.

Fremont basketry was distinctive. Members of this group wore leather moccasins instead of the sandals of yucca fibers worn by the Anasazi. Fremont potters used a unique recipe that combined granular rock or sand with wet clay.

The most compelling remains of the Fremont Indians is their rock art. Manlike beings dominate Fremont rock art, and one suspects that some drawings have religious significance. Though figures do appear in Anasazi rock art, game animals like bighorn sheep and birds are more abundant. Fremont rock art and unfired clay figurines have distinctive hair "boles" and necklaces.

MORMON HISTORY

Although some of Utah's state parks focus on Mormon history in the settling of Utah, it might be an advantage to have some prior information, especially since the Mormons are still a powerful group in the state.

The Mormon religion is a young one. It had its beginnings in 1823 with Joseph Smith when the angel Moroni revealed some gold plates for him to translate into *The Book of Mormon*. Smith published this in 1830 and founded the Church of Jesus Christ of Latter-Day Saints (LDS) in New York state.

Prosecution of the zealous Mormon followers, who were missionaries and practiced polygamy, soon followed. Tension and violence between Mormons and other people forced them to move first to Ohio and Missouri, and then they founded the city of Nauvoo, Illinois. In 1844, Joseph Smith declared his candidacy for president of the United States—to spread his religion—but this was cut short when Joseph and his brother Hyrum were arrested for the smashing of an anti-Mormon printing press and murdered while in jail. The president of the ruling body of LDS, Brigham Young, became the new Mormon leader.

In 1847, the Mormons—bringing many recent converts from other coun-

Collection of wagon wheels at Iron Mission State Park

tries—migrated 1,500 miles to Utah. This Is The Place State Park (originally Pioneer Trail State Park, which will acquire this new name along with a new visitor center in time for Utah's 1996 centennial celebration) tells of their arrival. Theirs was a group dream, not an individual one, not one of quick fortune but of helping each other. The Mormons' most common traits were colonizing, proselytizing, and self-sufficiency.

Unlike all other Western settlements, those in the "Mormon Corridor," a great swatch of land from southern Idaho through Utah and into Nevada and southern California, were the result of a planned, centrally controlled colonization. A Mormon village was a "heavenly city" laid out in a mile-square plan—never a Western shack-town. This social, economic, educational, and religious unit had small agricultural plots surrounding a central living area. A centralized system of irrigation ditches, where sidewalks would be today, accessed each house, with a constant murmuring of water. The farmers made the arid desert bloom.

In the Mormon culture, authority is respected and individual independence is not. Heaven is their destination. Laying on of hands, speaking in tongues, testimony meetings, perpetual patriarchs working miracles, polygamy (though this is outlawed now), and the belief that it is virtuous to bring waiting souls into the world are some of their practices. A woman's brood is her highest glory. A Mormon wife shares her husband's glory in heaven since it is his accomplishments that place him in the tiered heaven Mormons envision, so maybe it was better in the past to be the second wife of a great man. Some modern Mormons do not adhere to all of these beliefs.

HISTORY OF THE STATE PARKS

A valiant attempt was made seventy years ago to establish a state park system in Utah. In fact, the state legislature passed a bill to establish a State Board of Park Commissioners. Governor George Henry Dern signed it on May 12, 1925. The governor, the president of the Utah Agricultural College, and two others were to serve on this board for a term of four years, though without compensation.

This state board had the authority to accept gifts of land or money for parks and to buy lands deemed "of sufficient natural, historical, or lofty scenic quality to justify such action, if such an appropriation is available." Unfortunately, the legislature initially voted them no money to buy land. The only provision was that any monies from spare funds of the offices of the governor, the president of the state university, and the president of the agricultural college could be used for acquiring land.

As time passed, various individuals and groups made recommendations to purchase places in Utah that had special scenic, geological, or archaeological interest, such as Flaming Gorge, Capitol Reef, and the ice caves near Fillmore, but there was no follow-up to these suggested acquisitions. The State Board of Park Commissioners and the dream of a state park system were put on the back burner and seemed to be forgotten for several decades.

The dream resurfaced in 1957 to become reality when another legislature authorized the Utah State Parks Commission, appointed by Governor George Dewey Clyde. The instructions were to develop parks and recreation areas and to preserve and protect historical sites and scenic treasures. This enthusiastic group made a report that said, "We stand on the threshold of the greatest opportunity for recreation development that will ever be available to the people of Utah The nation is in the midst of a new era of recreation with $32 billion a year spent on recreation in America."

After considering possible park sites, the commission recommended 152 possibilities in a 1959 report. Some of these, however, were duplications under different categories, and the real number was 136 sites, though only a certain percentage of these were to become state parks.

State governments sometimes reorganize, and as part of a major administrative change in 1967, the Utah State Park Commission was dissolved and the Division of Parks and Recreation was created within the new Department of Natural Resources.

In the beginning, there were four Utah state parks. These were the old Utah State Prison site (now deleted from the system), the Territorial Statehouse, This Is The Place Monument, and Camp Floyd. Initial funds of $20,000 were furnished by a grant from the Rockefeller–Jackson Hole Preservation Foundation.

Individual park status was first shown on signs as state recreation areas, state beaches, and state historical monuments. Although not all signs reflect this legislative change, in 1985 they were officially named state parks, even undeveloped ones.

Today, the state park system encompasses some 100,000 acres of land. With the addition of two state parks in 1994, and one previous park now turned over to the Bureau of Land Management (BLM), there are forty-five developed and six undeveloped state parks in Utah. While money is often tight, parks are upgraded whenever possible.

The Division of Parks and Recreation has situated quite a few of its parks by waterways, which fits with its responsibility for enforcement of boating laws on all waters in Utah, which add up to more than a million surface-acres. This includes some 840 natural and man-made lakes and reservoirs large enough to count and 5,400 miles of streams. One can see why fishing offers considerable recreation in the state and is often possible year-round.

PARK CLASSIFICATIONS

The Utah Division of Parks and Recreation has classified its forty-five state parks under three categories: heritage, scenic, and recreation.

Of the ten **heritage** parks, Anasazi Indian Village and Edge of the Cedars feature artifacts and ruins of the Anasazi Indians, people who fitted their lives and homes into the landscape. Living in a similar time period, but with a few location and lifestyle differences, the Fremont Indian culture is the attraction at the park of the same name.

This Is The Place, Territorial Statehouse, and Iron Mission all deal with early Mormon history, from migration to Utah to the first government and mining operations for iron. The settling of one mountain man is commemorated at Fort Buenaventura. The Veterans Memorial honors Utah's dead. Camp Floyd/Stagecoach Inn was the site of a U.S. encampment, a pioneer settlement, and a stop on the Overland Stage and Pony Express lines.

The Utah Field House of Natural History encompasses a vast collection of artifacts and exhibits from the prehistoric times of dinosaurs through the times of Indian cultures and tales of explorers. Rocks, flora, and fauna of Utah enlighten us about today's environment, but probably the star of this museum is the Dinosaur Garden, where replicas seem almost real in their simulated natural setting.

Seven state parks are listed under the **scenic** classification, because their attractions are so extraordinary, yet they all have considerable recreational potential as well. Dead Horse Point and Goosenecks both have cliff over-looks of river meanders in desert country that are rated as outstanding. Goblin has captivating stone formations that tantalize children to fantasize and play among them.

Antelope Island is the largest piece of land that protrudes above the salty waters of the Great Salt Lake, making it wild country only a causeway drive or boat ride away from urban settings. Wasatch Mountain is a huge tract of forest and golf courses rimmed by peaks.

Kodachrome Basin is a grand example of Color Country at its best, with unique sand pipes and a lot of trails to explore—by horseback or on foot. For wandering in a slickrock landscape laced with lava flows and hidden canyons, the temperate year-round climate of Snow Canyon is an excellent destination.

Sign for Yuba State Park (recreation designation)

That leaves twenty-eight parks designated for **recreation**. Don't think that these are not scenic and varied, however, nor without their historical and geological aspects. For instance, Coral Pink Sand Dunes is a rare swatch of colored sand that is quite photogenic. It is also a place to study plants and dune formations or to ride an off-highway vehicle (OHV).

Two parks feature rivers. Jordan River is in the midst of Salt Lake City with trails bordering the river and launch points for canoes. Green River is in the backcountry and has accesses for river running into wilderness areas.

Three parks are natural lakes, though all in quite different terrains. Bear Lake is an azure lake in Rocky Mountain country adjacent to Idaho. Utah Lake is the end run of the Provo River where it descends to the valley. Great Salt Lake is a vast, unusual lake without an outlet, where one can sail or float upon salty waters, or play at beaches or the playground of Saltair.

Twenty-one of these recreation parks are reservoirs, products of dams built to irrigate the arid lands of Utah. Some reservoirs are quite large affairs not far from urban areas with significant numbers of visitors—Deer Creek, East Canyon, Jordanelle (the newest and most comprehensive in design), Rockport, Willard Bay, Hyrum, Yuba, Millsite, Huntington, and Quail Creek. Others are smaller or farther from population areas—Otter Creek, Scofield, Starvation, Steinaker, Red Fleet, Piute, Lost Creek, Gunlock, and Minersville. One reservoir—Palisade—doesn't allow motorized boats.

Though Escalante also has a reservoir, the petrified wood on its paths is its prime asset. One new park is the Historic Union Pacific Rail Trail State Park, a 30-mile trail for muscle-powered recreation, but no motorized vehicles.

21

Consider that Utah is the second driest of this country's states, yet most of its state parks feature water sports.

AMENITIES

Day-use Areas. Almost all of Utah's state parks have day-use areas with picnic tables, restrooms, and drinking water. A few do not, however, so take note of these. Gunlock and Lost Creek both have no tables or drinking water but do have vault toilets. East Side at Bear Lake, Goosenecks, Piute, and Painted Rocks at Yuba have picnic tables and vault toilets, but no drinking water. The new Historic Union Pacific Rail Trail does not now have picnic tables, vault toilets, or drinking water, though some of these facilities are planned for the future. One can, however, find facilities at access points along the trail.

Most of the parks charge a day-use fee. Only Veterans Memorial and the undeveloped parks of Goosenecks, Gunlock, Lost Creek, and Piute do not charge a fee for day use. Additional fees are charged for special facilities— golfing, boat mooring, ice skating, roller skating, group-use facilities, and reservations.

Some of the special events of individual parks are free, however, a worthy concession by the state, though some do require the regular park fee. For instance, winter lectures at the Utah Field House of Natural History, Hot Air Balloons at Snow Canyon, the Indian Powwow at Fremont Indian, and Free State Park Day (concurrent with Free Fishing Day, usually the second weekend in June) require no fees. For current information, check with the individual parks (see Appendix).

Putting green and fountain at Wasatch Mountain State Park

Campgrounds. Of the forty-five state parks, thirty-five of them allow camping. The facilities vary from primitive to campsites with full hookups, and include more than 1,600 designated sites, which does not include availability at the undeveloped parks where camping is allowed.

Primitive camping is found at East Side at Bear Lake, Goosenecks, Gunlock, Lost Creek, Piute, some areas at Starvation, and Painted Rocks at Yuba. None of these have drinking water available, so bring your own. All have vault toilets. Of these possibilities, only East Side and Starvation have private sites with tables adjacent to them. It is a matter of finding a place to park or pitch a tent at Goosenecks, Gunlock, Lost Creek, Piute, and Painted Rocks at Yuba.

Standard campsites have picnic tables, barbecue grills, flush toilets, culinary water, parking pads, and sewage disposal stations. A good percentage of these parks have showers, though not all of them. Dead Horse Point (water must be hauled to the park), Fremont Indian, Quail Creek, Red Fleet, and Steinaker do not have hot showers. Dead Horse Point, Minersville, and Snow Canyon have electrical hookups. Wasatch Mountain and Bear Lake have full utility hookups.

With the popularity of snow-based activities in Utah, all campgrounds except Deer Creek, Hyrum, Minersville, Scofield, and Steinaker (no facilities offered, but camping allowed in winter) are open year-round.

Camp only in designated sites unless it is a primitive campground. In developed campgrounds, vehicles must remain on paved sites. Though a few parks have firewood for sale (and it is noted in the description when they do), most do not and it is best to bring your own wood.

Most parks have a camping limit of 14 days in any one 30-day period, but Deer Creek and Wasatch Mountain allow only 10 days. Check-out time is usually 2:00 P.M. unless otherwise specified. If you have not reserved a site, it is imperative to check campsites to see if there's a reservation ticket on the site number post. In some parks, it is best to double-check with a ranger or camp host. Those sites not reserved are available on a first-come, first-served basis. Some parks close their gates at 10:00 P.M.

Camp fees cover a range of facilities from primitive to those with complete hookups. Extra vehicles are charged a fee. There is no fee for camping at Goosenecks, Gunlock, Lost Creek, or Piute. Since fees change periodically, obtain a fee schedule at any state park, regional office, or the administrative office in Salt Lake City.

Reservations for individual campsites may be made at all developed parks—by telephone or in person. Individual campsite reservations may be made from 3 to 120 days in advance. Group reservations may be made one year in advance, by telephone or in person. To make a reservation, call (801) 322-3770 or (800) 322-3770, from 8:00 A.M. to 5:00 P.M., Monday through Friday. A nonrefundable reservation fee is charged for each site reserved. Your site will be made available to other campers if you do not arrive by 3:00 P.M. on the day following your scheduled arrival. Cancellations forfeit the first night's camping fees if made less than 7 days before arrival date. A full refund, except for reservation fee, will be made for cancellations made more than 7 days in advance of the arrival date.

PARK GUIDELINES

Utah state parks are special places and will only be enjoyable sites of recreation if we respect their beauty, their amenities, and those who visit them. Make yours, and your neighbor's, a quality experience.

Quiet hours—no vehicles or generators running, or other disturbances—are usually between 10:00 P.M. and 7:00 A.M., though in Coral Pink Sand Dunes morning noise is not allowed before 9:00 A.M. Early risers do not appreciate late-night parties.

Campfires may be built in specified areas. Firewood collecting is not allowed in state parks.

Pets are allowed in most Utah state parks but must be confined or on a maximum 6-foot leash. Only seeing-eye dogs are allowed in park buildings. Pets are not permitted on developed beaches, in streams or lakes, or on golf courses. Please control your pet. Barking dogs can wreck others' enjoyment.

All plants, animals, minerals (don't pick up that tiny piece of petrified wood), and other natural features in state parks are protected. It is unlawful to mutilate or deface any natural feature or structure. Keep Utah's state parks beautiful.

Use of firearms, explosives, slingshots, fireworks, or firecrackers is not allowed in parks without special authorization by the park manager.

Unless otherwise posted, the speed limit on state park roads is 15 miles per hour.

Do not litter. Leave your site in better shape than you found it.

Fuller teasel plants at Willard Bay State Park

SPECIAL EVENTS AT THE PARKS

Utah has an extensive number of special events planned at many of its parks, which adds to the fun. Recreational parks on lakes often schedule fishing clinics. Channel Catfish Clinics, White Bass and Panfish Clinics, and Walleye Workshops are frequently held at Utah Lake State Park. Escalante holds a Wide Hollow Fishing Derby.

Fremont Indian State Park and This Is The Place State Park capitalize on the wealth of history associated with them by scheduling Indian Powwows, Harvest Days, Pioneer Artisan Workshops, Pottery Making Workshops, Pioneer Days, and a pioneer-style celebration that is part of their Christmas Candlelight Tours. Fort Buenaventura State Park and Bear Lake State Park keep alive the Mountain Man Rendezvous gatherings.

The scenic parks often have fun runs, kite flies, and beach days. Antelope Island has an impressive number of events planned each year now that it has reopened. Some of these feature bicycle or horseback races. Others celebrate the bison of the park by noting the annual release of calves and the fall roundup of buffalo.

HAVE A SAFE VISIT

Although experiences in Utah state parks will usually be safe and happy ones, park rangers can be helpful in case of an emergency. Or call 911. Most parks have phones.

Boating and Water Sports. Swimmers should never swim alone or during an electrical storm. Check the water depth before you dive. If swimming from a boat, be sure the boat is anchored and kept nearby by a knowledgeable operator. Nonswimmers should not go into deep water, even with a mattress or inner tube, and small children should be carefully supervised.

Do not drive a boat when under the influence of alcohol or drugs. Stay to the right when meeting another boat head-on and always yield the right-of-way to those boats on the right when crossing paths. Wakeless speed is required within 150 feet of another boat, buoy, dock, launching area, designated slow area, person, swimmer, skier, angler, or fishing equipment.

Coast Guard-approved personal flotation devices (PFD) are required for each person aboard a boat or being towed. Children under twelve must wear these at all times on board, except inside cabin areas of larger boats.

Boats with a sail or motor, except for sailboards, must be currently registered. Let people know where you are going when boating and how long you expect to be gone. If the boat capsizes, stay with the boat for easier rescue.

To pull a water skier, two people must be in the boat, one to drive and the other to observe and communicate with the skier. Signal the presence of a skier in the water with the international orange flag of at least 12 inches square. When assisting the skier back into the boat, stop the boat motor. Water skis, and other towed devices, are allowed only during daylight hours and users must wear the required PFD or ski belt.

In all water sports, remember not to panic if you are involved in an emergency situation. Calm, constructive thinking will give better results. Know your physical limits and don't overexert or overestimate your swimming ability. Be sure you remember to float if you become exhausted while swimming. Swimmer's cramps are frightening, but try to stretch the muscle while you float and remember you can still swim even with that cramp—it just won't be much fun.

For a comprehensive brochure on boating safety, contact the Utah Division of Parks and Recreation.

Hiking. Certain areas in Utah have rattlesnakes and other toxic reptiles, so be alert. Given a chance, though, these animals will try to get away. Cacti can also be hazardous so watch your step. Much of Utah is desert country and heat can be a problem. Know your limits, drink small amounts of water frequently, and rest when necessary.

If you are on a hike of any length or difficulty, it is best to be prepared for the unexpected, whether that is a change in weather, getting lost, or anything else. Take along drinking water, map, walking stick, suntan lotion, sweater, insect repellent, compass, sunglasses and/or sun hat, dry matches, compass, pocket knife, flashlight, a snack (add an extra high-energy bar just in case), and mini-first-aid kit (include bandages, aspirins, and forceps for tick removal).

Either know how to start a fire with wet wood or carry one of the commercial fire starters and cubes. New disposable gear that takes little room includes toe and hand heaters (flat 3-inch squares), ponchos (a flat 3 x 5 inches), and insulating blankets (2 x 4 inches).

One of the pleasures of outdoor recreation is a picnic at the foot of a waterfall or atop a viewpoint on slickrock. Needed items are easily carried, with hands free, in a knapsack on your back. Throw in an extra roll of film.

Bicycling. Wear a protective helmet and be sure your bicycle is in good operating condition. Carry a tire pump and patch kit. Be a defensive rider and follow the rules of the road. Remember that road conditions vary greatly in Utah so be prepared for the unexpected. Yield to hikers and equestrians.

Use sunscreen and carry adequate drinking water. Dress appropriately for the altitude and the weather, and carry emergency clothing in case of a change in temperature or conditions. Respect the land and its residents, including wildlife.

Off-highway Vehicles. Utah law requires that all OHV drivers from the age of eight until they receive a driver's license must complete a "Know Before You Go" training class given by the Utah Division of Parks and Recreation before they

Bicyclists on the first stretch of the Historic Union Pacific Rail Trail

can operate an OHV on public land. Those under eight cannot operate an OHV on public land. To become certified, minors must pass a written test and attend a half-day, hands-on class.

To prevent serious injury and even death, OHV operators should follow some basic safety tips. Before you ride, check the mechanical controls and safety devices on your vehicle for proper operation. While riding, at all times wear a safety-rated, properly fitted helmet, goggles, clothes that cover your arms and legs, and over-the-ankle boots. Do not take alcohol or drugs along for the ride. Ride only in designated areas, and be courteous to other riders. Do not carry passengers on single-passenger vehicles. Parents should always supervise children and inexperienced riders. Do not litter, chase wildlife, or damage vegetation.

A comprehensive brochure on the legalities and rules of OHV operation is available from Utah state parks.

OUTDOOR MANNERS

Rock Art and Ruins. Utah residents are justly proud of the state's profusion of rock art and Indian ruins, even the more recent remains of historic railroad trestles and Butch Cassidy's cabin. They share these treasures with the understanding that you will follow some guidelines. Some of this evidence of the past is threatened unintentionally, but education should help.

Look at rock art, but do not touch, trace, or make paper rubbings of it. The oils of human skin damage these fragile petroglyphs and pictographs. Do not chalk, paint, or mark with any kind of implement on rock art, including on an image that is becoming difficult to see.

Vandals who carve their initials or shoot bullet holes into rock art do more damage in a moment than weather has done in hundreds of years. This defacement is disrespectful to other cultures and a loss to future generations.

Stop and think before visiting a site to plan minimum impact while exploring. Do not walk through a midden—a trash pile left by the original occupants of the site. Stay on trails. Do not climb on roofs and walls. The smoke and high temperatures of fires can damage rock art and archaeological sites, so camp and cook outside of such areas.

A real concern today is removal of artifacts—whether it be potsherds or historic artifacts such as bottles, coins, and metal fragments—by unauthorized individuals. Removal is considered theft and is unlawful. Protection originated with the Antiquities Act of 1906, and the more recent Archaeological Resources Act of 1979 imposes stiffer penalties, plus a reward for information that leads to a conviction. Contact a ranger, other federal land management authorities, or the local sheriff should you discover any illegal activity.

Trails. Some trails in Utah, especially in red rock country, use cairns—stacks of tiny rocks—to mark trail routes. When you find one, sight the next one and head for it. Do not go too far without finding these route markers.

Rock art at Newspaper Rock (near Edge of the Cedars State Park)

In sandy terrain, footprints can be good markers for the return trip, so know the trace of your shoe soles.

On dirt trails, stay on the path and do not take shortcuts on switchbacks; it causes erosion, can start rocks falling, and can cause injury to others. Do not climb on crumbly rocks. Photograph the flowers, but do not trample or pick them. It is alright to hug a tree, but do not deface it or any other natural or constructed feature.

Nothing surpasses the joy of following a trail in solitude or quiet company, watching for wildlife, and seeing what nature is doing at the moment. This joy is easily destroyed by the loud noises of other trail users and/or their radios, or an unexpected, uncontrolled approach of a pet or a speeding mountain bike, just when you have discovered a fawn near the path. Please respect the enjoyment of others.

Litter along the trail mars the beauty of the surroundings. "Leave nothing but footsteps" cannot be said too often, it seems. Pack out your garbage. Even organic orange and banana peels are slow to decompose.

This general advice applies to hikers, bikers, horseback riders, and any nonmotorized trail users. Remember to show courtesy in meeting any of these trail travelers and don't travel or camp on private property without permission.

Wildlife. When we go outdoors for recreation, we invade habitats first populated by wildlife. If we go gently, with respect for both plants and animals, we can experience natural connections that are part of our heritage. Edward O. Wilson called the hunger for other life "biophilia," and believes it to be a basic part of the human psyche. Who would want to live in a world where we were the only life form?

So walk softly, speak gently, and be especially careful to avoid disturbing nesting birds or animals with young. Don't approach too closely animals that may be dangerous. This is not a Walt Disney world. And please do not feed the animals.

If you fish, practice gently releasing wild game fish to ensure future progeny. Fishing is open year-round in Utah. Check the Utah Division of Wildlife Resources Fishing Proclamation for specific regulations.

HOW TO USE THIS BOOK

To use this book as a guide to visiting Utah's state parks, I suggest the following approach:
1. Read the Introduction for general information about Utah—geology, human history, dinosaurs and fossils—and the park facilities, including rules, safety concerns, and outdoor manners.
2. Read the overviews to the nine regions to gain a perception of the terrain, a cursory acquaintance with the terminology of its highlights, some noteworthy history, recreational opportunities, and the climate factors.
3. Decide which of the nine regions to visit.
4. Scan the vital statistics at the beginning of specific park descriptions to choose attractions and facilities that interest you.
5. Read specific state parks' descriptions for more detailed information.
6. Check the Appendix and Index for additional information.
7. Plan routes and schedule to allow time to do the recreation you have selected, choose appropriate gear to take, and make reservations, if necessary.

Campers can travel throughout the state using state park campgrounds as base camps. Maps will help you plan your trip.

A NOTE ABOUT SAFETY

Safety is an important concern in all outdoor activities. No guidebook can alert you to every hazard or anticipate the limitations of every reader. Therefore, the descriptions of roads, trails, routes, and natural features in this book are not representations that a particular place or excursion will be safe for your party. When you follow any of the routes described in this book, you assume responsibility for your own safety. Under normal conditions, such excursions require the usual attention to traffic, road and trail conditions, weather, terrain, the capabilities of your party, and other factors. Keeping informed on current conditions and exercising common sense are the keys to a safe, enjoyable outing.

The Mountaineers

BRIDGER-LAND

Utah's smallest travel region is bounded on the western edge by the Wellsville Mountains, where the Wellsville Cone and Box Elder Peak rise over 9,000 feet from a narrow base. Cache Valley, where the Little Bear River meanders and world-famous Cache Valley cheese is produced, separates this high landscape from the Bear River Range that is east of Logan, where Mount Naomi and the Mount Naomi Wilderness are located.

An auto route slashes northeast through Logan Canyon and the Wasatch-Cache National Forest to popular Bear Lake and the Idaho border. When this forest was roadless, Jim Bridger liked to explore its lake country and mountain peaks where deer, elk, and moose still roam.

Jim Bridger was a legend because of his expertise as a mountain man and trapper. He excelled at following trails of any creature, including human, even at night when he touched the trail with his hands. From the moccasin track of an Indian he knew the tribe of the wearer. He wandered the West for so long that his linguistic gift enabled him to communicate in nearly a dozen Indian tongues as well as Spanish and French.

Now called Bridgerland, this region draws travelers to see the autumn colors of crimson maples in the Wellsville Mountains and the summer wildflower displays in the Tony Grove Recreation Area, accessed from the Logan Canyon Scenic Byway. A wealth of hiking and biking routes lets one take a more leisurely look at the surroundings. Rock climbers will find ample challenges and paddlers will enjoy birdwatching in quiet waterways by wetlands.

Though outdoor recreation and tourism are increasing in this area, about 90 percent of the land is used for ranching and agriculture. It is still terrain with some cowboy flavor.

Visit Logan for historical explorations into the lives of Mormon pioneers

Opposite: *Logan Canyon Scenic Byway on the way to Bear Lake*

at the Daughters of Utah Pioneers Museum, where craft demonstrations are featured. For an agricultural jaunt back in time, travel 5 miles south to the Ronald V. Jensen Living Historical Farm, which Utah State University operates exactly as Mormon pioneers would have in 1917.

The high elevation of this northeastern Utah country of the Logan and Bear Rivers has a pleasant summer climate, with temperatures in the eighties in the Cache Valley and the seventies in the Bear Lake Valley. Winters bring deep snow with uncrowded downhill skiing, snowmobiling, cross-country skiing, tubing, and sledding.

BEAR LAKE STATE PARK

Hours/Season: Overnight; year-round at Marina and East Side, April to September at Rendezvous Beach

Area: 906 acres

Facilities: Picnic tables; Marina has 13 campsites, wheelchair-accessible restrooms with showers, sewage disposal, group pavilion, visitor center, boat ramp, 220 transient boat slips; Rendezvous Beach has 138 campsites with utility hookups at 46 sites, wheelchair-accessible restrooms with showers, sewage disposal, group camping, boat rental; East Side has primitive sites, vault toilets, boat ramp, phone: (801) 946-3343

Attractions: Boating, fishing (ice fishing in winter), swimming, photography, snowmobiling, water skiing, scuba diving, windsurfing, cycling, birdwatching

Nearby: Logan Canyon Scenic Byway, Limber Pine Trail

Access: Marina is 2 miles north of Garden City on US 89, Rendezvous Beach is on the south shore near Laketown on State Route 30, East Side is 10 miles north of Laketown

If the light is right on arrival at Bear Lake, and it often is, the incredible turquoise color of the water makes one wonder if this is the Caribbean. Yet one is high in the Rocky Mountains (at 5,924 feet) in the extreme northeast corner of Utah, with almost half of the lake reaching into Idaho. The hypnotizing hue is the result of the suspension of limestone (calcium carbonate) particles in the lake. Utah's second-largest freshwater lake, Bear Lake is 20 miles long and 8 miles wide, covering 112 square miles.

Formed by earthquake action some 28,000 years ago, Bear Lake was separated from the Bear River about eight or ten thousand years ago by upheavals when the Bear River Plateau was uplifted on the east side of the lake. Originally, the river flowed from the edge of the High Uintas Wilderness area, via a circuitous route, into the north end of the lake via a system of swamps. Today a man-made canal connects Bear Lake to Mud Lake, which does unite with Bear River. Water flow via this canal can be regulated to flow into or out of Bear Lake, depending on river levels. Several small streams still flow into the lake.

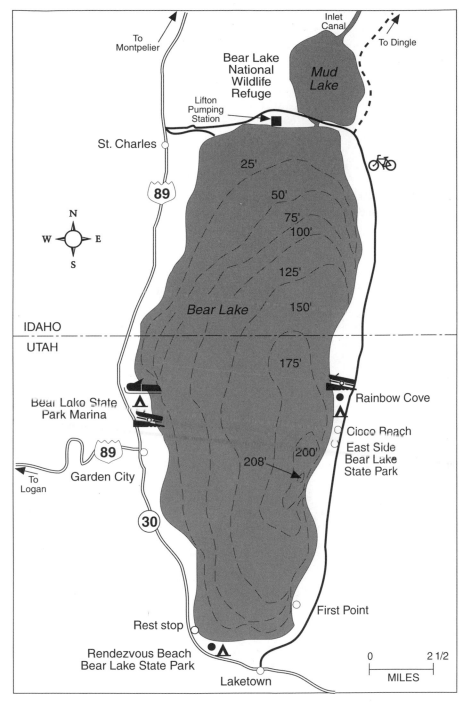

To
Montpelier

Inlet
Canal

To Dingle

Bear Lake
National
Wildlife
Refuge

*Mud
Lake*

Lifton
Pumping
Station

St. Charles

89

25'

50'

75'

100'

125'

150'

Bear Lake

N
W   E
S

IDAHO

UTAH

175'

Bear Lake State
Park Marina

Rainbow Cove

Cisco Beach

East Side
Bear Lake
State Park

89

Garden City

208'

200'

To
Logan

30

First Point

Rest stop

Rendezvous Beach
Bear Lake State Park

Laketown

0   2 1/2

MILES

Year-round recreation is popular at Bear Lake and public facilities are offered by the state park system on three sides of the lake.

The Marina, on the west side of the lake, is great for boaters who want slips. Camping sites are spaces marked off along one edge of the parking lot that overlooks the water. A narrow beach is reached on either side of the boat-basin jetties by walking through wetland areas that attract ducks and geese. Among the squirrel-tail barley and other wetland plants, there is open space for some private sun. A visitor center has information about local fish. Deer are often seen in the park. In winter, the extensive snowmobile trail system of the region connects with the Marina where camping is open.

East Side is located on the undeveloped shoreline of the lake. The Bear Lake Plateau, with semi-arid vegetation, rises abruptly above the water. Unless the water is unusually high, you can see the Cisco Beach underwater cliff, a shelf that goes out about 10 yards, before the water drops off to the deepest part of the lake, at 208 feet, and then gets progressively shallower from east to west.

En route in this section of the state park, one passes the Aquatics Camp with many small structures and tents on the hillside, a popular place for scuba divers, with sailboats parked along the water. The Cisco Beach area of the park is a short distance north, where several entry roads lead to camp-

Jet skier at Bear Lake State Park

sites and tables. Continue on to Rainbow Cove for a boat ramp and more choices of secluded picnicking and primitive camping with good views, accessed by bumpy, dirt roads. Consider camping at East Side, where there are no reservations, if other campgrounds are full.

Cisco Beach is named for the late January run of an endemic small fish called Bonneville cisco, a member of the whitefish family. For a week or 10 days, hardy outdoor people use dip nets to catch these fish when they come close to the surface to spawn near shore. If the lake is frozen, holes are chopped in the ice.

Rendezvous Beach, on the south shore, is the major camping and picnicking area of Bear Lake State Park. The sandy beaches are wide and the blue color is grand from this angle. Willow and cottonwood trees offer good shade in Big Creek Campground, where utility hookups are located. Those not needing hookups will find trees shading picnic tables and tent areas at Willow and Cottonwood campgrounds, but rigs are parked in lot spaces in the sun.

History suggested the name for Rendezvous Beach when a collection of over 1,000 people—mountain men, fur trappers, Indians, and supply caravans—came together to do some trading of furs and supplies at this site in 1827 and 1828. After long periods alone in the wilderness, these rendezvous gatherings were a time to renew acquaintances while attendees ate, drank, competed, and told stories. Jedediah Smith was present in 1827 when the campfires gave the appearance of a "lighted city." Today, an annual Mountain Men Rendezvous is held at this location each fall.

The first permanent settlement of whites in the area was at Garden City in 1864, between Rendezvous Beach and the Marina. Mormon pioneer Charles C. Rich built cabins on the shore of the lake for workers in his flour mill, and the addition of a sawmill, blacksmith shop, and wood-processing plant soon followed.

The flora and fauna of Bear Lake's ecosystem are diverse with four rare species found only here—the Bonneville cisco, Bear Lake whitefish, Bonneville whitefish, and Bear Lake sculpin. These fish are believed to be descendants of species that lived in ancient Lake Bonneville. Fishermen, however, usually go for the larger lake trout and Bear Lake cutthroat (a true native). Birdwatchers can observe white pelicans, sandhill cranes, egrets, herons, ducks, geese, western grebes, and many migratory waterfowl.

Bicyclists might want to do the 45-mile loop around the lake, an easy ride, mostly level, with small rolling hills and about 7 miles of gravel road. From the park marina, go south on US 89 and then take Utah 30 at Garden City to the outskirts of Laketown. Turn left on the county road and continue north into Idaho, staying near the lake until the road reconnects with US 89. Turn south back to the Marina. The loop provides spectacular scenery of the lake, mountains, and valleys. You might like to stop at the Bear Lake National Wildlife Preserve for some birding on the north side of the lake.

If you believe in rumors, keep an eye out for the Bear Lake monster. The Shoshone Indians cautioned the first white settlers about its ability to carry off braves or buffalo. The story was enough to convince a few early settlers who claimed they saw a huge serpentlike creature with legs and huge ears that swam very fast. Although it is good propaganda, the monster has not been seen recently.

Those visiting the area in early August will enjoy the Bear Lake Raspberry Festival with its rodeo, dancing, fireworks, chuckwagon breakfast, and crafts fair. The large berries lure visitors at this time of year, when they come to pick or purchase quantities for eating and preserving. Try a fresh raspberry milkshake.

If you approach or exit the state park via US 89 between Logan and Bear Lake, you'll find that this scenic byway includes interesting geological formations, a famous area for the study of Cambrian rocks and fossils. The color of the rock, mostly shades of gray, results from the inclusion of limestone and dolomite, typical marine decomposition products. Even with these drab hues, many scenic rock formations are seen along the drive.

From Bear Lake, it is exactly 7 miles (about 31 miles east of the Logan outskirts) southwest on this byway to the Limber Pine Reststop (no facilities except parking). This is the trailhead for the Limber Pine Loop, a highly recommended 1-mile hike. Beginning at an elevation of 7,800 feet in the Bear River Range, a northern spur of the Wasatch Mountains, the trail starts an easy ascent through Engelmann spruce and Douglas and subalpine fir forest with a few woodsy wildflowers. The path then enters open meadows with an exuberant display of varied and colorful species of summer wildflowers. The easy trail leads to a knoll overlooking great open slopes that fall into a valley with the curving highway below. A few shade trees crest the knoll with some huge striated rocks and smaller orange lichen-encrusted rocks scattered among the flowers that sprawl downhill, a wonderful picnic spot with birds adding to the charm.

A huge limber pine tree is located near the high point of the trail at 7,880 feet. Once thought to be the largest and oldest living specimen of this species at some 2,000 years, it is now known that it is five separate trees grown together and only about 560 years old, which is still rather impressive. Its seeds are scattered by Clark's nutcrackers.

Continuing on the trail, a view of Bear Lake backed by mountains is seen. Several benches along the trail let one savor the vistas. A trail guide tells about the ecosystem, including the water bears, or "tardigrades," that are microorganisms in moss on rocks, and the sapsuckers that drill straight lines of holes in trees.

After completing the loop trail and continuing west on the scenic byway, one passes the Bear Mountain Winter Sports Area in another 5 miles. Farther downhill through the Cache National Forest in Logan Canyon, stop at Rick's Springs where water pours into a cavelike rocky enclosure with ledges that entice one to explore. Continue on the road, following the bubbling Logan River downstream.

Many hiking trails of varied scenery and difficulty, as well as mountain and road-bike trails, are accessed from the scenic byway and lead to interesting destinations, like the 3,000 year-old Jardine juniper, Wind Cave, Naomi Peak, and Old Ephraim's Grave (Utah's last known grizzly bear).

Good brochures with maps for hiking and biking are put out by the Logan Ranger District of Cache National Forest and are available at ranger stations and the Chamber of Commerce in Logan. A string of forest camps lets you stay in the area to explore them.

Weather changes often during the changing elevation of this drive. One may begin in rain at Logan and arrive at Bear Lake in blue skies and white clouds. Logan, the home of Utah State University, is an appealing city with interesting shops, amenities, and good bookstores.

HYRUM STATE PARK

Hours/Season: Overnight; April through November
Area: 264 acres
Facilities: Picnic tables, 51 campsites, wheelchair-accessible restrooms
  with showers, group camping
Attractions: Swimming, water skiing, boating, cycling, fishing (ice fish-
  ing in winter), phone: (801) 245-6866
Nearby: Blacksmith Fork Canyon, Hardware Ranch
Access: In Hyrum, at 405 West 300 South, follow signs southwest to
  separate day-use area

Fed by the Little Bear River, Hyrum Reservoir, a 450-surface-acre lake at an elevation of 4,700 feet, was built in 1939 to provide irrigation water. Before the dam was built, Mormon settlers had to dig 9 miles of canal from the Little Bear River for farm irrigation to Hyrum, a town named after Hyrum Smith, the brother of the founder of the Mormon Church. Since the settlers had only hand tools, to assist in building this canal they devised an apparatus called a "go-devil" in which two split logs were fastened together at one end and shaped into a crude V that was pulled along by oxen to assist in digging.

Hyrum State Park was established in 1959 to administer recreation at this lake that is popular for water sports and entertainment for those relaxing along its banks. Though the park is not officially open in winter, most winters find ice fishermen and skaters attracted to the frozen lake.

At the entrance to Hyrum State Park, the road branches right and left to two areas of the campground, east and west, with the boat ramp in the central area. The roomy individual sites are in the west section, with several waterfront camping spots. Stairs or paths lead down the banks to the edge of the water where boats are sometimes beached. Though no indoor showers are found, an outdoor one for swimmers is useful. One wakes to the crowing of nearby roosters and sometimes the smell of cows in a morning rain.

The recently added day-use area is a mile southwest of the campground area, with parking both on the bluff and below close to the water (both require day-use entrance fees). A trail also leads down from the bluff to the beach and a nice roped-off swimming area.

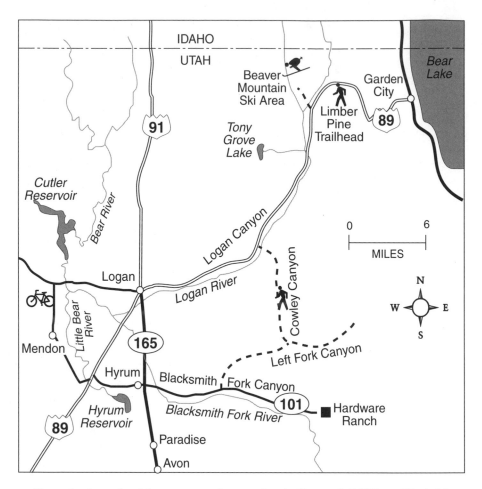

Years before the Mormon settlers arrived, General William H. Ashley stopped near what is now the edge of Hyrum Reservoir and cached about 150,000 dollars' worth of furs, mostly beaver, in the winter of 1825–26. These were safe in a cave dug in a clay bank until retrieved the following summer. Ashley returned then to transport the stash across the Wasatch Mountains by pack train and river raft to St. Louis. This bit of history resulted in the French-Canadian name of Cache Valley and Cache County.

The park campground is a good base for hikers, bikers, and auto tours. Bicyclists often do the nearby 8-mile road tour south on Utah 165. Two loop tours, the 12-mile Mount Sterling and the 24-mile Little Pyrenees, begin by going southwest from the campground and across the dam road. The latter tour goes through Mendon for good birdwatching at the nearby marshes. Check the details of these three routes in the Bridgerland Mountain and Roadbike Brochure (see Bear Lake).

A good road-bike or auto tour begins from the center of the town of Hyrum as Utah 101 continues east through Blacksmith Fork Canyon, which

Water sports at Hyrum State Park

follows the Blacksmith Fork River. More open at the beginning, the high rock walls become closer as the canyon narrows and the road follows a scenic corridor. One passes wildflowers, old small structures on wheels, summer homes, old beaver dams hardened with lime, and always the fast-flowing stream—a nice drive with excellent fishing (especially brown trout) and little traffic. Two hiking trails outlined in the hiking brochure, Leatham Hollow and Richards Hollow, are accessed from Left Hand Fork Road at about 6 miles. Continuing on Blacksmith Fork Road, Hyrum City Park and a couple of campgrounds are passed at 9 miles.

Hardware Ranch is located near the end of the highway. The primary function here is game management of the Rocky Mountain elk preserve, which is owned and operated by the Utah Division of Wildlife Resources. To prevent winter starvation and damage to nearby farmers' land, up to 700 elk in the vicinity are fed by employees. A visitor center and cafe are open from December 15 to March 15, with hot drinks and barbecue available. The winter activities include a tour and ride on a Clydesdale-drawn sleigh among the feeding elk. No reservations are needed except for group rides and special educational programs. Call (801) 245-3131 for recorded information.

GOLDEN SPIKE EMPIRE

A page of this country's history was written on May 10, 1869, when Central Pacific and Union Pacific locomotives pulled up to the one-rail gap in the first transcontinental railway. East and West were joined after the symbolic tapping of a golden spike, followed by a final iron spike. This event took place near the northeastern extremity of Utah's Great Salt Lake in the Promontory Mountains and precipitated the beginning of the end of the Western frontier.

The Golden Spike Empire is primarily basin and range country, an area dominated by the Great Salt Lake, the remains of what was once the much larger freshwater Lake Bonneville. Much of the terrain west of today's lake is the sagebrush and mirage land of the Great Salt Lake Desert. The lake itself is rimmed with many marshes that attract a great variety of migratory birds, a birdwatcher's paradise when conditions are right.

Antelope Island, the largest in the Great Salt Lake, is unique in this country, with desert and mountains rimmed with white, curving saltwater beaches. Though the history of this island contains some fascinating human drama, it is now owned by the state, a quiet place of wild buffalo, pronghorn antelope, and other fauna and flora.

The basin east of the lake curves upland dramatically to meet the Wasatch Front at the edge of mountains that rise just beyond the most populated cities of Utah. Residents of this area are within easy range of good skiing in these mountains. Utah is famous for its colder, drier powder snows, of Winter Olympics caliber, that attract skiers from all over the country. These snows are the result of storms from the North Pacific hitting the Wasatch Mountains after losing much of their moisture initially in the Sierra Nevada and Cascade Mountains to the west of Utah.

Opposite: *View from Sand Hill at Fort Buenaventura State Park*

Summer recreation seekers will find many trails, campgrounds, and fishing streams and lakes in the cool of the Wasatch National Forest. For colorful wildflower displays, visit the ski areas in May and June. Freshwater enthusiasts who want to stay in the warmer basin area, where temperatures are in the nineties, will find Willard Bay to their liking. Cyclists can choose from mountain rides or fairly level excursions in the basin area.

It was in this basin between lake and mountains that the first Anglo settlement was made at Fort Buenaventura, where the Weber River flows through on its way to the Great Salt Lake. Today this historic place is within the city of Ogden, part of the chain of settlements that run north-south and are bordered by good agricultural land.

Sample the fruit stands along US 89–91 between Pleasant View and Brigham City—called the "Fruitway"—for tasty seasonal delights. Or visit the horticultural research farm of Utah State University at Farmington to see the acres of flowers and plants.

The "Great Basin" is perhaps best visualized from lofty roads east of these metropolitan areas. The Bountiful Peak Scenic Backway is a steep, winding road between Bountiful and Farmington with a spectacular view of Great Salt Lake. The Ogden River Scenic Byway ascends narrow Ogden Canyon, passes Pineview Reservoir, and reaches the Monte Cristo summit in 33 miles, with great mountain and valley views. The drive from Henefer to Emigrant Canyon on Utah 65 follows the route of the first pioneers, including the Mormons, as they headed west.

WILLARD BAY STATE PARK

Hours/Season: Overnight; year-round at North Marina area, April to October at South Marina

Area: 2,673 acres

Facilities: Picnic tables; North Marina has 62 campsites, group camping, wheelchair-accessible restrooms with showers, group pavilion, sewage disposal, fish-cleaning stations, boat ramp and seasonal/transient boat slip rentals; South Marina has overnight room for 30 with vehicles but not specific campsites, wheelchair-accessible restrooms with showers, 1 boat ramp with 3 lanes, mooring, phone: (801) 734-9494

Attractions: Boating, fishing (ice fishing in winter), swimming, water skiing, birdwatching

Nearby: Golden Spike National Historic Site

Access: North Marina is 15 miles north of Ogden, just off Interstate 15-84 from exit 360; South Marina is 7 miles north of Ogden and 2 miles from exit 354 off Interstate 15

▲ Willard Bay Reservoir is a unique man-made body of freshwater reclaimed from the salt marshes of the Great Salt Lake by the Willard Bay Project, at an elevation of 4,200 feet. In 1966, land leased on its eastern shore from the Bureau of Reclamation became Willard Bay State Park.

Waterfront campsite at Willard Bay State Park

Within easy commuting distance of Utah's third largest city, Ogden, this park is visited frequently by locals and is popular with tourists as well for its water-oriented recreation and its diverse wildlife population. Stunning sunsets often illuminate the water and leave a warm glow of color on the Wasatch Mountains, which back the park to the east.

The Willow Creek Campground is adjacent to the entrance station of the North Marina area, the only area of the reservoir not diked. Some spacious waterfront sites are available with wide lawns where cottonwood and willow trees edge the water. Though there are some single campsites, many are large sites, a paved half-circle divided for two camping spots, so watch for numbers designating these. Lush wetland vegetation borders Willard Creek as it wanders through the campground on its way to the bay, and short trails access the creek.

A nature trail leads from site #48 to a wide sandy beach for swimmers and sunbathers; a road also connects. This walk passes through wooded areas, wetlands, and open areas with a tremendous number of Fuller's teasel plants. Footpaths branch east toward the water where ponds attract ducks and geese.

The boat ramp and several more campsites are located at the south end of the North Marina, a picturesque spot at the end of the road. Here a point of land projects out into the bay where sailboats are moored.

Boating is the major attraction at the South Marina, with camping a matter of picking a place in a large parking area to the north of Cold Springs Creek. This area near the Arthur V. Watkins Dam offers no beach.

43

Built mainly to store water for irrigation, the 15-mile-long dike for the reservoir was completed by the U.S. Bureau of Reclamation in 1964. Part of the Great Salt Lake flood plain, the dike separates 9,900 surface acres of freshwater from nearby saltwater. The Ogden and Weber rivers, a canal, and some small creeks supply the freshwater in the reservoir.

The dam was named to honor Arthur V. Watkins, in recognition of his lifelong service to water conservation. Watkins, with a law degree from Columbia University, had a varied career as a Mormon missionary, newspaper editor, farmer, and judge, and he became a U.S. senator in 1946. He achieved fame as the chairman of the "Select Committee to Study Censure Charges Against Senator Joseph McCarthy." He wrote about these happenings in one chapter of his American history book, *Enough Rope*, which was published in 1969.

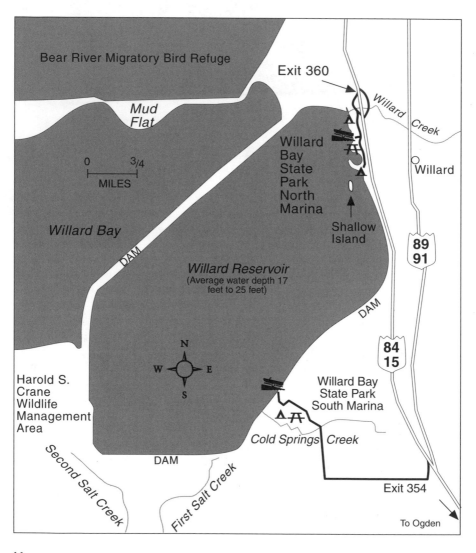

Boys fishing at the edge of Willard Bay

The name Willard, which designates the bay, the nearby town (originally Willow Creek), and a mountain peak, pays tribute to Mormon Willard Richards, who was with the advance guard that came to the Great Salt Lake Valley in 1847 under Brigham Young.

The wildlife of Willard Bay includes forty different mammals (most are nocturnal). Pocket gophers leave mounds from tunneling. Meadow voles make narrow runways in grassy areas. Muskrats are seen in marshy areas.

Ten of the sixteen species of fish found in the bay are game fish. Crappie, walleye, and channel catfish are stocked. A walleye run occurs in the spring. Large carp are easily observed in shallows and seen jumping out of the water not far from shore. Do have a fishing license.

Mosquitos, robber flies, damselflies, mayflies, and antlions are some of the common insects. There is some insect control in the park, so if you are concerned about exposure to chemical spraying, ask park staff about the spraying schedule.

Birders will be delighted, since over 200 species of birds can be seen. Stroll along the waterfront at dawn or evening to look for terns diving. Western grebes swim on the bay. American avocets and black-necked stilts are two common shorebirds with long legs and thin bills. Great blue herons are easy to spot in shallow water. Snowy egrets are the most common all-white wading bird. American coots are plentiful in marshy areas. White pelicans that nest on Gunnison Island in the Great Salt Lake come often to feed in the bay. Killdeer are common, and California gulls nest around the bay. Flocks of red-winged blackbirds are seen in the wetland vegetation. The most common falcon is the sparrow hawk, seen perched on utility poles or on wires while looking for insects.

The varied plant life includes 119 different species. The tallest grass is common reed (the most widely distributed plant in the world), which the Indians used for arrow shafts, mats, and other useful items. Sticky gumweed, with its pretty yellow flowers, is another plant utilized by the Indians, with parts used for medicine and tea. In late summer, look for the chrysalis of monarch butterflies on the milkweed. Morning glory, greasewood, prickly poppy, bee flower, and chicory are easily found.

Besides the cottonwoods and willows that hug the wet shore, oak, juniper, sagebrush, and grasses are hardy drought- and salt-resistant vegetation. Three exotic trees were planted in the camping area as ornamentals, wind breaks, and for shade—Russian olive, English elm, and Carolina poplar.

Harold S. Crane Wildlife Management Area is adjacent to the state park, to the west of the reservoir. On the north side of Willard Bay is located the Bear River Migratory Bird Refuge, which covers a vast complex system of dikes, ditches, and marsh. Prior to the rising of the Great Salt Lake in the mid- and late-1980s, as many as 60,000 tundra swans (formerly called whistling swans) were counted in the refuge between mid-October and mid-November, the single largest concentration of these migratory birds in North America. In November of 1985, only 259 were counted. A year later the number was down to three because of loss of habitat from flooding.

Replica of an early steam engine at Golden Spike National Historic Site (near Willard Bay State Park)

Humans did take a hand in artificially lowering the level of the water, and then the lake naturally retreated by the end of the 1980s and beckoned wild-life again.

Do take the time to visit the Golden Spike National Historic Site nearby. Go north on Interstate 15 and then west on Utah 83 from exit 368. It was here at Promontory Summit that the Central Pacific, from the west, and the Union Pacific, from the east, joined to complete the first transcontinental railroad tracks in 1869 and a symbolic golden spike was tapped. In summer, you can watch two exact replica steam locomotives, the "Jupiter" and the "119," as they run a short section of track relaid on the original roadbed.

An annual Railroader's Festival is held in August with a period-dress reenactment of the May 10, 1869, Golden Spike Ceremony. Food, live music, handcar rides, horse-drawn wagon rides, crafts, games, and contests are scheduled. Try your hand at spike driving, boiler stoking, greased pole climbing, railwalking, and buffalo chip throwing.

FORT BUENAVENTURA STATE PARK

Hours/Season: Day use; April to November
Area: 88 acres
Facilities: Picnic tables, group campsites (no single sites), wheelchair-accessible restrooms, visitor center, historical exhibits, canoe rentals, phone· (801) 621-4808
Attractions: Boating, fishing, history
Nearby: Davis County Bike Route
Access: At 2450 A Avenue, reached by following signs to park from exit 344 northbound and from exit 345 southbound off Interstate 15

▲ The site of the first permanent Anglo settlement in the Great Basin was preserved as Fort Buenaventura State Park in 1979. Miles Goodyear came to this place in the mid-1840s with his Ute Indian wife, Pomona (the daughter of an Indian chief), and built a cabin and eventually a trading post. He erected quarters for his partners and their families, planted a garden in the good soil, and enclosed it all with a stockade of tall cottonwood poles.

As a sixteen-year-old, Goodyear had left Connecticut for the West. Stopping to work for his room and board during the winters, he spent three summers walking until he met the missionary party of Marcus Whitman on the Oregon Trail in 1836. At that year's rendezvous of mountain men on the Green River in Wyoming he met the legendary trappers that had been part of his inspiration to aim west. The result was that he left Whitman's group at Fort Hall (now Pocatello), Idaho, to become a mountain man himself.

With a gift of two horses from Whitman, in gratitude for his help along the trail, Goodyear stayed in Idaho for several years to hunt and trap until he realized the fur trade was ending. From the two horses he built up a herd, began horse trading, and then moved to this location on the Weber

River in Utah that he named Fort Buenaventura (which means good venture in Spanish). This name had been used several times before for the Green River and other streams that were temporarily thought to be the mythical river that just had to be navigable all the way to San Francisco, since a waterway for transportation was so desired in those days. Such a river does not exist. Ogden-born writer Bernard DeVoto called this phenomenon "the geography of hope."

Goodyear's venture did not last long. When the Mormons arrived in 1847 to settle this area they were not happy to find people outside their church living in the vicinity. The upshot was that Goodyear's fort was bought by a Mormon and it became Brown's Fort, then Brownsville, and finally Ogden, to honor fur trapper Peter Skene Ogden (1794–1854), an expedition leader for the Hudson's Bay Company who had visited the area as early as 1825. Ready to move on west, Goodyear left with his 2,000 horses for California, where he enjoyed a short successful life as a horse trader and miner before he died in 1849 in the midst of the Gold Rush, at the age of thirty-two.

The original Fort Buenaventura burned to the ground in 1852, and the present state park is an authentic replica located at the same site as determined from letters, the known location of the flag pole, and an archaeological dig. The site is actually an island bounded by the Weber River and a slough.

Walk through the state park and envision a time when Goodyear had 2,000 head of cattle, 2,000 horses, and 1,000 Spanish goats. He built his cabin first with a fireplace and a sod roof. All of the present structures were built

Traders' Row cabin at Fort Buenaventura State Park

with the same wooden pegs and mortise-and-tenon joints to hold the cottonwood logs together. Considerable thought has been given to duplicating the furnishings. An elk skin serves as a blanket. The bed springs are of rope, and handmade as everything here is. Even the paint on chests is the old-style washable green milk paint that was made using a green pigment found in clay.

Spend time inside Traders' Row to see the variety of stores that reflect what was available in Goodyear's time— feathers, skins, beads, hardware for muzzleloaders, and much more. The stockade posts are of aspen and cottonwood. Corn is still planted in the garden. A pear tree exists that Miles Goodyear planted. Be sure to climb the Sand Hill, really an alluvial fan, for a splendid view of the surrounding area, including the Wasatch Mountains to the east. Since trees block out any evidence of today's civilization, it is easy to imagine Miles Goodyear seeing a similar view, though perhaps with horse riders and even Indians as part of the scene.

The quiet flow of the Weber River is a good place to put in canoes. This river begins at the edge of the High Uintas Wilderness Area and flows north past the park to empty into Willard Bay.

An annual event, the Labor Day Mountain Man Rendezvous, is held in the park to commemorate this historical meeting. Though usually held along the Green River of present-day Wyoming, four of the original get-togethers of trappers and suppliers were held in Utah, two at Bear Lake and two in the Cache Valley. The final rendezvous was in 1840. By that time, beaver skins were not so easy to get any more and silk arriving from the Orient was destined to become a new fad.

The present-day rendezvous celebrations are a time to see men and women in buckskins or furs doing Indian beadwork and stirring Dutch-oven meals while tanners, gunsmiths, leather workers, and hatmakers demonstrate old skills to the sound of Indian drums and chanting. The sound of muskets being fired may remind one of how the Indians traded vast numbers of beaver pelts (sometimes 2,000 dollars' worth) for a $17.50 gun.

Other events held at Fort Buenaventura State Park are the Spring Rendezvous held Easter weekend, the Pioneers Skills Show in July, the Indian Powwow in September, and a Turkey Shoot in November.

Cyclists might want to check out the Davis County Bike route, a dedicated bike lane that extends 35 miles from North Salt Lake to West Point City, which is just a few miles southwest of Ogden. This route connects eight city parks and offers views of the lake and the Wasatch Range.

ANTELOPE ISLAND STATE PARK

Hours/Season: Overnight; year-round
Area: 28,022 acres
Facilities: Picnic tables, group-use pavilion, wheelchair-accessible restrooms, showers, 11 tent campsites, room for 64 RVs in Bridger Bay

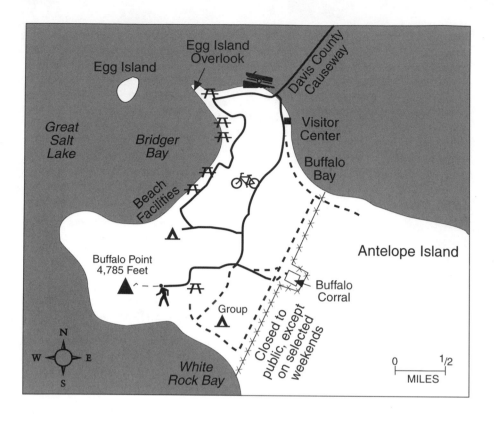

parking lot, 4 group camping areas at White Rock Bay, sewage disposal, marina, boat ramp, visitor center, concessionaire, overlooks, phone: (801) 773-2941

Attractions: Saltwater bathing, bicycling, birdwatching, hiking, horseback riding, boating, sunbathing, photography, wildlife viewing, parasailing

Access: By boat or causeway, 14 miles west of exit 335 on Interstate 15, via Utah 109 and Utah 127 to causeway

▲ The unique environment of Antelope Island State Park is that of the largest of ten islands in Great Salt Lake and the largest state park in Utah. In the past, only the northern 2,000-acre portion was open to the public, but this changed recently; the south end of the island is open on selected weekends. A network of four-wheel-drive roads will be converted to a trail system for nonmotorized visitors.

Great Salt Lake is the saltiest body of water in the world except for the Dead Sea, with an average salinity of 20 percent. (See Great Salt Lake State Park.) It measures some 75 by 30 miles for a total of 1,500 square miles at what is considered a normal level. The greatest depth is 40 feet, but the average is 14 feet. The average elevation is 4,200 feet with a record low in 1963 of 4,193 feet and a historic high in 1987 of 4,212 feet. The area covered by these two extremes was 1,000 square miles and 2,500 miles respectively, quite a difference.

Think about an extra 12-foot rise when you drive the 7.5-mile causeway across these salty waters and you will realize what would happen to the causeway and surrounding areas during a significant rise in water level—a lot of problems. Sixty million dollars were spent to pump water from the western shore of the lake to a low-lying desert area to the west called the "Newfoundland Evaporation Basin."

In 1983, rising waters inundated the causeway and forced closure of the park for ten years. Before that, in 1974 violent storms on the island had damaged the causeway and it was rebuilt two years later at a cost of $1.7 million. The causeway was refurbished and reopened July 1, 1993.

Watch for parasailing as you approach the island. A boat takes a person with a parachute across the water until he or she is lifted into the air. Attached by a long cord to the boat, the parasailor is wound in as the parachute descends, a little like water skiing except adventurers go up and down in the air instead of horizontally on the water.

On the island, the paved road follows the water's edge west past the new marina to the Egg Island Overlook, where gulls and other migratory birds can be seen at their island rookery. Gunnison Island, located across the lake to the northwest, is home for a colony of some 10,000 white pelicans. The number of islands seen in the lake depends on the water level, since many are connected at lower elevations.

The scenic drive continues downhill with good views of the large saltwater swimming beach, a cove of white sand by Bridger Bay. Swimmers find it is quite easy to float in this salty buoyancy. The camping area is soon reached via a spur road. A road to the southwest leads to the Buffalo Point Overlook, where a concessionaire sells buffalo burgers. A short trail climbs to the top of 4,785-foot-high Buffalo Point.

Most of the island land in the northern developed area is relatively flat with some hilly sections. It is a good bicycle destination, with wide shoulders along the causeway designated for safe riding as bike paths. There are 6 miles of pavement and 20 miles of gravel roads on the island. Cars should observe the speed limits of 25 miles per hour on the island and 40 miles per hour on the causeway.

The area of the island that was recently opened to certain activities contains a volcanic summit of 6,600 feet elevation, part of a north–south mountain range, and more varied terrain. Future plans include having a trail circle this southern part of the island, but it will be important to protect this fragile area. Maps of the entire island are available at the visitor center overlooking Buffalo Bay and the causeway.

At first, the island may appear barren and deserted, but it has long been the home for mule deer, coyotes, bobcats, many varieties of birds, waterfowl, a small herd of elk, and American bison, introduced in 1893 and in 1911, now numbering some 600 animals. Some of these, often with their young, may be seen by following the spur road to the buffalo corral. In winter you can watch the feeding of calves. The first buffalo hunt was held in

1921, and animals are culled periodically, with some ferried to the mainland and sold to ranches. A movie showing the buffalo herd, *The Covered Wagon*, was filmed on the island in 1922. An annual bison roundup is held each November when visitors can get a close-up look at techniques on a working buffalo ranch.

Though the island was originally home to pronghorn antelope, overgrazing, hunting, and range fires eliminated their population by the 1930s. Twenty-four pronghorns (fifteen bucks and nine does) were reintroduced from the Echo Reservoir area in early 1993 and soon numbered forty. Some of these antelope were equipped with radio transmitters for a five-year study. If this transplantation is successful, bighorn, more elk, and upland game birds may be introduced.

Antelope Island has a rich pioneer history. The Great Salt Lake was first discovered by James Bridger and Etienne Provost during their 1824–25 expedition. Then John C. Fremont explored from 1843 to 1845, when low water permitted him to arrive on horseback, and he named the island. In 1848, three Mormon groups drove their cattle to the island, and this was followed in 1856 by an LDS Church transport of 3,000 head of horses and other stock.

In 1897, Alice Frary, wife of homesteader George, died of a ruptured appendix before her husband could return with a doctor, and she is buried on the island. George Frary stayed to raise his family and spent considerable time exploring and taking depth soundings of the lake.

Bridger Bay beach area at Antelope Island State Park

Bison corral at Antelope Island State Park

Between 1925 and 1980, the island was used primarily for cattle ranching. The state of Utah purchased 2,000 acres, built the north causeway, and opened Antelope State Park in 1969. The remaining acres of the island were purchased by the State of Utah in 1981 for $4 million.

Now that the water level has normalized and the park is open again, many events are being scheduled during the year. Several bicycle races are offered, sometimes a moonlight ride, as well as kite flies and beach days. Endurance horse races are now held that travel into the southern part of the island, making a loop. The Bison Calf Release occurs in spring and the Annual Buffalo Round-up is held in late October to early November.

EAST CANYON STATE PARK

Hours/Season: Overnight; year-round
Area: 267 acres
Facilities: Picnic tables, 31 campsites with overflow area, wheelchair-accessible restrooms with showers, group camping, 2 group pavilions, sewage disposal, boat docks and ramp, fish cleaning station, concessionaire with snacks and boat rentals (summer only), phone: (801) 829-6866
Attractions: Boating, paddling, fishing (ice fishing in winter), water

skiing, swimming, water sports, snowmobiling, cross-country skiing
Access: Off Interstate 84 at exit 103, continue 12 miles south of Morgan on
Utah 66

▲ Several canyons—Deer Hollow, Big Dutch Hollow, Dead Ox Canyon,
Taylor Hollow and Dixie Hollow—feed running water into East Canyon
Creek as it flows from its origin just north of what is now Park City. An
earth-filled dam was constructed between 1963 and 1966 at the northern
end of this area, located near the intersection of Utah 65 and Utah 66, where
East Canyon veers to the northwest. As part of the Weber Basin Reclamation Project, East Canyon Reservoir has 680 surface acres. Below the dam,
the creek joins the Weber River at Morgan.

East Canyon State Park was established at this 5,700-foot elevation near
the dam in 1967. Sloping canyons, curving land projections, and low-slung
peaks provide a picturesque backdrop for the popular water activities on
the lake. Kayaks, rafts, motorboats, jet skis, and an occasional sailboat attract the viewer's attention.

The campground is on a hillside overlooking the water with pull-
through sites on gravel and a few scattered small trees. Though covered picnic tables are scattered throughout the day-use area, they are not shaded in
the campground. The restrooms are located at the bottom of the hill near the
water, and it is a steep downhill and return to your individual site. Since
water and garbage containers are in that same area, you might want to be

Waterfront scene at East Canyon State Park

organized. The showers are even farther away, near the concessionaire building, so do not be disappointed if you do not find them at first.

This park allows considerable overflow parking. Though there are no individual sites, campers can put their tents closer to the water on the grass and park their vehicles in the parking lot, and the facilities, including the covered tables, are more convenient.

The beach is essentially gritty dirt and mud. The day-use area and boat ramp are on the northwest end of the reservoir. A pier with individual boat docks provides ambulatory fishermen access to the water. Swimmers paddle out from water's edge.

Walkers might enjoy some exploring along the edge of the water or up the hillside and along the highway. The scrub growth is low and easily traversed. White poppies, yellow sunflowers, sage, and thistles grow on the rounded hills by the road, and even some red rock and hoodoos can be seen.

This park is accessible for winter activities if you approach from the north via Utah 65 or Utah 66. Utah 65 to the south is closed during this snowy season.

East Canyon and the surrounding area are rich in pioneer history, though this was a tough route for wagon trains. The Broad Hollow Historic Marker is just past the park on Utah 65. It relates how the Donner party turned right up Broad Hollow at this spot, climbed to the broad bench above, and then dropped down into East Canyon just above the present dam.

Historic marker along pioneer route at Broad Hollow, East Canyon State Park

The Donner party, also called the Donner-Reed group, was an assemblage of farmers from Iowa and Illinois going west to find fertile land to till. They passed through East Canyon near the creek in 1846, the first wagon train to pass this way, and had to hack a rough road through head-high brush and rocky obstacles, which slowed them down considerably.

The Donner party started west after talking to an adventurer, Lansford W. Hastings, who had traveled the way only once and on horseback in good weather, an altogether different experience from that of these eighty-seven men, women, and children with their oxen-drawn wagons. They had left Fort Bridger in southwest Wyoming on July 31, 1846, which was considerably late in the year for a trip to California.

After taking 19 days to chop their way through this area, they finally emerged at what is now called Emigration Canyon, just east of Salt Lake City. Continuing west, they had to cross 80 miles of waterless desert south of Great Salt Lake, which would have not been too difficult on horseback, but their three-day crossing killed many oxen and so weakened others that a week was needed to recover. From the banks of the Truckee River near present-day Reno, they continued on, not realizing the winter trek they had opted for over the Sierras. Their tragedy is well known, with only forty-seven of the original eighty-seven reaching California.

One year after the Donner party passed through East Canyon, Mormon pioneers followed their route to Emigration Canyon, but took only twelve days since the way was easier now. On July 19, 1847, Mormon scouts John Brown and Orson Pratt were the first Latter-Day Saints to climb 7,420-foot Big Mountain and see Salt Lake Valley. Brigham Young and his group of pioneers arrived at the same lookout 4 days later. By the time he arrived the advance party had already planted potatoes.

If one wants to hike a short portion of the Donner-Mormon route, the 4.3-mile Mormon Pioneer National Historic Trail begins south from Utah 65 and goes east at Big Mountain Pass. It ends at Big Mountain Flat where a historic marker is located.

Many people used the Donner-Mormon route over the next years, including the Overland Stage and the Pony Express.

LOST CREEK STATE PARK

Hours/Season: overnight; year-round
Area: 365 acres
Facilities: Primitive camping, vault toilets, boat ramp, *no water, no fee for park use*, phone: (801) 829-6866
Attractions: Fishing (ice fishing in winter), boating, water sports, swimming
Access: 10 miles northeast of Croydon on signed road

Lost Creek State Park is undeveloped, a place popular with trout fishermen who arrive at this reservoir via the paved road anxious to put lines into the water. To launch boats into the lake, take the gravel road across the dam and follow it at water's edge up a hill and then down to a hidden cove where the boat ramp is located. From the dam you can see trailers parked at water level there, though the ramp is not visible. This view helps you aim in the right direction. Many fishermen find the shore by the dam a convenient place to fish because there is a large parking lot at this 6,000-foot elevation.

Fishermen at Lost Creek Reservoir

The dam was constructed on Lost Creek—a tributary of the Weber River, which begins on the east slope of Horse Ridge—in the mid-1960s as part of the Weber Basin Project. The earth-filled dam impounds a 245-acre lake that stretches into the Wasatch-Cache National Forest.

A small primitive camping area is located in the trees off the entry road before the dam is reached, with a chemical toilet but no picnic tables. Other camping is possible along the west side of the reservoir just above the dam, where a boat can be launched fairly easily at the edge of the water. Trash is collected at the dam parking lot.

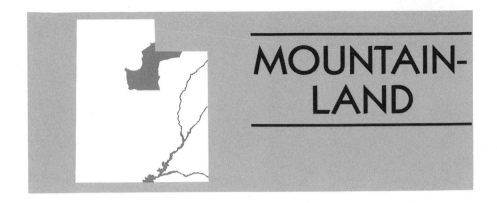

MOUNTAIN-LAND

Superlatives are easily tossed about when writing of the Mountainland region. For instance, the largest natural freshwater lake in the West is Utah Lake, situated in Utah Valley between the Wasatch Range and smack against the Lake Mountains, a place visited over 200 years ago by the Spanish expedition of Escalante and Dominguez.

Utah Valley lays claim to growing 75 percent of the state's fruit. The harvest of tart cherries from the southern end of the valley ranks third nationally.

West of Utah Lake is the ghost town of Fairfield, where the largest troop concentration in the United States spent three years occupying Camp Floyd. Still there is the Stagecoach Inn, once a stopover for the Overland Stage and the Pony Express, and now renovated and a state park attraction. A short distance northeast is the only veterans memorial park in Utah.

The region is replete with reservoirs that invite good fishing and numerous recreational choices, most with state parks along their shores. Deer Creek, Echo, Strawberry, Rockport, and brand new Jordanelle all capture flowing rivers from the mountains and temporarily turn them into lakes.

The Wasatch and Uinta mountains originally capture this moisture as snow and provide almost five months of "the greatest snow on Earth" for world-class skiing. Wasatch Mountain State Park (second largest in the state) offers the finest snowmobiling facility in the state and good cross-country skiing. In warmer months, the ski resorts entice mountain cyclists to ride their chairlifts and ride downhill on miles of trails. At the same time, Wasatch Mountain State Park opens its 27-hole golf course.

Two-thirds of Mountainland are covered with the Wasatch and Uinta

Opposite: *Discovery Trail along the Provo River in the Rock Cliff area of Jordanelle State Park*

national forests, timbered mountains with thousands of lakes, Rocky Mountain goats, and meadows of wildflowers. The many trails lure hikers and horseback riders to enjoy the cooler summer climate.

The Alpine Scenic Loop (Utah 92), in the Uinta National Forest, is reminiscent of the Swiss Alps as it passes Robert Redford's Sundance, snow-peaked Mount Timpanogos, Timpanogos Cave National Monument, and a spur road to Cascade Springs. Sundance has a summer theater under the stars.

The Mirror Lake Scenic Byway (Utah 150) travels through the Wasatch National Forest, the Uinta Mountains where many rivers originate, and heads northeast to Wyoming. It accesses mountain-bike trails, Provo River Falls, wildlife viewing areas (including moose), and scads of campgrounds.

At the lower elevation of Strawberry Valley, wildlife diversity is good. Alert observers can find spawning cutthroat trout, nesting sandhill cranes, rafts of white pelicans, herds of elk and mule deer, and raptors circling above.

For some different transportation, take the Bridal Veil Sky Tram in the Provo River Canyon. Or ride the steam-powered Heber Creeper railroad along the edge of Deer Creek Reservoir to the dam. Or ride a hot-air balloon in the resort town of Park City, which was once, supposedly, the world's greatest silver camp. On the way to becoming a ghost town until ski resorts were developed, Park City retains a smidgen of its historic Main Street, and also the highest-priced lift tickets in the country.

Utah's skinniest state park (only 135 feet wide) just opened, the Historic Union Pacific Rail Trail. It starts in Park City and runs nearly 30 miles to Echo Reservoir, a gravel hiking/biking/horseback riding/skiing route on the now defunct narrow-gauge railway that was built in 1880 and carried coal to Park City's silver mines.

The climate varies greatly with elevation in Mountainland. When it is ninety degrees in Provo in the Utah Valley, it may be eighty in the Heber Valley or Park City, and only sixty-five at Mirror Lake, where the elevation is 10,200 feet. Summer thunderstorms are frequent in late afternoon, so plan accordingly. Provo receives only moderate snow in winter. Ski resorts at Park City and Sundance average 300 inches of snow a year. Mirror Lake is snowbound at that time of year.

ROCKPORT STATE PARK

Hours/Season: Overnight; year-round
Area: 550 acres
Facilities: Picnic tables, campground with 86 campsites, group camping, wheelchair-accessible restrooms with showers, vault toilets, sewage disposal, boat ramp, boat storage, concessionaire, phone: (801) 336-2241
Attractions: Boating, windsurfing, water skiing, sailing, kayaking, fishing (ice fishing in winter), swimming, cross-country skiing, wildlife viewing

Access: Take exit 156 from Interstate 80 and travel 5 miles southeast on
  Utah 32

🌲 Rockport State Park takes its name from some mistake in translation
from the name of the settlement (of some 200 residents), Rock Fort,
which was purchased before being inundated by the reservoir construction.
When the first settler, Henry Reynolds, arrived in 1860, the village of Three
Mile Creek was founded. This was later changed to Crandall, and then took

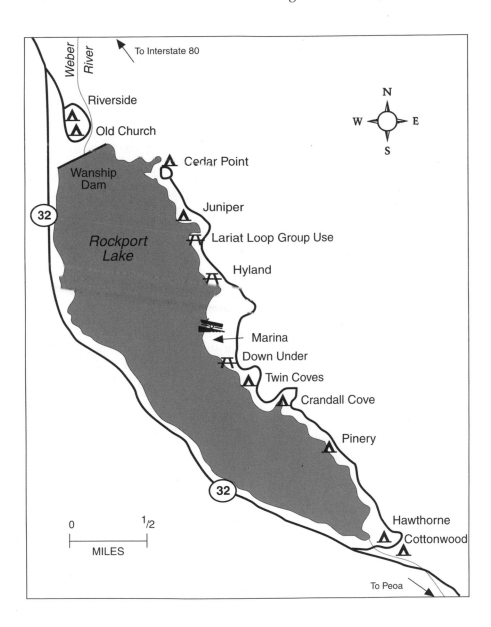

on the Mormon name, Enoch. In 1865, after Indian troubles provoked the construction of a protective fort—with 8-foot-high walls that were 2 feet thick—the town became known as Rock Fort.

Wanship Dam is at the north end of Rockport Lake. It was named after the town by the freeway exit. This village was settled just prior to Rock Fort, in 1859, when Robert Nixon built a cabin at the junction of Silver Creek and the Weber River. Wanship was the name of a friendly Indian chief who led a mixed tribe of Utes and Shoshones in the area. The town of Wanship got considerable traffic in the years before and shortly after the completion of the transcontinental railroad in 1869 because it was on the Overland Stage route.

At an elevation of 6,037 feet, Wanship Dam is a major water-storage and flood-control dam on the Weber River, which flows down from its headwaters in the Uinta Mountains. The reservoir is about 3 miles long and 0.5-mile wide, and covers over 1,000 acres. The land along its shores became a state park in 1966. This is sagebrush countryside with an occasional red rock formation.

Just north of Wanship Dam are two group campgrounds, Riverside and Old Church. The main area of the park is reached by driving the entire western length of the reservoir.

The park entry road crosses the Weber River, wetlands fringed by grassy lowlands, and continues for some 4 miles almost to the north end of the water, where the road ends. All of the development is between the road and the water, with good views of the popular water sports being enjoyed, except for the first campground area, one of nine campground choices that vary from primitive to developed in a variety of settings.

This first area with campsites is Cottonwood, and its scenic amenities include nice shade and individual sites along the frontage of the fast-flowing Weber River. This location includes a trail along the river where fishermen can enjoy quiet angling.

Going north, the next area is the Hawthorne Group Campground, a primitive area with vault toilets. Then another primitive campground, Pinery, occupies a somewhat sheltered cove, with good windsurfing and kayaking since it is away from the main stream of speeding boats. The Crandall Cove Campground follows with picnic sites, vault toilets, and recreational-vehicle parking, an area developed with donated materials. After passing another small day-use area on a bay inlet, the Twin Coves Campground, with vault toilets, overlooks easy water access.

Continuing north, a trail branches off through some of the upland area and also down to the water, where the Down Under day-use area has secluded picnicking. This is followed by the trailer dumping station and then the marina with its boat ramp, boat storage, restroom, marina store, and boat rentals.

In succession, one reaches the Hyland picnic area and then the Lariat Loop Group Day Use area, which has covered picnic tables by the water.

After passing another inlet, one arrives at Juniper Campground, the most developed in Rockport, and the only one with showers. These indi-

Campground overlooking reservoir at Rockport State Park

vidual sites are on the sloping hillside and all have great views, several adjacent to the water for easy entry. The last campground before the end of the road is Cedar Point, which is for tents only.

Individual reservations can be made for Juniper, Twin Coves, and Cottonwood campgrounds, and group reservations for Riverside, Old Church, and Hawthorne. All others are on a first-come, first-served basis.

Rockport is a popular park with year-round activities. In winter, bring your skis and ice-fishing gear. Cross-country skiing trails are maintained. They offer a contrast to more forested areas in the mountains with their more open sagebrush/juniper terrain and the better possibility of viewing wildlife from the trails.

Though juniper and sagebrush dominate the vegetation, cottonwoods and willows grow near water. Wildlife species are varied with mule deer, chipmunks, jackrabbits, cottontails, yellow-bellied marmots, badgers, raccoons, weasels, skunks, and Uinta ground squirrels. Not so common are the elk, moose, coyote, bobcat, and cougar that live in the area but are seldom seen. Birdwatchers should be able to spot Western grebes, Canada geese, whistling swans, great blue herons, ducks, red-tailed hawks, magpies, scrub jays, hummingbirds, great horned owls, golden eagles, and bald eagles.

HISTORIC UNION PACIFIC RAIL TRAIL STATE PARK

Hours/Season: Day use; year-round with no present hour limitations
Area: Not available
Facilities: Vault toilets, phone: (801) 645-8036
Attractions: Hiking, mountain biking, horseback riding, jogging, Nordic skiing, wildlife viewing
Access: *To reach trailhead at Prospector Park in Park City, from Salt Lake City* take exit 145 off Interstate 80, turn right on Utah 224, left on Kerns Boulevard (Utah 248), right on Bonanza Drive, left on Prospector Avenue, and park on right side of the street just past Park City Plaza. *To reach Park City via US 40*, take exit 4 to Utah 248, go left on Bonanza Drive, left on Prospector Avenue, and park on right side of street just past Park City Plaza; the *next trailhead* is 7 miles farther at Star Pointe, located east of Silver Creek Industrial Park, with access from US 40 at Silver Creek interchange; the *next trailhead* is 7 miles farther at Wanship (take exit 156 off Interstate 80 and find parking northeast of Spring Chicken Inn on US 189); the *next trailhead* is 8 miles farther at Coalville (take exit 164 off Interstate 80, veer right off ramp, proceed left on Main Street, and take a left on 200 North); another 5 miles takes you to the *terminus at Echo* with little or no parking at present

The Historic Union Pacific Rail Trail State Park has turned an abandoned railroad right-of-way into a recreational asset. Though not a new idea, it is a great way to create trails. During a visit, one can learn some of the interesting history of the area.

Two quite different cultures have interacted here in Summit County since the late 1850s. One group, mostly Mormons, farmed along the banks of the Weber River. A more rambunctious culture involved those who wove

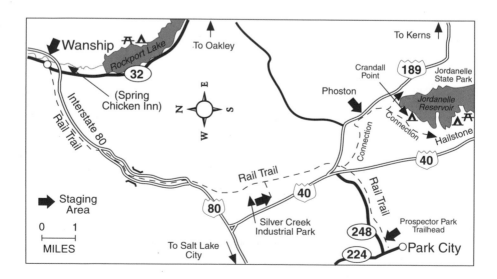

User regulations for the Historic Union Pacific Rail Trail

their lives around silver mines in the narrow mountain valley that became Park City.

The Park City mines needed the timber and coal resources of the neighboring communities, and a railroad provided transportation for these and other needs. To link up with the new Union Pacific line at Echo, only 5 miles away, the Coalville and Echo Railroad Company was organized in 1868. It would carry coal from mines near Coalville to Echo, and from there it would go to Wasatch Front communities. These plans were temporarily abandoned due to a shortage of track, though the grading was done and ties were prepared. In 1871, the increasing need for coal transport resulted in the formation of the Summit County Railroad Company, which by 1873 was moving coal along a narrow-gauge track between Coalville and Echo.

While this was happening, the silver mines created another market for coal, which was needed to run huge pumps to remove underground water from the mines. The newly organized Utah Eastern Railroad completed a narrow-gauge line in 1880 from Coalville to Park City. At the same time, the Union Pacific Railroad responded to the situation by completing a broad-gauge spur line to Park City.

The two narrow-gauge lines could not successfully compete with Union Pacific and went out of business within three years. For another hundred years, the Union Pacific spur served the Park City area until it was finally abandoned in 1989. Utah State Parks and a Utah-based salvage company entered into an agreement to convert the abandoned 135-foot right-of-way into a 30-mile recreational trail from Park City to Echo Reservoir. The salvage company removed the ties and rails and donated the property to Utah State Parks. Then the 1989 Utah Legislature appropriated funds for a hazardous-materials investigation and a master plan for the rail trail. Old mine tailings were found in some areas, and these will be capped with topsoil from the Jordanelle Reservoir site.

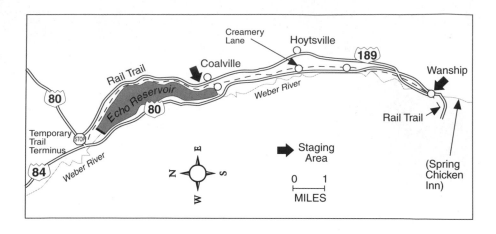

The approximately 15-foot-wide rail trail is now open to recreational uses that include hiking, jogging, cycling, horseback riding, and cross-country skiing. No motorized vehicles are allowed on the trail. The scenery includes mountain-framed meadows, the volcanic crags of Silver Creek Canyon, the Weber River, the shores of Echo Reservoir, and steep-walled Echo Canyon. Elevations vary from 5,280 to 6,900 feet.

A few livestock crossings are permitted. Users of the trail are asked to please respect private property by staying on the trail and packing out trash. No camping is allowed on the right-of-way, but facilities are available nearby. Restrooms, road-crossing controls, safety signs, and trash containers are located along the trail. Future plans call for the addition of picnic areas, benches, trees, trail improvements, mileage and interpretive signs (railroad history, human history, prehistory, and geology), and limited drinking-water and horse-watering facilities.

Trail users should be alert for wildlife. Mule deer are often seen at twilight and dawn. Elk or moose sightings are possible. Marmots can be found right along the trail.

In winter, birdwatchers can scan the cottonwood trees along the Weber River north of Wanship for roosting bald eagles. Other birds of prey and owls inhabit the area. Wetland meadows are habitat for sandhill cranes and waterfowl. Areas with willow, dogwood, and wild rose are good places to see songbirds.

Fish are visible in Silver Creek, which empties into the Weber River. During the time of the silver mines, the creek was known as Poison Creek, but the water quality has improved and trout species have returned.

Geology is of interest in the trail area. The Uinta Mountains and the Wasatch Range intersect here to make some fascinating geology. An extensive metallic mineral belt stretches west of Park City. Extensive fossil excavations in the Silver Creek Junction area revealed that mammoths, saber-tooth cats, camels, and other species lived in the region more than

Bicyclists and mountain vistas on the Historic Union Pacific Rail Trail

40,000 years ago. Ancient volcanic deposits are found near Wanship. The area around Coalville once looked like a swampy coastal plain.

Human history includes the habitation by Fremont Indians and later the Ute and Shoshone Indians. The northern end of the rail trail intersects the Mormon Pioneer National Historic Trail. A trail connection goes to Jordanelle State Park and another connection is proposed to Rockport State Park. A regional trail system with linkages to other trails is planned for the future.

This historic rail trail is a wonderful way to link communities in a more leisurely way and for users to see the land and its life forms up close. It also preserves this recreational strip from development.

JORDANELLE STATE PARK

Hours/Season: Overnight; year-round at Hailstone (open July 1995), April to September at Rock Cliff
Area: Not available
Facilities: Picnic tables, group pavilions, play areas, beach with safe swimming area, 100 trailer sites with full hookups, 60 campsites, 40 close walk-in campsites, primitive hike-in sites at Crandall Point, wheelchair-accessible restrooms with showers, laundry, sewage disposal, visitor center with theater, amphitheater, 76-slip marina with utility hookups, fuel dispensing, boat ramps, jet-ski ramp, wheelchair-accessible fishing deck, fish cleaning station, general store, restaurant, first-aid station, ranger station at Hailstone; picnic tables, group pavilions, nature center/environmental study area, 50 walk-in campsites (some for those with physical disabilities), wheelchair-accessible restrooms with showers, boardwalk interpretive trail, boat ramp for small

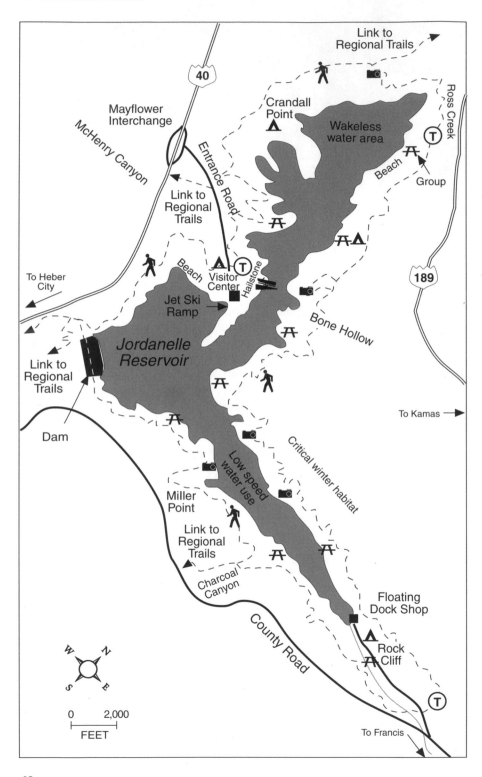

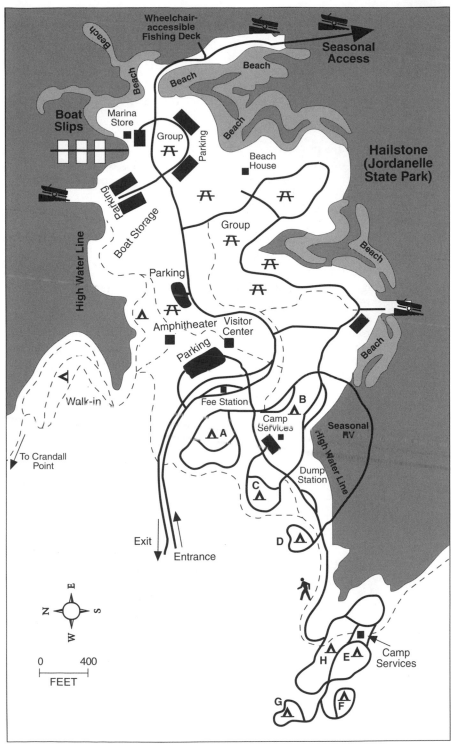

Wheelchair-accessible Fishing Deck

Seasonal Access

Beach

Beach

Beach

Beach

Boat Slips

Marina Store

Group

Parking

Beach House

Hailstone (Jordanelle State Park)

Parking

Boat Storage

Group

Beach

High Water Line

Parking

Amphitheater

Visitor Center

Beach

Parking

Walk-in

Fee Station

B

Camp Services

Seasonal RV

High Water Line

A

To Crandall Point

Dump Station

C

Exit

Entrance

D

N E S W

H

E

Camp Services

0   400

FEET

G

F

hand-launched watercraft, fish cleaning station, ranger station at Rock Cliff; phone: (801) 645-8036

Attractions: Boating, windsurfing, paddling, water skiing, sandy beaches, swimming, hiking, mountain biking, cross-country skiing, horseback riding, jogging, nature study, dining, fishing (ice fishing in winter), wildlife viewing

Access: *Hailstone* is 6 miles north of Heber off US 40. *Rock Cliff* is 2 miles west of Francis off Utah 32

Jordanelle, Utah's newest state park, is located on the shores of a brand new reservoir impounded by a dam on the Provo River, with waters also entering from Ross Creek, Drain Tunnel Creek, and other small tributaries. Part of the Central Utah Project, the reservoir and dam construction was a major project requiring relocation of several sections of highways and roads.

The dam is 296 feet high and contains water with a normal surface area of 3,068 acres at an elevation of 6,100 feet. Because of the deeper and steeper valleys that hold Jordanelle Reservoir, more water volume is contained. Irrigation storage at Jordanelle will stabilize twelve of the small reservoirs located on the Upper Provo River and enhance fishing and recreation on those lakes.

Completion of facilities for Jordanelle State Park is the result of a thirty-year project. Hailstone, the primary developed site, is on the west shore of the north arm of the lake, where the terrain is fairly flat and there is easy access from US 40.

Jordanelle Dam and Reservoir at Jordanelle State Park

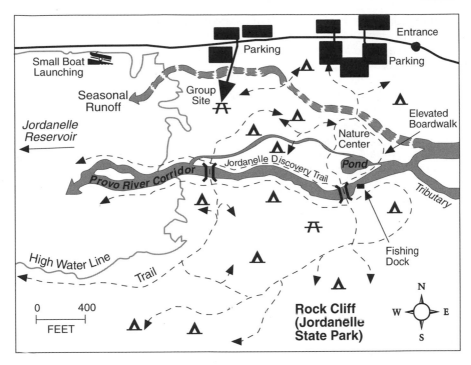

The high-quality facilities of Hailstone are clustered to simulate a village—with consistent architectural features—that has a marina as a focal point. This marina is located on the north side of Hailstone, in a protected cove, with a large boat ramp, boat slips, dock, and considerable trailer parking space.

Terraced beaches on the south and east sides of this peninsula are good for sunbathing, with day-use facilities and the wooded area of McHenry Canyon backing the beach areas. A wheelchair-accessible fishing deck, a couple of smaller boat docks, and a jet-ski ramp are located near the beach area. Windsurfing is good on the long expanses of water in both the north and east arms of the reservoir.

Several camping areas are available. Most are situated on the southwest end of the peninsula, some with hookups. Walk-in camping is adjacent to the amphitheater. Those wanting to move away from the crowd can choose primitive hike-in sites on Crandall Point, which is on the north side of the peninsula.

A good way to locate yourself in the park is with a visit to the Hailstone Visitor Center. A topographical model shows a detailed map of Jordanelle State Park and the adjacent area. A push-button display highlights recreation areas, points of interest, visitor services, and interpretive facilities. An electronic bulletin board with changing messages updates visitors on current information.

71

The main exhibit room presents an overview of human history in the Jordanelle area, including that of the native peoples who lived here long ago. You can also learn details about how the Central Utah Project moves water through mountains into arid countryside, and who benefits.

The Rock Cliff area includes both a Provo River section above the dam and a part of the reservoir. People interested in nature study and those wanting to launch a canoe will like this area. The Nature Center has maps, numerous environmental programs, exhibits on water and its endless cycle, information on the various habitats and their flora and fauna, plus some human activities that affect them, and an interactive display. The center is adjacent to a pond area that simulates a natural stream-fed pond, with a variety of life that varies with the seasons.

Because Rock Cliff is situated among numerous riparian wetlands, the sensitive nature of this habitat is preserved with a series of trails and elevated boardwalks. These connect with the Nature Center and other activity areas. Bridges cross waterways at four points. Fishing in the reservoir arm that backs up to the Rock Cliff site may prove to be the best in the lake, with catches of rainbow trout, browns, and smallmouth bass.

Camping at Rock Cliff is more nature oriented, with spacious walk-in campsites scattered through 100 acres of riparian habitat to give campers some seclusion. Some of these sites are for visitors with physical disabilities. Because of the abundant wildlife in this area, dogs are prohibited.

The Jordanelle Discovery Trail at Rock Cliff is a nature path with interpretive signs that winds through the Provo River riparian terrain, which

Nature Center in the Rock Cliff area of Jordanelle State Park

has various seasonal channels. The Provo River is a major Utah river that empties into Utah Lake. It was named for eighteenth-century fur trapper Etienne Provost. In this popular fishing stream, anglers catch rainbow, cutthroat, and a few brook trout. Another fish is the native whitefish that grows to 10 or 11 inches in length and is more difficult to catch than the trout.

The trees of the riparian community at Rock Cliff are primarily willow (soil-binding bank stabilizers) and narrowleaf cottonwoods that are tall and provide cooling shade and nesting places for eagles and other raptors. More than 160 bird species live or visit here. Take time to listen for their songs. The most obvious evidence of riparian animals is the beaver-chewed cottonwoods.

The hillsides of Jordanelle State Park are a drier terrain, with sagebrush and oak-brush, habitat for mule deer. Elk are occasionally seen within the park, and upland game birds frequent the hillside community.

For summer and winter use, Jordanelle has 27 miles of trails that encircle the entire reservoir. A variety of nonmotorized recreation seekers can use the trails—mountain bikers, joggers, hikers, horseback riders, and cross-country skiers. No motorized vehicles are allowed. When traveling the trail between Rock Cliff and the Ross Creek area, a critical winter-range area for mule deer is traversed. This section may be closed at the ranger's discretion to protect the wildlife. From Hailstone, a 2-mile spur connects to the Historic Union Pacific Rail Trail, with a staging area along US 189 called Phoston.

Future plans call for the Ross Creek site to be located on the north arm of the reservoir, with trail access for hikers and wakeless access for windsurfers, with a group picnic area as well.

WASATCH MOUNTAIN STATE PARK

Hours/Season: Overnight; year-round
Area: 21,592 acres
Facilities: Picnic tables, 139 campsites, wheelchair-accessible restrooms with showers, utility hookups, group camping, sewage disposal, group pavilions, visitor center, Chalet (group facilities), 27-hole golf course, full-service pro shop, driving range, practice greens, concessionaire, phone: (801) 654-1791 (visitor center), (801) 654-0532 (golf course)
Attractions: Hiking, golfing, fishing, cross-country skiing, snowmobiling, horseback riding, nature study, campfire program
Access: Take Utah 113 west from Heber City to center of Midway and then jog north on 200 W and jog again west on 200 N. Turn north on Homestead Drive. The visitor center sits where Homestead Drive becomes Snake Creek Road. The campground is reached by taking Warm Spring Road (on the east side of the visitor center) to intercept Pine Creek Road north. The golf-course road branches off just before the campground is reached. (This route is signed.) To reach the chalet

group-use area, continue on Utah 113 from Midway south to Tate Lane and take this to the chalet

▲ Wasatch Mountain is Utah's most developed state park. This vast landscape of almost 22,000 acres edges the Heber Valley on the east and climbs up into the Wasatch Mountain hinterlands to the west. Only Antelope Island, with a vast amount of undeveloped land, is a larger state park. Wasatch Mountain is the most visited of the parks with almost 900,000 visitors in 1993. It is both a summer and winter wonderland, where horseback riders will find plenty of room.

The visitor center is a good place to orient yourself if you are not familiar with the park. Here, at an elevation of 6,000 feet, is a helpful information resource—maps, brochures, travel guides, local material, and a bulletin board with current events, activities, and points of interest. A ranger will be glad to fill in any gaps.

A large pond is located near the visitor center. Children twelve years old and under are allowed to fish if they are chaperoned. Colorful red and green dragonflies whirl around the edge of the water.

The USGA-sanctioned, 27-hole golf course is the major attraction when weather permits. The par-72 course is framed by the Wasatch Mountains as they overlook Heber Valley, and the course is quite picturesque with ten lakes located throughout the tree-lined fairways. Since this is a busy focus of recreation, be sure to make reservations for tee times. A cafe and fountain add to the amenities.

Golfers at Wasatch Mountain State Park

Pine Creek Campground (with 122 of the campsites) is near the golf course for easy access. The on-site office has visitor information, and the staff has transplanted wildflowers to augment the small constructed pool in front of the building. Three loops—Cottonwood, Mahogany, and Oak Hollow—provide choices in campsites. Oak Hollow has tent pads. No tenting is allowed in Cottonwood or Mahogany. Water and electrical hookups are available to all sites, with 66 having sewer connections. Cottonwood has the best shade, with tall trees particularly near Pine Creek, which runs through this loop only. The east side of Cot-

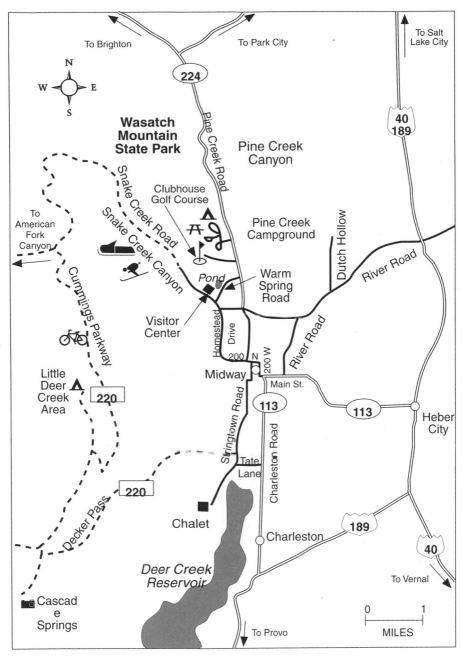

tonwood is more open with meadows containing a lot of wildflowers. Cattails are numerous in the wet areas near the creek. Hummingbirds, woodpeckers, and a variety of songbirds are frequently seen and heard. On summer weekends, the nearby amphitheater has campfire programs.

The two group-use pavilions (for up to 100 people each), Cottonwood and Oak, are near the campground area, with restrooms, parking, and volleyball and horseshoe-throwing recreational facilities.

Walkers can do considerable exploring from the campground area. A trail branches off behind campsite #17 in Cottonwood and comes out by the golf course. This same trail branches off north to connect to the other campground loops, the group pavilion parking lot, and eventually to the Pine Creek Nature Trail. Just past the trail from the pavilion parking lot, an old overgrown road that skirts the woods branches off and can be walked to the golf-course driving range. Except for the connecting path to the nature trail, these other paths and the road are not official trails, but they offer fine exploring.

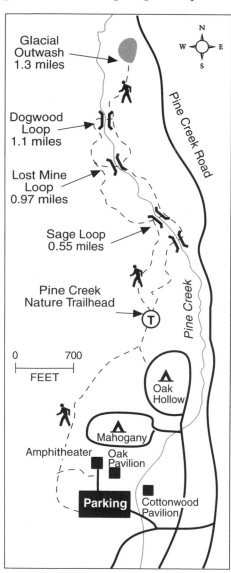

The Pine Creek Nature Trail, which takes off from the northwest corner of the Oak Hollow Campground loop, is very worthwhile, a delightful excursion into the natural world. It is a 1.3-mile loop if one takes the longest loop to the terminus at a glacial outwash, but several shorter loops are possible. The Sage Loop is 0.55 mile; the Lost Mine Loop is 0.97 mile; and the Dogwood Loop is 1.1 miles. The paths go on both sides of Pine Creek and cross it on bridges four times, so numerous variations are possible.

The beginning elevation is 6,100 feet, and the glacial wash is at 6,320 feet, but there are ups and downs at each bridge crossing. Rest areas are found along the trail and provide quiet times for observing wildlife. This is typical canyon riparian environment, where nature flourishes.

The trail is more open at first, gradually getting more into heavy shade, until the great boulders are seen at the terminal wash. Informative signs are found along the trail. Watch for mule deer tracks and their antler rubbings on smaller aspen trees. Gambel scrub oak is profuse in these foothills and canyons, with blazes of orange color in autumn. Other small trees are narrowleaf cottonwood, chokecherry, and quaking aspen. Common plants include big sagebrush, rabbitbrush, serviceberry, bracken fern, Oregon grape, and red-osier dogwood. You can find fresh puffball mushrooms even in the heat of August, and the sound of the creek is soothing.

Herbivores—rabbits, squirrels, and chipmunks—are attracted to this lush vegetation. Songbirds nest in the trees and birds of prey can be seen. Mammals are more elusive, but the area is habitat for fox, coyote, skunk, bobcat, and mountain lion.

A primitive group campground and picnicking area, Little Deer Creek is a remote, mountain facility located about 10 miles up a graded road. It has 17 tent sites, drinking water, modern restrooms, but no showers or electricity.

The chalet is another group-use facility that is located at the south end of the state park, on the upper side of Deer Creek Reservoir. This is a ranch-type building with kitchen (stove with oven, refrigerator, double sinks, and counter space), folding banquet tables and chairs (up to fifty people), fireplace, furnace, restrooms, but no showers or sleeping accommodations. Furnish your own cooking utensils and tableware. The facilities include a baseball diamond, volleyball standards, horseshoe pit, barbecue grills, open fire pit, and limited parking. There is space for some recreational vehicles (no hookups) and tent camping. Make reservations for a maximum stay of three nights. A path leads down to the water, a wetland place where sandhill cranes can be spotted.

Family at fishing pond, Wasatch Mountain State Park

Winter activities are not neglected at Wasatch Mountain State Park. It is considered the finest and most complete snowmobiling facility in Utah. Destinations include Pine Creek, Snake Creek, and American Fork canyons. Facilities include parking, restrooms, designated play areas, and about 90 miles of maintained snowmobile trails. Both the visitor center and the golf-course clubhouse are used as warming stations.

The golf course is groomed for skiing, with a 7.2-mile Nordic ski track with diagonal stride and skating lanes. Both flat and hilly terrain is found on this track, and the scenery includes farm and mountain views. Nordic skis, snowmobile equipment, and snowmobiles can be rented here. Snow-mobile tours are also available.

Advanced bicycle riders (Homestead Resort across from the park has rentals) can take the 25-mile loop that begins at the state park visitor center and continues northwest on Snake Creek Road, then connects with Cummings Parkway (Utah 220) going south. At the intersection to Cascade Springs, continue northeast on Utah 220, now Decker Pass, to Stringtown Road, and north to the center of Midway. Although some of this tour is paved, most is on dirt roads.

DEER CREEK STATE PARK

Hours/Season: Overnight; April to November
Area: 3,260 acres
Facilities: Picnic tables, 33 campsites, group camping, wheelchair-accessible restrooms with showers, group pavilion, sewage disposal, boat ramps, courtesy (loading) docks, fish cleaning stations, concessionaires, phone: (801) 654-0171
Attractions: Boating, sailing, windsurfing, fishing (ice fishing in winter), swimming, water skiing, concessionaire, dining
Nearby: Alpine Scenic Loop, Utah 92
Access: 7 miles southwest of Heber City on US 189

If you arrive at Deer Creek State Park from the southwest via US 189, you will cross the 1,304-foot-long top of the dam that was constructed between 1938 and 1940 as a federal project. The earth-filled structure is 235 feet high and impounds the water of the Provo River at an elevation of 5,400 feet in Deer Creek Reservoir. Its waters are used for culinary, fishery, agricultural, and recreational purposes.

In the southwest corner of the Heber Valley, the park is named after a major creek tributary below the dam, rather than the Provo River, whose waters originate in the high country of the Uinta Mountains at Trial Lake.

Established in 1971, the state park has several developed recreation areas along the long eastern edge of the reservoir. From the south, the first entry station is at the Main Boat Ramp and Sailboat Beach areas.

The campground in the Main Boat Ramp area has individual sites, with some trees for shade, that overlook the reservoir near Wallsburg Bay, a long finger of water that projects east and diverts the highway. Reservations are advised as this area is jumping on summer weekends with a flotilla of jet skiers, motorboaters, and water skiers. A few individual walk-in campsites are also available by reservation or on a first-come basis. These serve their purpose if you are pitching a tent, though users of the upper ones must access their spots by walking through the lower sites. If you sleep in your small rig, however, they are terrible, particularly since parking is on a sloping gravel lot, which is also a through road to group camping and water access. These sites are provided with grills and picnic tables but lack shade and are incredibly hot on a typical summer day. Picnic tables are scattered about the many viewpoints of the park.

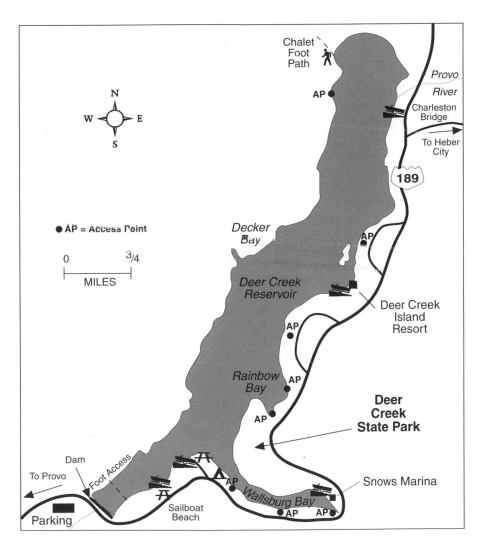

Campsite with a view of the Wasatch Mountains at Deer Creek State Park

This is not a quiet place due to the whine of motors on the water, though early rising before 7:00 A.M. rewards with quiet and some fishermen enjoying a peaceful float on the water.

A road continues south from this area to Sailboat Beach, where picnic tables and vault toilets are found. The canyon walls of the reservoir provide predictable afternoon winds for sailors. The mountain view from this area is of 11,750-foot, snow-peaked Mount Timpanogos, a splendid sight.

Several fishing spots are accessed from the highway, some with vault toilets, as you drive north along the water from this developed area. The major day-use area of the park is at Deer Creek Island Resort where one entrance station is located. Beach picnicking, restrooms, a boat ramp, boat rentals, sailboard rental and instruction, and the Dock of the Bay Restaurant are located here.

At the upper or north end of the reservoir, the Charleston Bridge day-use area is popular with fishermen wanting some quiet along this wetland terminus where sandhill cranes and great blue herons are often spotted. A boat ramp and vault toilet are found, but no picnic tables.

Each year, the reservoir is stocked with 170,000 rainbow trout. Yellow perch, brown trout, largemouth bass, walleye, carp, and crayfish naturally reproduce in these waters.

In 1984, the quality of the treated water, which over 763,000 people drink, was not good, as it was polluted by excessive nutrients, primarily phosphorus. This stimulated algae growth, gave the water a foul odor and taste, increased water-treatment costs, and depleted the oxygen supply needed for fish survival. Cleanup is underway, however, as a result of combined efforts. A new $15 million sewage treatment system has been installed, and new health regulations are strictly enforced. Local dairies did their part by building animal-waste storage facilities. The Midway Fish Hatchery constructed a new settling pond. New restrooms were built along the water, and public education has helped.

For several scenic attractions, travel south of the dam along the Provo River to Utah 92, the 24-mile Alpine Scenic Loop, and take this route over the mountains to Interstate 15. This is a paved road, but rather narrow and winding with caution particularly advised on busy weekends.

Sundance is 3 miles uphill. This is the product of Robert Redford's vision of a community of recreation, the arts, and a commitment to the environment. The setting is superb, with a rushing mountain stream between structures that marry comfortably to the wilderness surroundings and some cottages peeking out from high up in the woods. In winter, Sundance is a ski resort.

Another 7 miles and the Cascade Scenic Drive heads off to the right and leads travelers to a series of springs in a lush wetland area.

Back on the main route, and 9 miles past Sundance, is the trailhead to the top of 11,750-foot Mount Timpanogos. Very popular, this 15-mile round-trip hike is long but not overly strenuous, if you're in good condition and can handle the high elevation. Or you can sample a short section by hiking 1.5 miles to a rustic overlook with a view of Scout Falls.

Past this trail, the drive through American Fork Canyon has grand scenery and passes Timpanogos Cave National Monument, a very busy place on summer weekends.

According to legend, the name Timpanogos came about by combining the names of ill-fated lovers: Timpanac and Ucanogos. Timpanac was a member of the Nez Perce Indians from the north who originally met Ucanogos when he traveled south to barter furs for food in a year of drought. When it was time for Ucanogos to marry, she asked her father to hold a contest, hoping that Timpanac, who she sent word to, would win. The final contest was to climb to the top of a high mountain, a skill that her favorite possessed. Instead, his opponents hid at the steepest part of the climb, before the contest started, and pushed Timpanac off the mountain to his death. In her sadness, Ucanogos threw herself off the mountain after praying to the Great Spirit to join her soul with Timpanac's, and it is said that this happened and their two hearts hang as one in the heart of Timpanogos Cave.

Utah Lake State Park

Hours/Season: Overnight; year-round
Area: 308 acres
Facilities: Picnic tables, 3 group picnic sites, 73 campsites, group camp-

ing, wheelchair-accessible restrooms with showers, visitor center, sewage disposal, marina with 78 boat slips, 4 boat ramps, fish cleaning stations, wheelchair-accessible fishing area, Olympic-size ice rink (December to March), phone: (801) 375-0731

Attractions: Boating, sailing, paddling, windsurfing, swimming, fishing (ice fishing in winter), wildlife viewing, ice skating, roller skating

Access: 3 miles west of Interstate 15, from exit 268

At an elevation of 4,500 feet, Utah Lake State Park lies on the eastern shore of the largest natural freshwater lake west of the Mississippi River. The park was originally the Provo Boat Harbor before it was donated to the state park system in 1967. Though large in area (96,000 acres), Utah Lake is not deep. Today it averages about 10 feet in depth, with the greatest depth about 18 feet. Because of its shallowness, the waters do not appear really clear since the wave action stirs up sediments, though it seems fine for swimming, fishing, and water skiing.

At least the level of the lake is fairly stable now, which wasn't so in the past. It once varied greatly between being a mudhole or at flood stage, but it is now artificially maintained with diversion of the lake's water by a vast network of canals between the lake and Great Salt Lake. The natural outlet is the Jordan River. Actually, the building of these canals provoked considerable debates between farmers and industrialists. At one time during a drought, there was only a foot of water in places and all the fish died. Since the 1970s, however, an emphasis on recreation has kept the level fairly consistent, except during the severe flooding in 1982–83, which destroyed the state park. It has been restored to full operating status and is the fourth most popular state park.

The Cedar Valley Mountains rise above the western shore of the lake, and the Wasatch Mountains provide vistas to the north and east. The American Fork River feeds the lake farther north of the park. The Provo River flows into Utah Lake on the edge of the developed area of the park, a very pleasant wetland landscape that abuts the grassy lawn of several of the campsites. The city of Provo and the river are named after Etienne Provost, one of the Anglo discoverers of Great Salt Lake.

The park entry goes past wide expanses of green picnic areas to a large paved parking lot where spaces are marked off for camping. Some campsites front the interior harbor; others front the Provo River.

Roads connect to breakwaters where piers are located on both sides of the harbor area. Fishing is for channel catfish, walleye, white bass, black bass, and several different species of panfish. A remnant of ancient Lake Bonneville, the lake has been a major fishery off and on since prehistoric times. The Channel Catfish Clinic is held annually at the park in mid-July. In late July, the Utah Lake Walleye Workshop is held here. White bass and panfish clinics are also held in the summer.

Utah State Park is unusual in having an Olympic-size ice rink that is open to ice skaters from December through March. In summer, however, nature is the entertainer and wonderful masses of swallows scavenge for insects while other wildlife can be seen while exploring. A lot of ducks find the Provo River to their liking, and some belligerent geese can be quite defensive of their wetland territory. The white pelicans in the vicinity are always crowd or individual pleasers. A bridge crosses the water for further exploring. The river is a good place to paddle a canoe.

Little indigenous vegetation survives, except for some long-leaf poplar trees, but a major landscaping effort has supplied greenery of cork-screw willow, dome willow, weeping willow, hybrid cottonwood, maple, blue and green spruce, Lombardi poplar, mountain ash, birch, and flowering plum.

Possible wildlife sightings include skunks, weasels, opossums, raccoons, beavers, muskrats, pheasants, quail, great horned owls, red-tailed hawks, Cooper's hawks, and a variety of shorebirds. Canada geese, mallards, pintails, wood ducks, teals, redheads, canvasbacks, and other ducks such as the goldeneye and ruddy migrate in and out of the area. A sharp eye may spot an occasional bald or golden eagle.

It was on the eastern shore of Utah Lake where Ute Indians became acquainted with Father Silvestre Velez de Escalante and Father Francisco Atanasio Dominguez in 1776. At that time the lake was called Timpanogos (meaning "the stone one"). The Spanish needed a trade route from Santa Fe to California, and they thought there was a waterway in Utah that might give them that. Also expected to scout out Indian settlements for missionary work, the expedition included six other explorers and a mapmaker. Several Indian scouts were added along the way. These Native Americans told the missionaries of Great Salt Lake to the north a tantalizing tale of the River Tizon that was said to flow from that lake to the Pacific. Unfortunately, the missionaries were out of supplies and time, so they returned to New Mexico by heading south. The Utes liked these explorers and wanted them to return, and though the Fathers tried to get missionaries sent back to them, the Spanish leaders decided against it. These explorers were probably the first Europeans to visit what is now Utah.

The Escalante-Dominguez Expedition was not successful in its goals. There were no converts made and no route to the sea found, yet their trip was an extraordinary feat in traversing the

Marina at Utah Lake State Park

rugged country of Utah, which included the Paria Canyon area, Split Mountain on the Green River, and the Wasatch Range. The mapmaker, Don Bernardo Miera y Pacheco, charted the first Utah maps.

Contemplate the course of history if the Spanish had stayed and been in Utah when the Mormons decided to come west. But that didn't happen, and the first church to settle Utah was the Mormon Church, not the Catholic one.

For a closer look at today's environment around Utah Lake, bicyclists can take the 100-mile loop around the lake by following either the highway or low-traffic frontage roads. This fairly easy route on mostly level terrain passes farms and harbor areas and goes through small towns.

VETERANS MEMORIAL STATE PARK

Hours/Season: Day use; year-round
Area: 30 acres
Facilities: Museum, wheelchair-accessible restrooms, phone: (801) 254-9036
Attractions: Cemetery, wall of honor, chapel
Access: On Utah 68, 3 miles south of Bluffdale at 17111 Camp Williams Road

▲ Until four years ago, Utah did not have a Utah Veterans Memorial Park, a facility that was needed. That omission was remedied when Utah Veterans Memorial State Park was conceived, constructed, and then dedicated on May 28, 1990. A generous donation of his services by architect Kevin Scholz helped make this park possible. Scholz did this to honor his father, Carl Scholz, a Marine who died on active duty.

The chapel is a very striking and innovative structure five stories high that seats 200 people in concentric circles around the clergy and the deceased. This arrangement fosters a feeling of sharing and togetherness.

Several purposes are served with this memorial state park. An honored burial ground is available to eligible Utah veterans, their spouses, and dependent children. The chapel can be used for memorial services, funerals, and meditation. It honors and memorializes Armed Forces veterans of all wars. It pays tribute to national, state, military, and other leaders. It houses a museum of military artifacts, uniforms, and related memorabilia.

A special feature of the park is the Wall of Honor. Besides holding vertical squares with the names of deceased veterans and loved ones, it contains the names of contributors to the construction and development of Memorial Park. Names of individuals, organizations, and businesses can still be added. Names are engraved on the Granite Wall for a donation of $100, the Bronze Wall for $500.

Some have called this park the "Arlington of the West." Simple government headstones/markers are used on the open lawn backed by distant mountains. Those marking graves in Plat A are flat, light-gray granite ones, while upright white marble stones are used in Plat B.

CAMP FLOYD/STAGECOACH INN STATE PARK

Hours/Season: Day use; 11:00 A.M. to 5:00 P.M. daily, Easter weekend to October 15
Area: 42 acres
Facilities: Picnic tables, museum, restrooms, Stagecoach Inn (visitor center), military cemetery; camping on Easter and Memorial Day weekends near cemetery, phone: (801) 768-8932
Attractions: History exhibits, military cemetery, stop on Overland Stage and Pony Express routes, interpretive tours
Access: 25 miles southwest of Lehi on Utah 73

As one arrives at Camp Floyd/Stagecoach Inn State Park, after crossing a desert that seems scarcely inhabited, it takes some imagination to see why Mormon John Carson and a small group of settlers picked this spot to found the village of Fairfield in 1855. Consider, however, that these pioneers found water and saw tall waving grasses, not today's desert of sagebrush, saltbush, greasewood, and rabbitbrush.

When John Charles Fremont was exploring this country, grasslands covered three-fourths of the Great Basin, but today's overgrazed rangeland is dominated by sagebrush, even though it is not very palatable to cattle. Sagebrush has the largest range of any ecosystem in the western United States, nearly 300 million acres. The most important herbivore of sagebrush desert is the black-tailed jackrabbit, an animal that has adapted to this desert by using vasodilation to withstand hyperthermia.

The pioneers viewed a different landscape from that of today. To defend themselves from Indian attacks, they constructed a square stone fort (66 feet on each side) and built log and adobe houses inside it. They cultivated some land and planted trees at this elevation of 4,900 feet.

If today this place seems isolated, then it is thought-provoking that from 1858 to 1861 this location quartered the largest troop concentration in the United States. From Fort Leavenworth, Kansas, a United States Army detachment marched toward Utah with 3,500 men, 586 horses, 500 wagons, and 3,000 mules—infantry, cavalry, artillery, engineers, ambulances, brass bands, and supply trains—in response to orders from President Buchanan.

It is not clear from conflicting sources exactly why the Army was ordered here, but the rumors were that the Mormons of Utah might rebel against the government of the United States. Before the marchers reached Utah, further orders instructed the Army not to harm the Mormons unless there were problems. Brigham Young, in turn, promised no resistance if the Army was peaceful and did not remain in the Salt Lake City area. Young helped to maintain peace by essentially evacuating that city, except for a few watchmen at strategic points.

Under the command of Albert Sydney Johnston, the Army descended Emigration Canyon—the route of the Mormon pioneers—and marched straight across the city without incident, stepping to the band's playing of

"One-Eyed Riley." The soldiers continued on to Fairfield, where pasture for the animals and supplies of water and wood were found, though little else. And so they were stationed 1,100 miles from food and other essentials, which had to be freighted to them.

The Army was busy that year building between 300 and 400 structures. Barracks, mess halls, stables, warehouses, officers quarters, headquarters buildings, blacksmith shops, and corrals were erected immediately south of the little stream that separated the village and the Army post.

When construction was completed on November 9, 1858, General Johnston ordered a full-dress military review. The flag was hoisted during the playing of the "Star-Spangled Banner," and the post was officially named Camp Floyd after the Secretary of War at the time.

Fairfield changed. Hard cash was something not usually found in the vicinity of the Rocky Mountains at this time. The Army payroll enticed a great influx of people—including tradespeople, mechanics, craftspeople, saloonkeepers, gamblers, and women. The population swelled to 7,000 or more, almost half that of Salt Lake City at the time.

The stone fort became obsolete and was taken down. The two-story frame-and-adobe Stagecoach Inn that still stands today was built by John Carson. In the Mormon tradition, it was a place of morality, with no liquor allowed, in contrast to the wild ways elsewhere in town, where there were seventeen saloons.

The camp was finished before the time of the Overland Stage and the Pony Express, but both soon arrived, and the first Overland Stage station out of Salt Lake City was established at the Carson Inn of Fairfield in 1858. The Pony Express stopped here during its daring runs from April 3, 1860 to October 26, 1861, when the telegraph made it obsolete. Young men (preferably orphans because of the risks involved) rode from one station to the next.

The Carson Inn, now known as the Stagecoach Inn, was respectable and had prominent visitors. Mark Twain, Horace Greeley, and many well-known actors and actresses stopped on their way to San Francisco.

The camp was well-disciplined and also had its cultural attractions. A theater was built and plays were held regularly. Other amusements included a German singing club, a circus company, a billiard hall, dances and balls, and the first Masonic Lodge in Utah. More reckless entertainment was just across the creek at Fairfield, often called "Frogtown."

Camp Floyd was also a historic site for journalism. The first non-Mormon newspaper, the *Valley Tan*, was conceived here. Founder Kirk Anderson made it an opposition newspaper, though a later publisher supported Mormon politics.

There was no Mormon rebellion. Instead, the troops were gradually called East when the Civil War threatened. General Johnston was replaced in August of 1860 by Colonel Philip St. George Cooke, who changed the name of the camp to Fort Crittenden, since Floyd had defected to the Confederacy.

Buildings were torn down, hauled away, or burned. Too dangerous to be moved quickly, or to get into Confederate hands, the accumulation of mu-

Stagecoach Inn at Camp Floyd/Stagecoach Inn State Park

nitions and weaponry was set on fire, ending the occupation with a great explosion. By July 27, 1861, the Army was gone and 4 million dollars' worth of Army surplus was auctioned off for $100,000. By September 2, 1861, the village shrank to eighteen families.

Visitors to the state park today can tour the restored Stagecoach Inn, complete with period furnishings. Enclosed by a picket fence, the grounds of the inn are a cool, shady delight in the midst of arid desert. An awesome huge, old willow tree in the center of green lawn is just one of the many shade trees. A covered picnic pavilion and restrooms edge the lawn. The day I was there, the only other people were a few children and a young girl swirling around the green, enjoying themselves immensely.

During the years of 1993 and 1994, the Stagecoach Inn was again renovated and closed for repairs. A new roof, new floors, and a radiant-type heating system were installed. The facility will be operational again for the 1995–96 season.

Across the street, the only surviving Army building is the commissary. A reminder of earlier times, the Camp Floyd cemetery remains and is 0.5 mile northwest, via a road. Through the efforts of the Utah Historical Society and the American Legion, this final resting place has been rehabilitated and markers have been placed for each of the eighty-four graves there. A gentle breeze blows among the old willows and Russian olive trees in the cemetery.

Camping is allowed on Easter and Memorial Day weekends in the large parking lot of the cemetery. Picnic tables are available.

GREAT SALT LAKE COUNTRY

▲Almost the mirror image of the Golden Spike Empire, Great Salt Lake Country contains half of Great Salt Lake and half of the Great Salt Lake Desert, yet there is a whole set of additional scenic attractions.

West of the lake, where traveling between Salt Lake Valley and San Francisco was once a dreaded experience, daring people come to race the fastest of machines on the Bonneville Salt Flats, the bottom of prehistoric Lake Bonneville. Record speeds of over 600 miles per hour have been set on the smooth salt surface of the Bonneville Speedway.

The seemingly hard surface of the salt flats does collect water, however, in spring and winter, and sometimes mires unwary amateurs in the gray-green mud. Yet by the time this water is blown away by the wind and evaporates, it has smoothed the surface and fashioned a better raceway. The salt flats are also a place where one can see the curvature of the Earth over dry land.

Road and mountain bikers can tour the less crowded terrain of Tooele County, which stretches from the south end of Great Salt Lake west to Nevada. Routes lead to dazzling deserts, the forested Oquirrh Mountains, the Kennecott Mine overlook, Ophir Canyon, Stansbury Island, ghost towns, and the old Pony Express Trail. Rockhounders will be interested to know that the Dugway Mountains, southwest of Tooele, are known for their geodes.

Between the popular recreational edge of Great Salt Lake and the forested slopes of the Wasatch Front lies the broad Salt Lake Valley, which the Mormons picked to be their "Zion." Salt Lake City, the state's largest metropolis, is a cultural center complete with the Utah State Capitol, Mormon Temple and Salt Lake Tabernacle, and the famed genealogical records at the Mormon Family History Library.

Opposite: *Covered-wagon ride at This Is The Place State Park*

A short distance southeast of Salt Lake City, Little Cottonwood Canyon Scenic Byway is a 7-mile drive into the Wasatch Range to two ski and summer resorts, Alta and Snowbird. Seasonal pluses in this rugged glacier-carved canyon are fishing in Little Cottonwood Creek, fields of wildflowers, great autumn colors, and many hiking trails, including wheelchair-accessible ones.

With the vastly different terrains of the region, activities can revolve around selected climates. Summer days are usually over ninety degrees in the valleys, though cool at night, and winter daytimes are in the thirties, with only moderate snowfall. The mountains, of course, are cooler in summer and often hazardous from winter snowstorms.

GREAT SALT LAKE STATE PARK

Hours/Season: Overnight; year-round
Area: 3,115 acres
Facilities: Picnic tables, group pavilion, primitive camping, visitor center, restrooms, vault toilets, open showers, 240-slip marina, concessionaire, phone: (801) 250-1898
Attractions: Boating, swimming, sandy beach, wildlife viewing
Access: Off exit 104 on Interstate 80, 16 miles west of Salt Lake City

It is not surprising that Great Salt Lake is the second most visited of Utah's state parks. It is a place of sunsets and vistas, boundless mud flats, Franklin sea gulls, isolated islands, easy floating for swimmers, and year-round boating on a saltwater lake that never freezes. If the lake is low, newly exposed rocks, driftwood, and weeds will have a coating of stunning salt crystals.

Historically, the lake's salinity has varied between 5 and 27 percent, depending on the amount of water the lake contains. Water flows in from the Bear River (its greatest source), the Jordan River, and the Weber River, and a considerable amount comes from precipitation. It does not flow out anywhere, though. It has no outlet, because it is on the floor of the Great Basin, and hence salts accumulate from inflowing water. Evaporation of water intensifies the situation. Besides common sodium chloride, there are fifteen other salts.

Great Salt Lake is a shrunken remnant of ancient Lake Bonneville, a great freshwater sea that covered more than 20,000 square miles (roughly ten times the present area) and about a third of Utah, with an extreme depth of 1,100 feet. Geologists point out the terraces or benches, about 1,000 feet above the level of Great Salt Lake, that were carved along the eastern edge of the basin (on the Wasatch Range to the east) by the waves of the old Ice Age lake.

When John Charles Fremont explored this area, searching for the mythical river from the Rockies to the ocean, he saw that it was a vast area of in-

Saltair Pavilion at Great Salt Lake State Park

ternal drainage, with no outlet, and named it the "Great Basin" in 1843. It should be noted, however, as Wallace Stegner points out in his book *Mormon Country*, that "the first Anglo-American tracks in a large part of the Mormon Country were the tracks of Jed Smith," and what he did sure helped Fremont. Jed Smith was one of the best of the mountain men, an intelligent explorer who knew the West and had already established that the mythical river did not exist.

It is interesting that when eastern Utah was still under water some 65 million years ago, western Utah was a vast highland. Then it collapsed along hundreds of faults, and erosion modified the structural blocks into what is today "basin and range" topography, or the Great Basin, a large, imperfect bowl of ridges and valleys. Today this basin is lower than the Colorado Plateau of eastern Utah. Many mineral ore deposits (mostly copper, gold, and silver) were pushed upward during the period of collapsing and volcanic intrusions.

Upon exiting the freeway to visit this park, the first view is of the Saltair Pavilion, a modern mini-replica of the Moorish-style original. It is impressive, really quite beautiful, as it seems to float in the foreground of the lake. The pavilion was closed during high water, when sailboats were moored in the 8 to 10 feet of salt water that is now the land side of Saltair Beach. Its reopening coincided with the 100-year anniversary of the original resort.

A concessionaire now operates various fun activities in front of the pavilion. Round rubber rafts offer riders the chance to bump into each other in a huge pool of water. There are camel rides for children, and a small

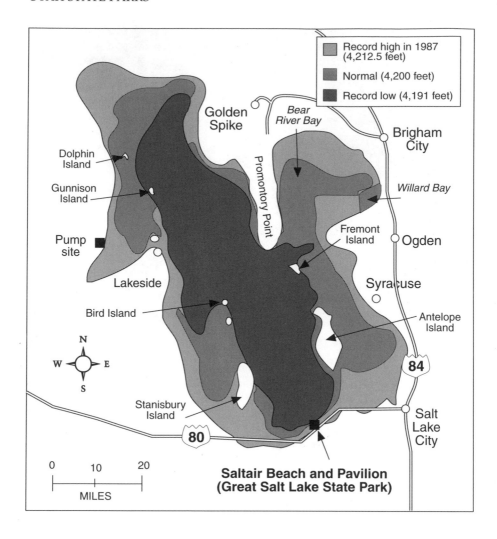

Legend:
- Record high in 1987 (4,212.5 feet)
- Normal (4,200 feet)
- Record low (4,191 feet)

Golden Spike

Bear River Bay

Brigham City

Dolphin Island

Gunnison Island

Promontory Point

Willard Bay

Pump site

Fremont Island

Ogden

Lakeside

Syracuse

Bird Island

Antelope Island

N
W E
S

84

Stanisbury Island

Salt Lake City

80

0   10   20
MILES

**Saltair Beach and Pavilion
(Great Salt Lake State Park)**

paddleboat floating on a pond serves as a gift shop. A couple of old railroad cars are souvenir stores.

Inside the pavilion is a vast open central area with a high ceiling, tables and chairs, and informational video shows. Snack bars provide food and drink. Upon entering, a sign says that no food or drink is allowed inside. The only picnic tables are outside between the railroad cars.

One can walk through the pavilion to access the lake. Bathers in swimsuits are able to walk a long distance out into the saltwater, rippling the small waves, before it gets very deep. Gnatlike insects, called brine flies, cluster in dense mats along the shore in July and August and can be disconcerting, though they do not bite. One stirs them up just walking along the beach.

The salty water of the lake normally supports only three kinds of life, blue-green algae, larvae of the brine flies, and orange brine shrimp. (Some 12 million pounds of brine shrimp eggs are harvested from the lake and sold each year as tropical fish food.) When water levels rose above normal in the 1980s, biologists discovered that tiny fish called rainwater-killifish had taken up residence temporarily where warm-water springs diluted the salt concentration.

The camping area of the state park is located 1.5 miles east of Saltair. There are no specific sites, just a gravel lot, vault toilets, and no vegetation or trees. A wide expanse of salty beach offers a lot of room for sunbathing and access to open water.

The beach here is not composed of the usual mineral grains tossed ashore but rather small pellets that are cast out by the brine shrimp digestive system and coated with calcium carbonate from the water. These gray to yellowish gray grains are called oolites, meaning fish eggs, because of their spherical shape. Swimmers find that after bathing their skin looks white as salt crystals dry on them. No one wants to swim underwater with the high concentration of salt.

The state park yacht harbor and marina is about a mile west of Saltair, not far from Lake Point. In the past, lakeside resorts, hot-dog stands, eateries, and roller coasters were spread along the lakefront from here north to Syracuse, but not any more. Besides destruction by fires, the water level fluctuations made commercial operations a chancy affair, and they have become a thing of the past. The marina has covered picnic tables, restrooms, and a yacht club office. Many sailboats are parked at slips, photogenic

Marina at Great Salt Lake State Park

shapes in the foreground of the distant mountains across the lake. Sailboat races are held each Wednesday in summer, and many sailors are on the water on weekends.

The first person to promote tourism along the shores of Great Salt Lake was John W. Young, the third of Brigham Young's twenty-five sons. He built a resort named Lake Side near the railroad stop of Farmington. Jeter Clinton followed with a resort on the south shore called Lake Point. One of the attractions at both resorts was steamboat rides. Then one of the steamboat skippers built another lake resort, Lake Park, which had a large dance pavilion, covered pier, elegant dressing rooms, restaurant, saloon, and the best sandy beach. But, after fifty years of footprints in the sand, it turned to mud and the resort failed, finally burning to the ground in 1904.

These resorts were a prelude to the birth of the original Saltair, built in 1893 on 2,500 pilings driven into the lake bottom that supported a large two-story pavilion with mosquelike towers and a tall dome. On the ground floor was a restaurant and picnic tables that overlooked the water. On the upper floor was what some called "the world's largest outdoor dance floor." Bathers stepped into the lake, and amusement park rides entertained.

By 1904, Saltair was the only resort until the lake level dropped in the early 1930s and two new resorts braved the water-fluctuation odds. Tourists flocked by railroad and auto to these three resorts until after World War II, when the popularity of ballroom dancing declined. Saltair was destroyed by fire in 1970.

In 1981, John Silver tried his resort luck by building the Saltair replica, ill-starred timing just prior to inundation of the site by flood waters that also covered the airport, railroad line, and the interstate highway to Nevada. With the lowering of the lake's water level, Saltair is once again open to the public.

JORDAN RIVER STATE PARK

Hours/Season: Day use; year-round
Area: 440 acres
Facilities: Picnic tables and wheelchair-accessible restrooms at 1700 South, 800 South, and Cottonwood Park, group pavilion, docks, vault toilets, model port, 9-hole golf course, 200-acre off-highway-vehicle riding park, phone: (801) 533-4496 (office), (801) 533-4527 (golf course)
Attractions: Boating, fishing, hiking, paddling, golfing, off-highway-vehicle riding area, wheelchair exercise, wildlife viewing, jogging/exercise course, bicycling, radio-control aircraft, horseback riding
Nearby: Bicycle loop of Salt Lake City landmarks
Access: Within city of Great Salt Lake, see map

Jordan River State Park was a dream in the mind's eye of planners decades before blueprints began to be translated into a recreational waterway for Salt Lake City. In the beginning, the quality of the water needed improvement. It tended to be polluted with debris and sewage from the industries and communities along its course. The river runs smack through the center of the city on its route from Utah Lake to empty into Great Salt Lake. In 1967, the State Department of Natural Resources said of the Jordan, "What could be Utah's greatest asset has become its greatest liability, an open sewer unfit for aquatic life and recreation."

Another concern was flood control, since the river had been known to increase its flow tenfold in some spring runoffs. Realization of a dream seemed possible in 1973 when the state legislature appropriated funds to construct a sloping greenbelt, or berm, along the edge of the river to prevent flooding. Shrubs, grass, and trees were planted to increase the ambiance. So far, the berm has done its job against the increased spring flow of water. In 1980, the Jordan River Parkway Foundation stepped in to aid in long-term responsibility for improvements, and in 1986 extra monies were provided by the state.

Do take your map to this park unless you are familiar with the area because signs were few in 1993. The state park follows the river in an 8.5-mile corridor from 1700 South to the Davis County line, with various put-in and take-out points for canoes and kayaks. Parking is available at 1700 South at the city's Glendale Park, where Raging Waters (with wave pool and waterslides) is operated by a concessionaire. This is an excellent place to launch canoes and head north on the tree-lined Jordan

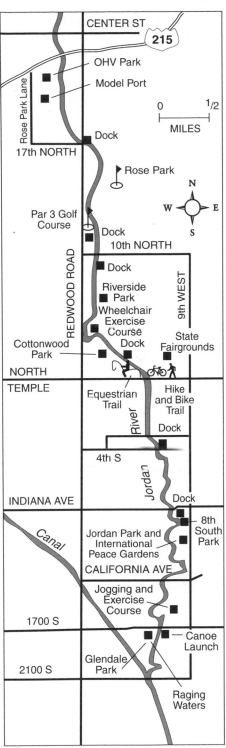

River. The Exchange Club has donated a nice ramp at this canoe marina.

Cross 1700 South to access the 1.25-mile jogging and exercise course between this street and California Avenue. Another mile north, the park passes the long-established Jordan Park and the International Peace Gardens, an arboretum with representative flora from many nations. Continuing north, 8th South Park is another picnic area near Indiana Avenue. At North Temple and 1000 West (another mile), the park traverses the Utah State Fairgrounds, where there is a dock and a sign designating the state park. A 3-mile equestrian trail and 2-mile paved hike-and-bike trail begin here. About midway between North Temple and 10th North, the river passes Cottonwood Park and a wheelchair exercise course. Hiking trails will eventually rim the waterway.

The 9-hole, par-3 golf course is accessed from Redwood Road just north of 10th North and adjacent to the park office. The northern end of the river corridor has both a model port (financed by hobby enthusiasts) and an off-highway-vehicle riding area off Rose Park Lane.

Canoeists paddle along the most popular canoeing area between 1700 South and 1000 North from June through October, a surprisingly peaceful ride through the city, but some paddlers continue on to Great Salt Lake. Another navigable stretch is from 6400 South to 4500 South in the city of Murray. Other parts of the river can be dangerous because of low bridges and irrigation dams. For experts only, a whitewater section passes through the Jordan River Narrows north of Utah Lake, where kayakers have a wild 2- to 3-mile ride if the water level is right.

Jordan River just north of Glendale Park (Jordan River State Park)

Bicyclists who want to see some of Salt Lake City's most famous landmarks can take a short loop that begins at the corner of State and South Temple streets in front of the Beehive House, former residence of Mormon leader Brigham Young. Ride on South Temple west past the Brigham Young monument and Temple Square, which frames the Mormon Temple and the Salt Lake Tabernacle. Turn right onto West Temple, then follow North Temple and State streets to the State Capitol Building. Take 300 North, East Capitol Boulevard, and West Bonneville Boulevard to City Creek Nature Preserve. Head through Memory Grove, and follow Second Avenue and State Street back to the start.

Geese at Jordan River State Park

THIS IS THE PLACE STATE PARK

Hours/Season: Day use; year-round
Area: 1,645 acres
Facilities: Picnic tables, group pavilion, visitor center, wheelchair-accessible restrooms, concessionaire, phone: (801) 584-8391
Attractions: Cross-country skiing, walking tour of historic buildings, wildlife viewing, This Is The Place Monument
Access: From Utah 186 in Salt Lake City, go east to 2601 Sunnyside Avenue, across from Hogle Zoo

A A unique opportunity to visualize Mormon pioneer life is part of the appeal as visitors stroll through the town of Old Deseret in This Is The Place State Park at 4,900-foot elevation. The buildings represent a period of development from 1847 to 1869, when the railroad arrived.

It was on July 22, 1847, that the advance party of Mormon pioneers arrived here at the mouth of Emigration Canyon. Two days later an ill Brigham Young came in his carriage. He scanned the valley below, where the Great Salt Lake glimmered and the Jordan River meandered, and said, "This is the place." He had headed vaguely for the Great Basin after reading John C. Fremont's account of the area and talking with Father De Smet. He had wanted a land that would be bypassed by pioneers headed for Oregon and California, a land that no one else wanted.

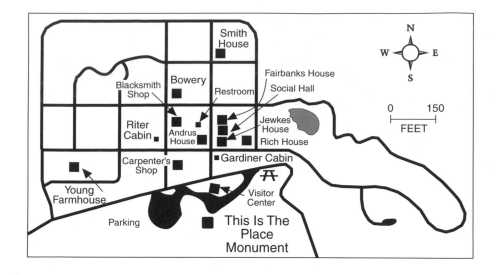

To commemorate the 100-year anniversary of this auspicious decision to settle here, the "This Is The Place" monument was erected at the site in 1947. A tall granite and bronze sculpture, on the National Register, the monument was designed by Brigham's grandson, Mahonri M. Young. Three clusters of bronze figures honor people of historical importance. At the bottom are Spanish priests and explorers Escalante and Dominguez and a grouping of trappers and fur traders. Atop the monument are sculptures of Mormon leaders Brigham Young, Heber C. Kimball, and Wilford Woodruff as they look out over Salt Lake Valley.

The Mormons were industrious pioneers and they named their destination the State of Deseret, though it later became the Utah Territory. Deseret means honey bee, a symbolic insect to the Mormons. Today the state is known as the Beehive State since Utahns take their work seriously.

So it is fitting to call this living-history museum "Old Deseret." The state park was one of the four original parks established in 1957 and is now the sixth most visited. The visitor center offers an audio presentation, a gift shop, and a three-wall mural, painted by Utah artist Lynn Fausett, that illustrates the 1,300-mile migration of Mormon pioneers from Nauvoo, Illinois, to the Great Salt Lake Valley.

The walking tour of the buildings begins north of the visitor center, and guided tours are available from Memorial Day weekend to Labor Day weekend. One may also wander freely. Volunteers are trained each spring to staff the buildings. Wearing period costumes, they greet arrivals at individual buildings and present interesting history about the Indians, explorers, mountain men, and everyday life of the Mormons. In summer and on holidays, the volunteers demonstrate the skills of butter churning, lacemaking, quilting, weaving, soapmaking, blacksmithing, open-hearth cooking, spinning, candlemaking, gardening, carpentry, and rugmaking.

Across from the visitor center is the John W. Gardiner Log Cabin, a one-room structure with a sleeping loft (furnished with a straw mattress and homemade quilts) that was accessed from outside. It was built in 1864 in Pleasant Grove and relocated here in 1980.

Cross the street to enter the Samuel Jewkes House, built in 1860 using traditional mortise-and-tenon construction. Inside are a spinning wheel and various colored yarns of flax, cotton, wool, and silk. Herbs to dye the natural fibers were grown in the garden. An interesting display shows eggs decorated with flowers that were made using a special technique of wrapping with yarn before dyeing.

Next door is the reconstruction of the Social Hall that was built in Salt Lake City in 1852–53 of adobe and sandstone. An important meeting place, dances, plays, and lectures were held in this two-story structure.

A few steps north is the two-story John Boyleston Fairbanks House, built of adobe in the 1850s with a kitchen and two wings added some years later, and later relocated from Paysen. Displays show carving, bobbin lace, hooked rugs, tatting, and a quilt in progress.

The Milo Andrus House is a large frame building put up in 1858 that now represents a combined general store and residence. Many old items hint at pioneer life. A cup-and-ball toy, button games, "Game of Graces," bonnets, baskets, candy, herbs, jams, rag rugs, kegs, candleholders, and colorful candles are some of possible purchases of the time. Courting couples used special candles to time visits. When the candles burned down to the rings, suitors had to leave.

Outside, visitors can take a ride around the state park in one of the horse-

This Is The Place Monument

Brigham Young Forest Farmhouse at This Is The Place State Park

drawn covered wagons, getting more information en route. Across the way is a farmyard complete with pigs, sheep, and garden. One of the oldest surviving pioneer cabins, built in 1847 inside a fort, is now at Old Deseret. A blacksmith shop, a carpenter's shop, and an example of the home of a polygamous family may also be seen.

New pioneer structures—the Hickman Cabin and a pioneer dugout—were added in the spring of 1994. William Adams Hickman came to Utah from Kentucky with the pioneers in 1849, served as a U.S. Territorial Marshal, and took part in the Utah War. His cabin was built in Fairfield in 1854 and served as the Fairfield Pony Express station in 1861. He lived there with his seventh wife, Margaret, a Shoshone Indian. The pioneer dugout is the type of temporary structure that often housed pioneers until more permanent homes could be built.

The Brigham Young Forest Farmhouse is set apart from the other buildings, with its own parking lot. This restored large frame and stucco house was built 4 miles southeast of Salt Lake City by Brigham Young on a 640-acre farm that supplied dairy products for Young's large family. Sugar beets, silkworms, and alfalfa were also raised as agricultural experiments on this private farm.

This historic building is shown only on twenty-minute tours, with doors locked in between, when a guide with a full-length, flowered dress with lace and a tatted collar, hair held in place by a snood, ushers visitors into the dining room where the table is always set, since it served as a cupboard. The laundry and washroom were without running water, and the heavy irons had to be heated. A lantern with a candle was ready to be taken outdoors. As in the typical large kitchen, a Mormon couch could let the cook tend sick children while she worked. (No children were allowed, however, on this particular farm.)

There was a ballroom because there were so many dances. A merry bunch, the Mormons often had affairs that started with brunch and continued into dinner, followed by dancing and perhaps an overnight stay. When not used for entertaining, the ballroom served as a workroom, where sounds of "pop goes the weasel" were heard as skeins of yarn were measured on the weasel. There was also an "up" parlor and a domestics room.

After your walking tour, relax and enjoy a lunch in the picnic area while you ponder Mormon pioneer life in this valley. The state park also includes considerable recreation space and the beginning of a 36-mile trail, now part of the National Trail System, that goes from the edge of the park to Henefer, following the final part of the Mormon trek here. The park also allows cross-country skiing on Old Deseret's streets in winter.

Special events are scheduled at This Is The Place State Park: Old Deseret Days on Memorial Day weekend; Pioneer Independence Day on the 4th of July; Pioneer Days in late July; Harvest Days over Labor Day weekend; Pumpkin Harvest (carving included) in late October; and Candlelight Christmas Tours in mid-December. A new visitor center is scheduled for completion in 1996 to coincide with Utah's centennial celebration.

DINOSAUR-LAND

▲ Try to visualize a time 145 million years ago when dinosaurs roamed a lush, semitropical, low-lying plain with several large rivers where crocodiles, clams, and turtles lived. The place was this northeast corner of Utah. These often gigantic animals that so intrigue us left clues about their shapes and lives, sometimes in fossilized footprints, often in their bones. Touch base across the ages by visiting Dinosaur National Monument and the Utah Field House of Natural History.

In the different geological surroundings of today, two natural features dominate the regional map of Dinosaurland: the Green River and the Uinta (*you-in-tah*) Mountains. Near the spine of these mountains is the highest point in Utah, 13,528-foot King's Peak. Located a short distance south of the Utah–Wyoming border, this mountain range is the largest east-west range in the Western Hemisphere.

Ashley National Forest encompasses the mountains and their foothills, a backpacking and horsepacking paradise with trails and hundreds of glacial lakes, many stocked with trout. Timbered slopes, rushing streams, green meadows, solitude, over 200 species of summer wildflowers, and the rugged High Uintas Wilderness Area are found in this forest, which was named after fur trader William H. Ashley. The snowmelt from this high country runs downhill to eventually empty into the Colorado River drainage and to fill the reservoirs of the Uinta Basin. Three of these—Starvation, Steinaker, and Red Fleet—are the nucleus of state parks and recreation centers.

The southern portion of Flaming Gorge National Recreation Area pokes into Utah, a vast, colorful meeting of canyon walls and the dammed Green River. It was in this area that Ashley attended the first mountain man rendezvous of the Old West in July of 1825. In that same year Ashley floated

Opposite: *Tyrannosaurus in front of Utah Field House of Natural History*

103

down the Green River through Flaming Gorge, but it was explorer/scientist John Wesley Powell who named the gorge in 1869 and continued on to explore the vast, dangerous waters of the Colorado River. The Flaming Gorge Recreation Area offers good wildlife viewing, with pronghorn, bighorn sheep, elk, moose, and nesting ospreys.

Excellent fly fishing is found on the river below the dam. The river soon becomes a place for whitewater rafting. Several put-in and take-out points for river running occur in the long diagonal slash of the Green River across this region. Some trips require good whitewater skills; some are placid affairs. Some stretches are in open desert country; some in spectacular canyons.

Those traveling via roads, either by vehicle or bicycle, will find the 67-mile Flaming Gorge–Uintas Scenic Byway between Vernal and the brilliant canyon to be fine scenery. In autumn, fall foliage colors add to the charm.

Long before Ashley and Powell explored this region, the Fremont Indians lived here. Impressive examples of their rock art are found in Nine Mile Canyon south of Myton. More recently, the Utes and Shoshones roamed and hunted here. Today, several large chunks of Dinosaurland are occupied by the Uintah and Ouray Indian Reservation. The Ute Indians are a proud people who enjoy sharing their cultural heritage during the July Powwow held at Fort Duchesne.

Another major Dinosaurland event is the Outlaw Trail Festival, held in June and July in Vernal, a reflection of the days when the Wild Bunch and other desperados hid in these canyonlands.

The warmest temperatures in this region are in the lower elevations of Dinosaur National Monument, where the average high is over ninety degrees in July and August. Vernal is a few degrees cooler, and Flaming Gorge is in the low eighties during the hottest months. The mountains offer a range from pleasant summer days to near freezing at night in the highest altitudes, though night temperatures in winter are below zero with highs of about twenty-five degrees. The winter valleys range from five to thirty degrees. Snow is widespread, with heavy amounts in the mountains. Several cross-country skiing trails are found in the Ashley National Forest north of Vernal.

STARVATION STATE PARK

Hours/Season: Overnight; year-round
Area: 3,310 acres
Facilities: Picnic tables, 54 campsites, wheelchair-accessible restrooms with showers, sewage disposal, boat ramp, primitive campsites with vault toilets, group camping, fish cleaning station, group pavilion, playground, concessionaire, phone: (801) 738-2326
Attractions: Boating, fishing (ice fishing in winter), swimming, windsurfing, water skiing, wildlife viewing, photography
Access: 4 miles northwest of Duchesne off US 40

There is a conflict in rumors about the naming of Starvation State Park. It appears that a cache of food was probably buried in caves and rocky holes near the southwest shore of what is now Starvation Reservoir and that a group who did not plant that cache used it, leaving the original, foresighted ones to starve. The two groups involved are fur trappers and Indians. The conflict occurs over who hid the food and who stole it, and the story varies.

At the time the Escalante-Dominguez Expedition passed through this countryside, in 1776, it looked considerably different from how it looks today and travel through it was not easy. This party came from New Mexico through what is now Dinosaur National Monument, and headed west. Crossing the Strawberry River was the problem, wrote Escalante in his journal,

Windsurfer picks up a breeze at Starvation State Park

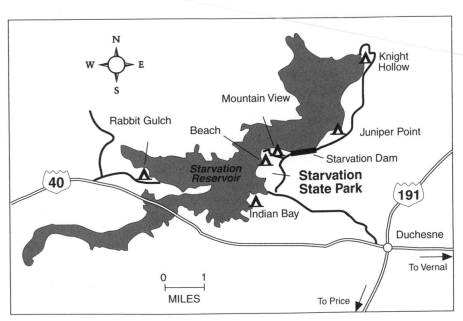

because of rocky terrain, precipices, and thick vegetation. A horse was injured and the party had to backtrack about a mile and try at another meadow by the river, yet that way was thick with bamboo reed and willow and was slow. The expedition finally took the channel bed of an arroyo and climbed out of the canyon. This place is memorialized at the Escalante-Dominguez Overlook on US 40, where an arm of lake is crossed.

That terrain was obliterated to build the dam completed in 1970 on this area of the Strawberry River as part of the Central Utah Project for conservation and flood control. At 5,720-foot elevation, the reservoir impounds 3,495 surface acres of water with 23 miles of shoreline. The area became a state park in 1972.

The main developed part of the park has a sandy beach and two campgrounds, one of which is by the water. The Beach Campground is popular with tenters and is close to boat launching and the concession building. The Mountain View Campground is more private, located on a nearby bluff with good views of the reservoir and the impressive Uinta Mountains in the background. Individual back-in sites each include a covered picnic table. A trail connects the two camping areas. The large covered pavilion, with its group-size barbecue grills, is popular for family reunions. Gathering firewood is prohibited.

Boy fishing at Indian Bay, Starvation State Park

Four primitive camping areas provide further choices, all with vault toilets, but many of these are new, though no culinary water is available, so be prepared. Juniper Point and Knight Hollow are accessed by crossing the dam, with 100 acres of sandy hills for OHV riding at the latter (know the regulations). Rabbit Gulch, with a sewage-disposal station, is reached by traveling west past the bridge on US 40 that crosses the arm of the reservoir and then taking a road northeast.

The fourth primitive area is at Indian Bay, just west of the main park area, and is a very special place. Take time to explore the several coves here. You can often find a wonderful, expansive private site with picnic table; some sites have stone fireplaces, most have some scrubby trees and vegetation. These are places one would like to stay for a while, for a feeling of connectedness with the outdoors without that hemmed-in feeling of some campgrounds. An old boat ramp is found near the entrance area.

This very scenic waterfront campground has rocky terraces that project into the water for easy wading, sandy beaches, rocky projections to fish from, and curving boulders that enclose swimming holes. Children can easily dive in and swim across to another section of the sandy beach backed by rocks. Windsurfers find privacy for practice glides across the water. Boats and water skiers do venture around from the main boat ramp. One can explore on foot, venturing to huge expanses of climbable rock or to grassy wetland habitats.

Snowy rivulets still top the Uinta Mountains to the north in August. Summer thunderstorms frequently devour the white cumulus clouds of the blue-sky afternoons and replace them with swirlings of satiny grays that look like bubbles smashing, followed by vivid patches of sunset reds. The clear water reverberates in the shimmer of the last glow of the day's light.

The flora of Starvation State Park includes juniper, pinyon, rabbitbrush, agave, sagebrush, and a variety of desert plants. The fauna is more elusive, but mule deer, cottontail, jackrabbit, lizard, beaver, badger, chipmunk, prairie dog, coyote, fox, bobcat, and elk all live in the area.

Mountain bluebird, scrub jay, magpie, sparrow, great blue heron, Canada goose, an assortment of ducks, and occasional bald and golden eagles are some of the bird species. The walleye fishery is good, and there are smallmouth bass and brown trout.

UTAH FIELD HOUSE OF NATURAL HISTORY STATE PARK

Hours/Season: Day use; year-round, except Thanksgiving, Christmas, and New Year's Day
Area: 1.66 acres
Facilities: Picnic tables, dinosaur garden, amphitheater, museum, gift shop, visitor center, restrooms, playground, phone: (801) 789-3799
Attractions: Geology, paleontology, Indian prehistory, natural history, educational programs, science reference library, research
Nearby: Dinosaur National Monument
Access: In Vernal, at 235 East Main Street

When Earl Douglass first looked for fossils in northeastern Utah, he found a *Diplodocus* (the longest of dinosaurs) thigh bone and heard tales of sheepherders finding colossal bones. He returned to the Carnegie Museum in Pittsburgh, Pennsylvania, speculating that he could find a dinosaur quarry in the Split Mountain area near the Green River. The timing was perfect. Andrew Carnegie needed something "as big as a barn" to fill the new wing of the museum that was to be the great Hall of Vertebrate Paleontology. He sent Douglass back to Utah to find it.

Douglass returned to what is now Dinosaur National Monument in 1909,

Utah Field House of Natural History

and his speculations became reality when he discovered one of the world's finest concentrations of fossil dinosaur remains.

The local community, led by Arthur G. Nord, was reluctant to see the area's prehistoric wealth continue to be carted back East and formulated the concept of a local field house. As a result, the Utah Legislature established the Utah Field House of Natural History, in 1945, to house and display "the fossil remains of ancient plant and animal life and other objects of natural history." This opened in 1948 and became a state park in 1959.

Located in the Uinta Basin adjacent to the Uinta Mountains, the field house has lived up to its goals and has a wide variety of exhibits about the area. Uinta County and Uinta Basin have a wealth of twenty-six major formations, of which twenty-one contain fossils, and a 600-million-year geological history.

Certainly the dinosaur is the star of the exhibits at the field house, and there is an extensive history of the dinosaur ages. A huge wall diagram—the landscape done by Ernest Untermann, with geology by C. E. Untermann and B. R. Untermann—shows the geological layers, with animals placed in the strata and time that they lived. Jim Matson, former state paleontologist, is in the process of assembling a dinosaur replica of *Diplodocus* out of extruded polyester to place inside the museum. Exhibits show various dinosaur parts—vertebra, skulls, claws, legs, and feet. Fossil remains include leaves, algae, insects, fish, various teeth, shells, and three-toed dinosaur tracks.

Indian exhibits tell what is known of the Fremont culture from A.D. 700 to 1250. Desert survival and culture displays are of basketry, food gathering, metates, rock art, and many arrowheads. Artifacts of the more recent American Indians—the Utes—include baskets, beaded boots, coats, gloves, moccasins, ceremonial dress, vests, cradles, and a painting of the Sun Dance.

Explorer history tells of the Dominguez-Escalante Expedition, the first white men who came through this area in 1776 from New Mexico, and how they mapped and recorded what they saw. Mountain men are not neglected in this look at Utah's history.

The natural-history room contains a variety of stuffed animals and birds that inhabit the landscape today, plus a butterfly collection and mounted trophies. One fascinating exhibit asks the viewer to match definitions with objects in a grouping of plants, birds, fish, and a skull.

Rockhounders, and others, will delight in the mineral room. In addition to a geological map of the state with sedimentary structures detailed, the individual rocks invite close inspection. The Oregon agate is particularly colorful and beautiful. One section is a darkroom with ultraviolet light shining on the rocks that contain fluorescent minerals.

Anyone who remembers playing with toy soldiers will be excited to find an extensive collection of Herm Hoops toy soldiers in the video room.

Winged Pteranodon in Dinosaur Garden, Utah Field House of Natural History State Park

Outdoors, the Dinosaur Garden (added in 1978) is extremely popular, a wonderful grouping of dinosaur replicas—one of the finest collections in the world—in a natural setting of ponds and vegetation. It is one thing to read about the dinosaur ages, but this garden lets you stroll around and pretend that you're living back then, though stuck in a time warp where the dinosaurs don't move.

A recent addition in February 1994 of a model of a small dinosaur, *Coelophysis bauri*, brings the number of prehistoric animals in the garden to seventeen. *Coelophysis* was created by David Thomas of Albuquerque, New Mexico. It is the first model exhibited of the Triassic Period, which was the earliest time of the dinosaurs.

The eight-ton, life-size replica of the 20-foot *Tyrannosaurus*, with its 6-inch, knifelike teeth, is the king of dinosaurs and was the largest of the meat eaters. Here also are the horned *Triceratops*; the six-ton *Stegosaurus* (which had a brain no larger than a kitten's); the gigantic, more than 80-foot-long, plant-eating *Diplodocus*; the winged *Pteranodon* (one of the largest flying creatures ever with a wingspan of 25 or more feet); the *Edaphosaurus* (a fin-backed reptile); and the huge, birdlike *Ornithomimus*. Off in a corner is the woolly mammoth with its huge, curving tusks.

Utah Sculptor Elbert Porter created many of these replicas over a period of fourteen years. After traveling the country and researching dinosaurs, Porter came home to make one-twelfth life-size models first. Then he developed a technique of molding fiberglass over plywood frames to make the full-size replicas. The replicas were displayed in the West for a time before the state parks system acquired them for this garden in 1977. Three concrete dinosaurs by sculptor Millard F. Malin are part of the garden display.

Lectures are held in the garden amphitheater in summer. Children will want to buy pieces of dinosaur bones, books, or fossils at the museum gift shop. The museum building also houses a visitor center with information on the surrounding country.

The picnic area is located behind the museum structure, where tables are scattered beneath tall shade trees. A playground is nearby.

Continue your study of dinosaurs by taking a trip to Dinosaur National Monument, about 20 miles east of Vernal. Paleontologists are still extracting and reassembling dinosaur bones from the quarry that Douglass discovered, a "sandbar cemetery" on an ancient riverbed. In time, as sandstone formed, silica percolated through the strata and mineralized the bones within the 145-million-year-old Morrison Formation. Thousands of bones have been found here already, including many almost complete skeletons.

The quarry is now encased inside the visitor center as a working laboratory where visitors could, until recently, watch technicians use jackhammers, chisels, and ice picks to expose fossil bones. Rangers will answer questions and tell about the time when dinosaurs roamed a green, lush semitropical area, when ferns and tall conifers grew in the wetter climate. Now it is arid desert.

For a look at the Green River and today's desert, drive 3 miles to Split

Mountain Gorge and take the 2-mile nature trail, preferably in the cool of early morning if it is summer. An informative trail brochure instructs about the geology, plants, and animals.

STEINAKER STATE PARK

Hours/Season: Overnight; April to October
Area: 2,283 acres
Facilities: Picnic tables, 31 campsites, wheelchair-accessible restrooms, group pavilions, sewage disposal, boat ramp, phone: (801) 789-4432
Attractions: Boating, paddling, fishing (ice fishing in winter), swimming, hiking, windsurfing, water skiing, photography, nature study
Nearby: Moonshine Arch, the Green River
Access: 7 miles north of Vernal off US 191

On relatively level ground at 5,520-foot elevation, Steinaker State Park is a desert oasis in the midst of the Uinta Basin, a distinctly bowl-shaped geological feature at the northern edge of the Colorado Plateau.

The dam for Steinaker Reservoir was built in 1961, an unusual water-storage facility since the lake is supplied via a canal from a diversion dam on Ashley Creek, which is several miles to the west. The reservoir was

Fisherman boating on the reservoir at Steinaker State Park

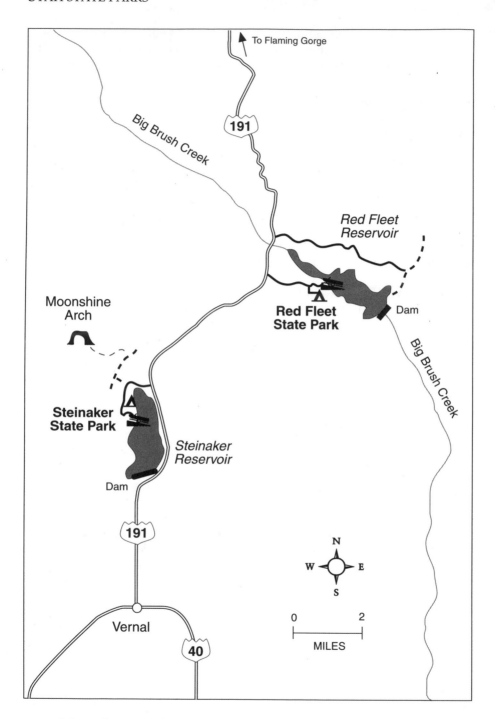

named for John Steinaker, an 81-year-old member of a pioneer ranching
family at the time of the groundbreaking for the dam.

The surface waters of the reservoir reach a comfortable summer temperature of about seventy degrees Fahrenheit, which makes water sports great fun. Yet, the deep portions of the lake, 130 feet in places, are cold enough to support a prime recreational fishery of rainbow trout, bluegill, largemouth bass, and an occasional brown trout.

The campground is situated on the northwest side of the reservoir. Campers have a choice of high lakeview sites; pull-through, level sites near the restroom; or sites that front the upper wetlands that are shaded by huge, old cottonwood trees. If conditions are right, a walk out into the wetland often is rewarded with patches of photogenic squirrel-tail barley. Paths meander along the bluffs above the reservoir south to the boat ramp and day-use area, or one can take the road.

Another day-use area, undeveloped except for a vault toilet, is seen along the entry road. From here, an old road leading toward the upper end of the reservoir provides a good walkway for exploring. A lot of vegetation is nourished by this wet edge, and it provides good hiding places for wildlife. Watch for great blue herons up high, where you would not expect to see them.

The wildlife species are many and varied. Mule deer, jackrabbits, cottontail rabbits, lizards, porcupines, golden-mantled squirrels, even elk, coyote, and bobcat are spotted at rare times. Bird life is interesting with pinyon jays fluttering around the cottonwoods and sightings that can include magpies, scrub jays, pheasants, western grebes, loons, ducks, Canada geese, turkey vultures, ospreys, and golden eagles.

Though sagebrush and juniper predominate in the desert terrain of the park, spring brings a blossoming of wildflowers. Larkspur, penstemon, Indian paintbrush, globe mallow, sunflower, and the beautiful sego lily (Utah's state flower) provide spots of color.

The park holds the Dinosaur Triathalon in late July. Steinaker frequently serves as a base for people visiting Dinosaur National Monument or en route to Flaming Gorge National Monument. It is also used as a training ground and campsite for rafters. Kayakers take their vessels to the calm waters of the reservoir to practice rolling over in the water, a safety preparation. Then they head for the launch site at Sand Wash Ranger Station on the Green River, southwest of Steinaker State Park. From there, they go downstream through the roadless area of Desolation/Gray Canyons until the take-out just before Nefertiti Rapids, above the town of Green River. This is a river run (Class II–III) of 75 miles that takes four to five days, a scenic whitewater trip with sixty-seven rapids.

Hikers visiting the state park have a chance to hike through desert terrain to the relatively unknown Moonshine Arch. Walk west on the dirt road (an OHV road with some room for parking) that branches off from the sharp bend in the entry road. Proceed about 0.7 mile to an intersection of dirt roads with a steep, sandy truck-climb hill in front of you. Turn right and walk between 0.8 and 0.9 mile (you are on an aqueduct road) to a V-fork in the road (a huge sandy mound is on the right). Take the left fork and walk only about 0.1 mile to where you make a sharp left and go another 0.1 mile to the end of the dirt road. A roadblock is here, with vehicles prohibited past this point. Continue uphill past this sign and over sandy terrain that edges slickrock for about 0.5 mile to where the arch is almost hidden among rock formations on your right. This is a nice arch, backed by a cavelike structure.

If you head out of the park going north on US 191, be alert for the highway signs denoting the various geological formations and the fossils found in them. Called the "Drive Through the Ages," the highway gradually climbs to 9,500 feet at Flaming Gorge as it reveals newer formations at higher elevations.

Directly opposite the state park is a bank of the Morrison Formation, a layer of strata that was deposited 140 million years ago during the Jurassic Period when dinosaurs roamed the Earth. The Curtis Formation contains fossilized squid. Other fossils include oysters, clams, and other shellfish of ancient seas. Obsidian chips and arrowheads are found in the adjacent hills. The region is of great interest to geologists, historians, and collectors of artifacts.

RED FLEET STATE PARK

Hours/Season: Overnight; year-round
Area: 1,963 acres
Facilities: Picnic tables, 29 campsites, restrooms, fish cleaning station, sewage disposal, boat ramp, phone: (801) 789-4432
Attractions: Boating, fishing (ice fishing in winter), water skiing, sandy beach, swimming, sailing, windsurfing, dinosaur exhibit, photography
Nearby: Ouray National Wildlife Refuge
Access: 10 miles north of Vernal off US 191

As visitors approach Red Fleet Reservoir on the 2-mile entry spur, huge red sandstone rock formations loom above the water. They resemble a fleet of ships moving through the sea, hence the name "Red Fleet."

The reservoir collects the waters of Big Brush Creek as it descends from the Uinta Mountains. On its downhill journey, the entire flow of this creek enters Brush Creek Cave, about 18 miles north of Vernal. Caves are a not unusual occurrence in the Mississippi Formation found in the area.

A fluid blue nestled in a magnificent setting of red slickrock country, Red Fleet Reservoir contains 750 surface acres of water impounded in 1980 as another part of the Central Utah Project. It provides culinary water for Vernal and irrigation water to area farms and ranches. Its waters lure fishermen with rainbow trout, largemouth bass, and a few brown trout.

Views of the reservoir and surrounding terrain are good from all campground sites, but the spaces are rectangles in a parking lot. An adjacent expanse of lawn offers good tenting and covered picnic tables. The back row of spaces edges a bluff with more private tenting and picnicking areas atop the hillside.

The bluff at the edge of the reservoir has good picnicking spots where

Rock formations resembling the prows of ships at Red Fleet State Park

one can watch the action of water skiing, boating, and swimming. An orange-colored slanted shelf slopes into the water across from the boat ramp. This is a favorite destination for boaters and swimmers (the distance is not far) because they can sit on the ledge or look for the dinosaur footprints that have been found here recently.

Almost 200 million years ago, dinosaurs crossed this area. In doing so, they left their footprints in the wet sand and mud along the shore of a small desert lake. Paleontologists can tell from these tracks now preserved in Navajo Sandstone that the dinosaurs were three-toed (tridactyl) and walked on two legs (bipedal). The tracks range in size from 3 to 17 inches. A second site of about forty dinosaur tracks of 4 to 5 inches, in the more recent Carmel Formation, has been found in the area, but the species has not yet been identified.

A trail for exploring some of the dinosaur tracks can be reached via a road on the north side of the reservoir. Check with the park ranger for detailed access information.

Paths on the developed side of the reservoir lead to interesting coves along the water, both to the left and to the right of the boat ramp. Walkers might want to explore along the entry road, particularly early and late in the day when chances of seeing wildlife are better. This is sagebrush terrain that provides a winter range for deer and some elk. Coyote, bobcat, prairie dog, skunk, rabbit, bald eagle, golden eagle, hawks, magpie, mourning dove, prairie falcon, and pinyon jay are species to sight. Mountain bluebirds are frequent visitors near the campsites.

If the weather is right, and you are interested in birdwatching, travel 28 miles southwest of Vernal on US 191 and then Utah 88 to the road going east into the Ouray National Wildlife Refuge, 11,826 acres of choice nesting, resting, and feeding habitat for migrating birds. In a short distance, you will come to the refuge headquarters, where a map and brochure are available.

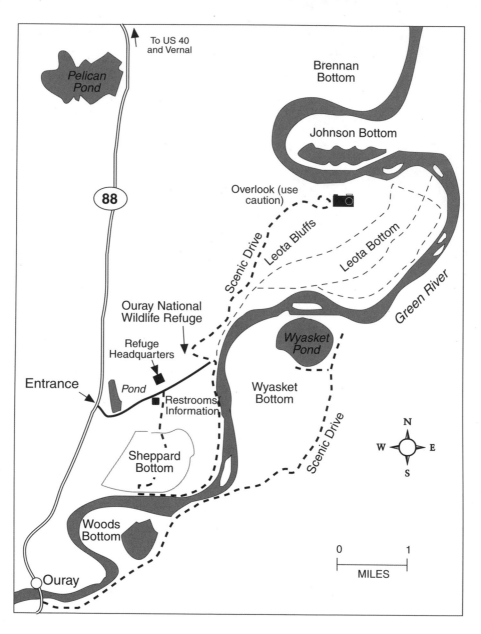

A 9-mile auto-tour route with marked stops passes an observation tower, bottomland, and wetlands along the meandering Green River, the Leota Bluffs, and an overlook. Areas of interest may be explored on foot. The refuge roads are passable only in dry weather, and some are closed during the fall hunting season. Pelican Lake, which is passed on the way in via Utah 88, has good wetland vegetation and also attracts a considerable number of birds.

Dinosaur tracks are found near this slanting rock formation at Red Fleet State Park

CASTLE COUNTRY

Look at a map of Castle Country and you'll find a landscape of few towns, an untamed but captivating chunk of Utah that appeals to the adventurous, to those who want new and exciting experiences. Yet there are special places for family activities as well.

Castle Country's major city, with a population of less than 9,000 inhabitants, is Price. Situated on the Price River, the monumental stone formations guarding the mouth of Price Canyon have given the name to this travel region.

Most of the small cities sprang forth in Castle Valley, bordered on the west by the sheer escarpment that marks the edge of the Wasatch Plateau. Manti-La Sal National Forest climbs to the top of this plateau that rises over 11,000 feet and forms the western side of the region.

Hikers will find mountain trails under conifers and aspens that follow creeks and ridges of the forest where wildlife viewing is good. Anglers find rainbow trout in the creeks and reservoirs—Ferron, Electric, Joe's Valley, and Scofield—fed by snowmelt. From Castle Valley, several roads, including the Huntington Scenic Byway, access the Skyline Drive that follows the ridge of the Wasatch Plateau, also called the Manti Top.

Those wanting easier destinations for good family recreation will take note of the three state parks—Scofield, Huntington, and Millsite—that are in Castle Valley, all on reservoirs fed by the waterways off the plateau.

To the north in the region, Indian Canyon Scenic Byway, US 191, follows an old Indian Trail—passing the beginning of the Roan and Book Cliff formations—into Ashley National Forest and then down to the Uinta Basin. Another auto tour in this area, going north near Price, is Nine Mile Canyon.

Opposite: *Natural sculpture resembling a giant mushroom at Goblin Valley State Park*

This route accesses some of the best ancient rock art in the West. Throughout Castle Country, be alert for significant examples of petroglyphs and evidence of the ancient Fremont Indians.

In the middle of Castle Country, east of Huntington, is the Cleveland-Lloyd Dinosaur Quarry, of interest to amateur and professional geologists. With a history of vast numbers of dinosaur and other bones excavated, this is still an active quarry for research digs. Visitors are welcome.

Those wanting to hunt for rocks will find that this region is famous for such collectibles as agate, jasper, geodes, and petrified wood, among others. A favorite destination for rockhounding is Cedar Mountain, southeast of Cleveland. The minerals and the mines that were worked around them brought an influx of ethnically diverse miners to Castle Country. That diversity endures. Greeks, in particular, play a major role in the area, and Greek Days are celebrated each July in Price.

Those who want to run rivers head east to where the Green River flows along the north–south boundary of Castle Country. The only town along this waterway is Green River, but it will supply you with the essentials for rafting down the river, plus detailed information and guides. Except for an aerial trip, the water route, with launchings at Green River State Park, is the only way to see scenic Labyrinth and Stillwater canyons. Visit the John Wesley Powell River History Museum while in town.

Last, but definitely not least, a famous lure of Castle Country is the San Rafael Swell and the San Rafael Reef, which occupies much of the southern half of the region. Butch Cassidy, that accomplished but errant cowboy who wanted more adventure in his life, made trails across the wildness of the San Rafael Swell with his Wild Bunch. Today, some dirt roads meander around, but most of this landscape still requires considerable know-how for survival. Yet many are willing to try their hand at exploring it, whether by horseback, off-highway vehicle, hiking, or mountain bike. Even those on auto tours can see good snatches of the San Rafael Swell by taking Interstate 70 across it, stopping at the many viewpoints to savor and photograph it. Don't miss taking the children to Goblin Valley State Park, at the edge of the San Rafael Reef, to wander among the intricate creatures carved by nature.

Castle Country has put out a special Trail Guide for mountain bikers that fits easily into a hip pocket. Detailed information on ten routes is given, plus it addresses ethical and ecological concerns. Included are trails in the Manti-La Sal National Forest and Nine Mile Canyon, one on a railroad grade, and many in the San Rafael Swell area.

The climate of the desert areas of Castle Country, which includes much of the San Rafael Swell, is downright hot in summer, at least in the nineties, so the best time to visit is in spring and autumn. Summer is the season to head for the Manti Top where it is about twenty degrees cooler. This is also the place for winter action; cross-country skiing and snowmobiling are both quite popular.

SCOFIELD STATE PARK

Hours/Season: Overnight; May to November (open to day-use activities in winter)

Area: 418 acres

Facilities: Picnic tables, 40 campsites, group camping, group pavilion, restrooms with showers, sewage disposal, and boat ramp at Madsen Bay; picnic tables, 34 campsites, wheelchair-accessible restrooms with showers, vault toilets, boat ramp and docks, and sewage disposal at Mountain View; no firewood, phone: (801) 448-9449 (summer), (801) 637-8497 (winter)

Attractions: High mountain lake, boating, fishing (ice fishing in winter), swimming, snowmobiling, cross-country skiing

Access: Off Utah 96, Mountain View is 3 miles north of the town of Scofield, Madsen Bay is 4 miles north of Scofield

At 7,600 feet above sea level, Scofield is Utah's highest state park. Located in the Manti-La Sal National Forest on the Wasatch Plateau, the main attraction is the 2,800-acre Scofield Reservoir. Upper Price River was dammed in the 1940s for farm irrigation downstream. Circling the lake are high ridges broken by several canyons that empty creeks into the reservoir that filled part of Paradise Valley.

Boat launch in Mountain View area of Scofield State Park

The developed area called Mountain View has a campground on a small hillside above the lake, with back-in sites separated by wooden post dividers and shaded by aspen trees. The boat ramp is directly below the campground. A small day-use area with a picnic table overlooks the water.

Madsen Bay has half-circle campsites at water level, new modern restrooms, but not many shade trees, though this is not so crucial at this altitude. The camping arrangement is more spread out and a better choice for reunions and groups. To get to the boat ramp, a road skirts this edge of the reservoir, where a narrow finger of water flows down from Lost Creek. This is a lush wetland spot with vegetation that attracts birds. Continue past this to the west side of the water and to the ramp, extremely popular as there are frequent launchings on early summer mornings. Some anglers fish from shore.

The cold waters of the reservoir are good habitat for the stocked rainbow trout, and fishermen also catch wild cutthroat. Because of the water temperature, the swimming and water skiing is a little chilly, but the state lists these as recreation choices.

The park is busy enough in summer that the campground is sometimes full. Camping is not available in winter, but the park is open for ice fishing and is a good base for snowmobiling and cross-country skiing in season.

The state park and reservoir are obviously named after the nearby town of Scofield, but that town was first known as Pleasant Valley in the 1870s. Later the name was changed to honor General Charles W. Scofield, an area timber contractor after the Civil War who became president of the company that operated the state's first commercial coal mine near the town. A terrible disaster occurred when there was a vast explosion at the Winters Quarters mine in 1900 that took 199 lives. A good percentage of the dead were recent immigrants from Europe. Most of the men were buried in the Scofield Cemetery, now a National Historic Site. This tragedy led to widespread concern for improved safety in mines, but many of the miners at Scofield who remained in the area refused to go back when the mine reopened and moved away. The town's population peaked in the 1920s and has since declined.

HUNTINGTON STATE PARK

Hours/Season: Overnight; year-round
Area: 111 acres
Facilities: Picnic tables, 22 campsites, group pavilion, wheelchair-accessible restrooms with showers, sewage disposal, boat ramp and dock, phone: (801) 687-2491
Attractions: Boating, paddling, fishing (ice fishing in winter), water skiing, windsurfing, swimming, lawn games, photography, birdwatching
Nearby: Cleveland-Lloyd Dinosaur Quarry
Access: Off Utah 10, 2 miles north of town of Huntington, 0.25 mile north on Mohrland Canyon Road to park

Cliff reflections at Huntington State Park

Pull into Huntington State Park at the right time and the tropical blue color of the reservoir water will seduce you to stay. At an elevation of 5,840 feet, the lake is in Castle Valley, at the base of the Wasatch Plateau. Your view is enhanced by the chiseled peaks and slopes of sandstone cliffs in the distance. This undulating rocky ridge forms a symmetrical reflection on the water surface in the morning as boats launch and head across the reservoir.

This park has expansive green lawns and is a favorite for groups and reunions, an oasis in an arid landscape, a place to relax, to picnic, to read a book and listen for birds, glancing occasionally at the scenery. Campsites are both back-in and pull-through, with several overlooking the lake.

This is also a place for active water sports, for cooling off in the summer heat. A shallow, covelike area south of the boat ramp makes a splendid swimming and wading area and the sounds of happy children are often heard as they splash around. The 237-acre, warm-water reservoir is good for water skiing and boating. The opposite shore is undeveloped. Solitude is only a boat ride away.

Huntington Reservoir was completed in 1966 as part of an Emery County irrigation and recreation project. Its water is routed here from Joe's Valley and Huntington Creek via a canal system. Since completion, the shoreline has been managed as a state park.

The name of both the town and the reservoir honors the three Huntington brothers who first explored this area in 1855—Oliver, William R., and Dimick. Dimick was an interpreter for the local Indians; William was famed as a scout and explorer; and Oliver was an official recorder for the unsuc-

Picnicking at Huntington State Park

cessful Elk Mountain Mission to Moab. The town of Huntington was founded in 1877.

The lake has a good warm-water fishery, with largemouth bass and bluegill the most noteworthy. It is also a good place to catch crawdads, an especially popular activity for children.

Many migratory birds, particularly waterfowl, are sighted here. A walk north of the campsites, past the boat ramp, to the north edge of the reservoir will most likely lead to sandpipers, killdeer, and a variety of ducks in a vegetated wetland with some flowers. Though a little muddy, this edge of the reservoir is obviously good hunting for crawdads, as seen by their remains along the shore.

From the town of Huntington, Huntington Canyon Scenic Byway, Utah 31, climbs high up onto the Wasatch Plateau and into Manti-La Sal National Forest. This 48-mile paved road to Fairview passes high-elevation lakes, interesting geology, and many hiking trails. Stop at the Price Ranger District for handouts on individual trails and a map. The 4-mile Left Fork of Huntington Canyon Trail #131, a National Recreation Trail, is particularly recommended for foot and horse use only and makes a good day hike, with waterfalls, creek, and angling.

A short distance east of Huntington, reached via the town of Cleveland, is the Cleveland-Lloyd Dinosaur Quarry, a National Natural Landmark because of the incredible number of bones and fossils excavated in the area. William Stokes, Utah's pioneering geologist, came home from his studies at Princeton to find a dinosaur skeleton—an *Allosaurus*—for that school in this quarry area in the Morrison Formation. That was the beginning of many such finds for him and resulted in eight fossils being named for him by others; he refused to so honor himself. A visitor center and nature trail are open to the public.

MILLSITE STATE PARK

Hours/Season: Overnight; year-round
Area: 638 acres
Facilities: Picnic tables, 20 campsites, 2 group pavilions, wheelchair-

accessible restrooms with showers, vault toilets, sewage disposal, boat ramp, boat docks, sandy beach, phone: (801) 687-2491

Attractions: Paddling, boating, fishing (ice fishing in winter), windsurfing, water skiing, swimming, hiking, mountain biking, adjacent 9-hole golf course, photography

Access: Off Utah 10 at Ferron, 4 miles west on Ferron Canyon Road

Millsite State Park is along the shore of a particularly scenic reservoir at the mouth of Ferron Canyon. The developed areas of the park are on flat, curving arms of landscaped land with poplar trees on the southwest edge of the lake. Almost twice the size of Huntington Reservoir, at 435 acres, the northern shore of the lake runs smack into 2,000-foot-high cliffs. These are topped with striated sandstone with soft hues of gold and rose, but their feet are badlands eroding at water's edge. An early morning view might be of sun shining intermittently through steel-gray clouds, with raindrops waltzing around canyon walls, illuminating first the reds, then a patch of green on ochre.

One camping area has a section of parallel pull-through sites that are quite close together, but most of the sites are spacious—both back-ins and pull-through circulars—and spread out along the irregular shoreline. Tents are put up on the grassy lawn, and there is access to beach privacy and coves to launch sailboards. The covered group pavilions have large-size grills that enhance the amenities of group picnics. This facility is adjacent to the boat ramp. Supervised groups are frequently brought here to learn how

Cliffs, cove, and reservoir at Millsite State Park

to canoe, and they have considerable fun in the process as they swish softly across the water.

Desert explorers will find foot paths around the water and expanses of natural terrain for walking, with a nature trail for plant interpretation. Tamarisks grow by the water. Mountain bluebirds flit among the trees, and golden-mantled squirrels are seen. Winter visitors at the park have a good chance of seeing some of the big-game herds of deer, elk, and moose that have their wintering grounds in the area. The reservoir is used at this time of year for ice fishing and skating, though the entry road is not plowed.

The Millsite Reservoir is part of the Ferron Watershed Project, a multi-purpose water containment at 6,100 feet completed in 1970 with the combined efforts of several agencies. Before the dam was built, there was an old dam at the site to service a flour mill, hence the reservoir name. The lake provides water for farm irrigation, domestic use for the city of Ferron, and recreation. The dam is deep enough to provide cold water for the rainbow and cutthroat trout populations.

Immediately east of the state park is a 9-hole golf course constructed by the city of Ferron and Emery County. It adds to the recreational possibilities while using the state park as a camping base.

Ferron Canyon Road continues past the park, though now a gravel road, and leads to many points of interest as it climbs to the top of the Wasatch Plateau, locally called the Manti Top or Manti Mountains. First seen along this route is the wetland vegetation at the upper end of the reservoir, where a variety of ducks hang out. As one follows the pretty creek uphill and onto Manti-La Sal National Forest land, the sandstone walls—jumbled forma-

Young canoeists practice at Millsite State Park

tions with numerous flat surfaces—close in. This nearby stretch is good scouting country for rock art, which is found quite often in this area a few miles northwest of the state park. More recent graffiti, of pioneer times, is also seen. Check with a park ranger for exact locations. This route (closed in winter except to skiers and snowmobilers) continues on to high country, past Black Canyon, Slide Hollow, Willow Lake, and Ferron Reservoir, and connects to the unpaved section of Skyline Drive. It eventually goes downhill again to reach US 89 at Gunnison.

GREEN RIVER STATE PARK

Hours/Season: Overnight; year-round
Area: 53 acres
Facilities: Picnic tables, 42 campsites, group camping, group pavilion, wheelchair-accessible restrooms with showers, sewage disposal, boat ramp, amphitheater, phone: (801) 564-3633
Attractions: Boating, hiking, fishing, paddling, birdwatching
Nearby: John Wesley Powell Memorial Museum
Access: At the eastern edge of the town of Green River, just off Interstate 70, on the western bank of the river

Although known early to the Indians as *Seedskadee* (meaning prairie hen), this waterway has been called the Green River since General William Ashley's fur-trapping days, and possibly as early as when Spanish explorers roamed these parts. In the town of Green River, Green River State Park is on the banks of that river at a hot summer elevation of only 4,100 feet.

The town is known for its fine-tasting watermelons, which are honored with a Melon Days festival in September. The park is near the only vehicle crossing of the Green River for approximately 300 miles. This crossing was originally used as a postal station along this route by a man named Blake who won a United States mail contract in 1876. It evolved into a town, later named to coincide with the name of the railway station here on the Denver and Rio Grande Western Railroad.

The state park is a green place of tall cottonwoods and well-manicured lawns, a favorite embarkation place for putting into the river, though the campground is seldom full. The Green is wide and quiet in this open stretch of river, a fine stretch of flatwater for canoes. Walkers have room to stroll along an old road that edges the water. Few parks have shadier campsites. An amphitheater has interpretive programs for campers.

A good variety of birds can be sighted at certain times—kingbirds, mourning doves, egrets, herons, hawks, owls, and numerous species of warblers. Astute observers will spot beaver and/or muskrat in the river in the dim light of morning or evening.

Anglers come to catch catfish and carp, and they can also snag one of the four unique native fish that are threatened with extinction and protected—Colorado squawfish, razorback sucker, humpback chub, and bonytail chub. Fishermen are requested to release any of these alive and to report their catch to the Utah Division of Wildlife Resources, Nongame Section, 1596 W. North Temple, Salt Lake City, Utah 84116, phone: (801) 538-4700. If the fish is tagged, report the number and type of the tag.

For over thirty years, an annual Friendship Cruise has started at this state park. This powerboat trip takes two or three days and covers nearly 200 miles, first going down the Green River to the Colorado and then traveling upstream on that river to the take-out point at Moab.

The Green River originates in Wyoming, where it flows 291 miles before entering the state of Utah. Though it jogs for 42 miles into Colorado, its journey through Utah, until it connects with the Colorado River, is about 397 miles. Running this long river has become a popular adventure trip, and a quota of floaters has been put into effect. Permits are required.

Green River State Park is the put-in point for the 123-mile float through Labyrinth and Stillwater canyons to the Green's confluence with the Colorado River in Canyonlands National Park. No vehicle access, however, is available at that point. This section is rated beginner to intermediate for canoe, kayak, and raft. Some rafters go on to the more demanding experience of Cataract Canyon and exit at Lake Powell. Those wanting a shorter, calmer trip with a take-out point can float 70 miles downstream from the state park through Labyrinth Canyon, but not Stillwater, leaving the river at

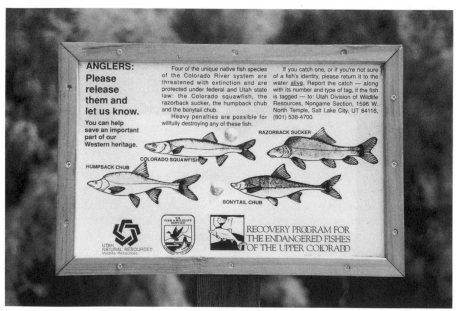

Sign describing recovery program for endangered native fish at Green River State Park

The only bridge within a 300-mile stretch of the Green River (near Green River State Park)

Mineral Bottoms near the north boundary of Canyonlands National Park, where a primitive road connects to Utah 313 and eventually Moab. One-day rafting trips are also a possibility near the town of Green River.

To learn more about Utah's river history and heritage, and especially the accomplishments of nineteenth-century explorer John Wesley Powell, visit the John Wesley Powell River History Museum in the town of Green River, with its interpretive exhibits, art displays, river runners' hall of fame, full-size boat replicas, and multimedia presentation.

Powell was an extraordinary individual of great intelligence and deductive powers, besides being a courageous one-armed man who ran the Colorado and Green rivers while sitting on an armchair lashed to a wooden flatboat. A sandstone frieze at the museum depicts him navigating a rapids on the Green River from this unusual perch. He lost his right forearm in the Civil War battle of Shiloh, yet he went on to name some of the wildest sections of the Green and Colorado rivers—Desolation, Westwater, and Cataract canyons.

A self-taught man, after the war he became professor of geology and natural history at Illinois State Normal University and then collected funding for his 1869 river explorations. He went on to become father of half of today's federal scientific bureaus and realized how proper water management would become so important in the settlement of the arid West, with water rights and land titles coupled together. Powell's firsthand study of American Indian philosophy helped shaped his conservation concerns, and if his early advice on how to treat and educate Indians to fit into a modern world had been followed, their history might have been a happier one. His ideas on forest use, irrigation projects, and setting aside public lands for its citizens were considerably ahead of his time.

Mountain bicyclists may want to do the 10-mile ride from the town of Green River to Crystal Geyser, located along the river bank. This feature shoots water into the air several times a day and bubbles away in between eruptions, spilling down stone terraces stained by minerals and algae and rimmed with salt deposits.

Those traveling Interstate 70 west of Green River should plan more time than is usually allowed for freeway travel. The almost 70-mile stretch of highway west to Utah 10 goes through a vast primitive area in the midst of the San Rafael Swell and San Rafael Reef, spectacular scenery that deserves frequent stops. The highway system has been kind enough to include many rest stops along the way. Why not take a picnic along?

GOBLIN VALLEY STATE PARK

Hours/Season: Overnight; year-round
Area: 3,014 acres
Facilities: Picnic tables, 21 campsites, group camping, group pavilion, wheelchair-accessible restrooms with showers, vault toilets, sewage disposal, exhibit information, phone: (801) 564-3633
Attractions: Intricately eroded formations, geology, hiking, photography
Nearby: San Rafael Reef and San Rafael Swell
Access: 19.5 miles north of Hanksville on Utah 24 to the Temple Mountain junction, then 5 miles west on signed paved road, and 7 miles south on gravel road to park

The desert and millions of years of geological happenings work in strange ways. Nothing in Utah is quite like Goblin Valley State Park.

Imagine a sea bottom that became exposed when the climate became drier. This layer of sediments gradually hardened into Entrada Sandstone, and uneven weathering began to shape strange creatures. Softer areas were removed by wind and rain, and the more resistant components were smoothed by windblown dust to look like hardened mud. One almost needs to invoke the magic of a sorcerer's apprentice, who somehow invents new tricks, new shapes that we appropriately call goblins.

Goblin Valley was late in being discovered. Though an occasional cowhand probably searched for lost cattle among the weird shapes, it was not until Arthur Chaffin traveled through the area in the late 1920s and named it Mushroom Valley that anyone showed much interest in the place. From a high viewpoint, Chaffin and two companions were fascinated by a vista that included five buttes and a valley of strange-shaped rock formations surrounded by eroded cliffs. Chaffin didn't forget what he saw; it sim-

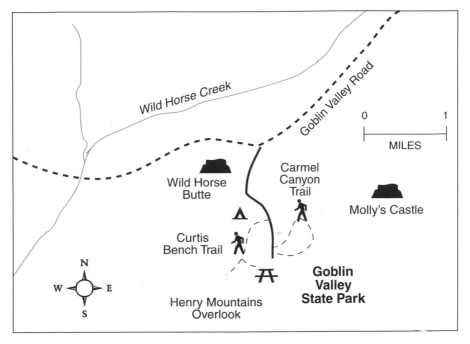

mered in the back of his mind until he brought a party to explore and photograph the valley for several days in 1949. Times change, and Chaffin, the
owner-operator of the old Hite Ferry, became a promoter of Utah's scenic
wonders. He brought Goblin Valley to the public's attention, and it became
protected in 1954, a state park in 1964.

About Goblin Valley State Park is a place for the imagination, but it is also a
destination best visited in April and May—or even winter—not in the swel-
tering heat of August. At an elevation of 5,200 feet, the campground is
backed by sandstone walls, and hoodoos and spires, that reflect more heat
than what comes from direct rays. There are no trees in the camping area,
nor any shade in the midday sun. The parking for the campsites is just one
big strip of paved lot with an adjacent picnic table (not covered) and grill on
the desert surface. (One is a little surprised that no trees were planted in the
campground when the ranger's residence has such nice tall ones.)

About 2 miles down the paved road is the covered observation shelter
overlooking Goblin Valley and its fun trails. The shelter includes picnic
tables and an information exhibit about the park's geology.

Short paths lead down into the goblin arena, where the route is up to the
individual. Just wander about or aim for any distant formation that you
want to inspect closer. These natural sculptures range in height from 10 to
200 hundred feet. It is easy to find mushroom shapes of all sizes. Some of
the intricate shapes look like creatures from outer space, or a band of dwarfs
huddled against the wind, or comic-strip shmoos, or even the head of a

steer, complete with horns and eye sockets. Some even resemble hamburgers on pedestals. Yet the smell is of the desert, not a fast-food restaurant. In the distance, the higher greenish white Curtis Formation stands out in sharp contrast to the red siltstone of the cliffs and goblins.

Children will love playing hide-and-seek in this valley of creatures zapped still. If a rainstorm happens along, don't leave the area; wait to see the chocolate-colored rivers flow between the figures. Then, like more wizardry, these dry quickly in the warmth and sun and abracadabra! New characters arrive. Change happens often here. Some characters grow, some fall away. *Bicycles and OHVs are not allowed inside this area of Goblin Valley.*

The hot, sandblown area of the goblins is pretty devoid of plants. Some sparse desert vegetation is seen in the surrounding San Rafael Desert and consists of wild onion, Russian thistle, tumbleweed, shadscale, winterfat, larkspur, cacti, Mormon tea, and Indian rice grass.

The wildlife is mostly nocturnal and seldom seen, but spotted skunk, porcupine, kangaroo rat, kit fox, coyote, bobcat, jackrabbit, badger, gopher, chuckwalla lizard, and scorpion species do reside here.

Besides Goblin Valley wandering, two other trails are part of the state park. Carmel Canyon Loop goes off from the northeast corner of the observation parking lot for 1.5 miles, descends into a canyon, winds through some badlands and toward an impressive butte called Molly's Castle, then enters a short narrows section before climbing back to road. The 2-mile

An impressive butte called Molly's Castle backs the sculptures at Goblin Valley State Park

Curtis Bench Trail begins at the campground and is more interesting, with many ups and downs. A spur from this trail offers a view of the Henry Mountains to the south.

The facilities at the park are powered by solar energy, converted by photovoltaic (PV) cells into electricity for both the two ranger residences and the campground restroom. Twenty-eight of the silicon PV cells make up an array that faces south at an angle to collect maximum energy from the sunlight. This creates direct current that is stored in large, deep cycle batteries in an adjacent building. A power inverter converts this electricity into alternating current, enough for three days without sun. Some RVers are beginning to use PV cells to power their rigs.

The hot water for showers is solar heated, with collectors on the restroom roof. Antifreeze in coils behind the collectors is heated and pumped into a heat exchanger to heat water, and then the antifreeze is recycled.

When visiting Goblin Valley State Park, you might want to look for the Indian writings that are near Temple Mountain, reached by continuing on Temple Mountain Road before turning south to the park. Though paved initially, this soon becomes a dirt road.

Located at the southeastern corner of the San Rafael Reef, the state park is a good base for exploring the primitive areas of both the Reef and the San Rafael Swell. The reef is a near-vertical sawtooth ridge at the eastern edge of the San Rafael Swell where it meets the San Rafael Desert. It is a classic monocline, a sudden tilt or jog in the plane of sedimentary rock strata.

Named by Spanish explorers, the San Rafael Swell is a great anticlinal, kidney-shaped upwarp lying entirely within Emery County, roughly 75 miles long by 30 miles wide. It was formed millions of years ago when underground forces pushed upward and the overlying rock strata was deformed. The central area is of late Paleozoic outcrops, with surrounding hard and soft formations of Triassic, Jurassic, and Cretaceous ages. Cliffs enclose the central area called Sinbad.

Since this geological upheaval, weathering has beaten away at this jumble of rock called the San Rafael Swell and fractured it into an unusual array of mesas, buttes, pinnacles, seldom-visited streams, deep canyons, and panoramic vistas. Except for the slash of Interstate 70 through it, some inactive uranium mines, a network of dirt roads, and a few livestock facilities, the Swell is an undeveloped area, and visitors should travel with topographic maps and information, including safety precautions, available from the Bureau of Land Management.

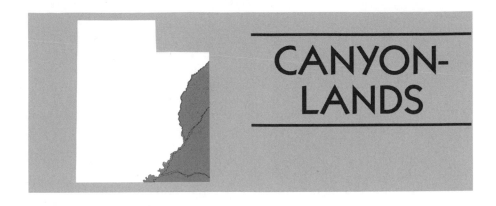

CANYON-LANDS

▲ Utah's land east of the Colorado and Green rivers from the Book Cliffs in the north to the Arizona border constitutes the travel region of Canyonlands. The influence of these two rivers upon the landscape has laced canyon after canyon across the land. Dead Horse Point State Park offers a bird's-eye view of some of the results.

For more evidence of erosion, visit Arches National Park near Moab to see the densest collection of natural stone arches, where rock formations have cracked and split and chipped away until fins of porous sandstone became arches. These vary in size and shape from Landscape Arch (longest natural span in the world) to Double Window to Delicate Arch, with its framing of the snow-peaked La Sal Mountains.

If you get an urge for green forests and mountain lakes, drive the 37-mile La Sal Loop. Besides the opportunity to discover a couple of lakes, wildlife, trails, and wildflowers, one gets an eagle's view of the red rock terrain around Moab on the rise to higher elevations.

Canyonlands National Park shows erosion and geology at its most diverse. Spires and needles and mazes form a three-dimensional puzzle of rock formations that only the hardiest trekkers, cyclists, rock climbers, and rafters can penetrate to its innermost secrets. The Canyon Rims Recreation Area to the east of this park provides additional views and exploration possibilities.

As the Colorado continues southwest it begins to widen, to spread fingers out into any crevice in the surrounding rock walls as it backs up from its unnatural damming to become Lake Powell. The river becomes a broad waterway for fishing and water sports in the Glen Canyon National Recreation Area.

Opposite: *Hikers take in a view that stretches from Dead Horse Point to Canyonlands National Park*

The world's largest natural bridge is a sacred place called *Nennezoshia* ("rainbow of stone") by the Navajo Indians. Boats from marinas in the Glen Canyon National Recreation Area can travel to Forbidding Canyon, from where it is only a 0.25-mile hike to Rainbow Bridge National Monument. The bridge was reached only by a 14-mile hike or horseback ride when the river was still wild. One can still do that trail. Formed by the erosive action of streams, other natural bridges are found at Natural Bridges National Monument, though no stream flows under one of the three bridges any longer.

Just south of these bridges is the Grand Gulch Primitive Area, a place where backpackers can hike past many Anasazi ruins, petroglyphs, and pictograms. Indians used to farm on these canyon floors.

This region is rich in evidence of the ancient Anasazi and Fremont Indians. Edge of the Cedars State Park contains excavated ruins and a museum of artifacts. Horseshoe Canyon in Canyonlands National Park has possibly the best prehistoric rock art in North America. Indian culture is still viable in the extreme south of the region, on the Navajo Reservation.

Much of the northern boundary of Navajo land is the San Juan River, which curves into a section of entrenched meanders at Goosenecks State Park. Constrained by high rock walls, these loopings of the river are easily seen at the park viewpoint.

This part of the Colorado Plateau frequently experiences summer temperatures over one hundred degrees during the day, though nights cool down to the fifties. Spring and fall—with pleasant days—are good times to explore. Winter weather varies with the elevation and terrain, with some places getting some snow (particularly the mountains), and temperatures at night below twenty degrees. Water is hard to find outside cities, so carry it with you.

It does rain sometimes. Mystery writer Tony Hillerman says that the Navajos call "the brief, noisy, violent thunderstorm 'male rain'... and the slower, enduring, soaking shower 'female rain'."

DEAD HORSE POINT STATE PARK

Hours/Season: Overnight; year-round
Area: 5,082 acres
Facilities: Picnic tables, 21 campsites, group camping, group pavilion, visitor center, interpretive museum, gift shop, sewage disposal, electric hookups, amphitheater, observation shelter, *limited water so fill RV tanks before arrival (reason for no showers)*, phone: (801) 259-2614
Attractions: Hiking trails, photography, nature study, geology, potholes, wildlife viewing, summer evening programs
Nearby: Canyonlands' Island in the Sky District
Access: 11 miles northwest of Moab on US 191 and then 23 miles southwest on Utah 313 to the end of the highway

136

William Lee Stokes wrote, "One formation stands out as the greatest scene-maker of the western United States, the Navajo Sandstone." He goes on to list places where this is the chief attraction, and Dead Horse Point State Park is on that list. His words have authority, too, because as a geologist at the University of Utah Dr. Stokes taught an extremely popular course entitled Geology and Scenery of Utah. His book, *Geology of Utah*, has a 360-degree photographic image of the vista at Dead Horse Point State Park that wraps around the cover and is breathtaking. This hints at the visual attraction of this park.

When *National Geographic Traveler* ran a feature on the country's top fifty state parks in the spring of 1994, Dead Horse Point State Park shared the honors. Three of these parks were featured by *CBS Morning News* on location, and this was one of those selected. That event increased the popularity of this already much-visited park.

The park's name is another story. The promontory so named had a 30-yard neck that became a natural corral for rounding up wild mustangs. All it needed was a bit of fencing and a gate. Cowboys chose the better horses after roping and breaking them for either personal use or sale. The culls or "broomtails" were left behind. The story goes that the gate was supposedly left open to let the "broomtails" run free off the point, but for some reason they all stayed there and died of thirst.

When entering the park, stop at the visitor center for information. If you

Potholes in slickrock provide a unique opportunity for nature study at Dead Horse Point State Park

are camping, check in with the ranger for site openings. This facility has exhibits, publications, souvenirs, and snacks.

Kayenta Campground, a short distance past the visitor center, has individual sites with tent pads among the juniper trees with picnic tables that are covered and enclosed on two sides. There is a storage cupboard that can be padlocked and an overhead light. Although there are modern restrooms, water is trucked from Moab and there are no showers. *Please limit your water use.*

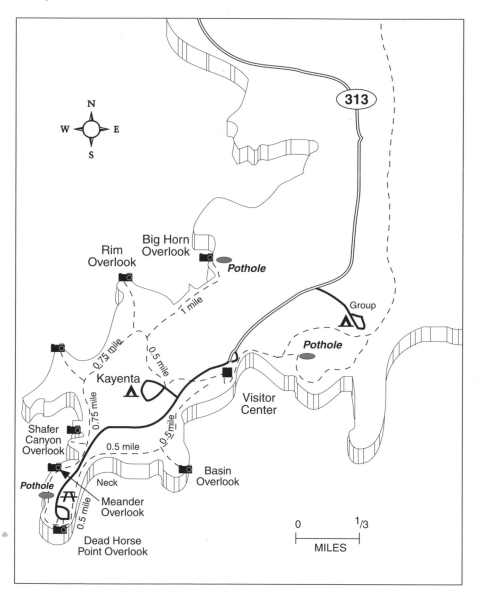

Kayenta Campground is open April through October, but winter camping is allowed on the point. The winter season is short with little snow, and although nights are cold, daytime temperatures are pleasant. At 6,000 feet, this arid desert landscape of stark and magnificent geological beauty has an average of 10 inches of rainfall annually.

Although a road goes to the Dead Horse Point Overlook, hiking trails will let you savor the environment on the way. The main trail starts at the visitor center and follows the southeast edge of this high mesa that drops off sheerly on both sides and the point. At 0.5 mile there is a short trail to the basin overlook. Notice the brilliant turquoise pools far below in the valley. These are solar evaporation ponds containing potash that is mined near Moab. Another 0.5 mile and the trail reaches the neck, the natural boundary of the mustang corral. From here it is another 0.5 mile to the point. This is an easy trail but watch the weather. It is not a place to be when a summer thunderstorm strikes because you will be the tallest object.

The day-use area is at the point and includes a large observation shelter and scattered picnic tables. Take your time to savor each foot of the views around the point and consider the forces at work here over the ages.

Two thousand feet below the point, the Colorado River loops and winds through the Colorado River Gorge as it sends its hoard of drainage water toward Canyonlands National Park. To the southwest is Sky Mesa, wedged between the Green and Colorado rivers. South of Sky Mesa, the rivers converge. During the period of uplift, which accelerated river erosion and canyon carving, even small tributaries left their cutting patterns as swiggles seen upon the distant rocky landscape.

Below the rivers is the 300-million-year-old Paradox Formation. Just above that lies the Honaker Trail Formation at a level with the Colorado River. Stacked above are the layers of sedimentary rock slashed through by the rivers—Cutler, White Rim, Moenkopi, Chinle, Wingate—until finally the Kayenta Sandstone that you stand on, surrounded by patches of Navajo sandstone that still remain. Time and erosion and rivers have exposed these layers of rock.

A return hike from the point can be made in reverse order or by way of a continuing trail on the other side of the mesa. Trail following is somewhat more difficult here, with some route finding and slickrock maneuvering (with cairns to mark the way), but it is a more interesting hike. Outcroppings of rock are varied, and there are views of buttes, pinnacles, and benchlands in this bedrock vista. Several short hikes lead to rim overlooks.

Nature study is better on this side also. Watch for deer tracks, skittish chipmunks, and jackrabbits, which are small and friendly. Lichens color many of the rocks, and spring finds yellow and red wildflowers blooming. This trail returns via the campground, with a short trail continuing on to the visitor center.

Another trail heads off on the other side of the visitor center and goes east for some distance to an area of potholes. These are concave areas, caused by erosion of softer rock, in large slabs of slickrock that contain pools of water that vary according to the weather—rainwater pockets. Look for life that manages to inhabit these, tadpoles and fairy shrimp, for instance. The trail is in the process of being extended to the east and north of this pothole area to the entrance of the park, probably another 4 miles or so.

Another interesting feature of this desert area are the microbiotic crusts. These are crunchy surfaces in sandy soils that contain many living creatures, living patches of soil that play an important role in this ecosystem. Though dominated by cyanobacteria (the oldest form of life known), this soil also contains lichens, mosses, green algae, microfungi, and other bacteria. In desert soil, cyanobacteria are filamentous bacteria that leave trails of sticky mucilage that form webbings of fiber throughout the soil when moistened. As a result, this soil is held together against erosion. This sticky soil also stores water. These patches of microbiotic crust are rich in nutrients and provide benefits for vascular plants. When exploring, watch for these and try to avoid stepping on them. They are easy to spot with their dark, crusty appearance.

In August, the Annual Dead Horse Point Square Dance is held at the visitor center.

It would be a shame to travel Utah 313 to the park and not continue the next few miles to the Island in the Sky section of Canyonlands National Park. (The state park can serve as an overnight base). If nothing else, drive across "The Neck" of Sky Mesa to the end of the road at Grand View Point. This was described by explorer John Wesley Powell: "What a world of grandeur is spread before us! Below is the canyon through which the Colorado runs. We can trace its route for miles, and at points catch glimpses of the river. From the northwest comes the Green in a narrow winding gorge."

Walk the mile to the tip of the rim of this island for a panoramic survey of this national park, with the Henry, La Sal, and Abajo mountains behind the convoluted canyons. With more time, do the 0.5-mile loop trail to Mesa Arch, and take a side road to Upheaval Dome. Mountain bikers might want to consider riding down into the canyon on the Shafer Trail road to White Rim. Canyonlands is a place of quiet backcountry wilderness and solitude, with little development in the park.

Hikers and mountain bikers will find a variety of trails in the Moab area. Pick up information at the Moab Visitor Center at 805 N. Main Street. The Slickrock Bike Trail is a challenging, advanced experience of 10.3 miles, with an adjacent practice loop. Other trails are easier and pass great scenery, even petroglyphs. Check on the very popular Canyonlands Fat-Tire Festival held in Moab in autumn.

Moab is also a center for rafters since the Colorado River is next door. Utah's most popular one-day river trip for kayakers and rafters is launched 21 miles northeast of Moab at Hittle Bottom. It is 13 miles to Takeout Beach and requires intermediate skills, more challenging in high water.

EDGE OF THE CEDARS STATE PARK

Hours/Season: Day use; year-round, except for Thanksgiving, Christmas, New Year's Day, Civil Rights Day, and Presidents Day
Area: 16 acres
Facilities: Picnic tables, museum, gift shop, wheelchair-accessible restrooms, phone: (801) 678-2238
Attractions: Prehistoric ruins, history, interpretive trails, Anasazi artifacts, historic films, slide shows
Nearby: Newspaper Rock
Access: Follow signs from US 191 in the city limits of Blanding for 1 mile to park

▲Edge of the Cedars State Park, located at an elevation of 4,800 feet, is misnamed. Mormons chose this area to settle because water was available in Westwater Canyon, a tributary of the San Juan River that eventually reaches Lake Powell. On this fertile White Mesa, they found Utah juniper trees and thought they were cedars, hence the name. The trees, however, were satisfactory for chests, fence posts, and shingles.

The Mormons raised hay and grain, cattle, horses, and pinto beans in Grayson, a town they named after a pioneer. Then an Easterner named Thomas D. Bicknell offered to build a library for any town that would be named after him. Two Utah towns took him up on it, so he split the library fund:

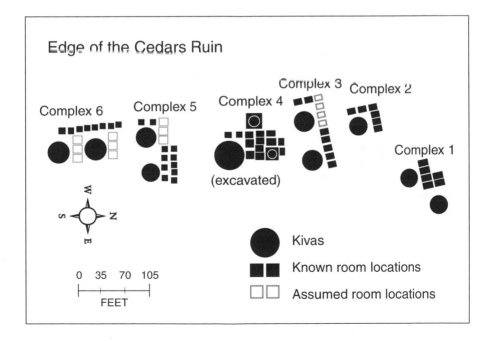

141

Anasazi ruins at Edge of the Cedars State Park

Grayson became Blanding (after his wife's maiden name) and Thurber became Bicknell.

Inhabitants of Blanding found evidence of ancient ruins near the town, but it was not until the late 1960s that Weber State College of Ogden sent out an archaeological team on a dig. For three years they excavated Complex 4 and part of Complex 6. To preserve the exposed ruins, they capped the walls with cement mortar. Other walls and mortar are the originals.

This site, which covers a linear distance of 586 feet, was the home of several Anasazi Indian families from about A.D. 700 to 1220. Archaeologists have identified six living and ceremonial complexes made of stone and adobe on this ridge above Westwater Canyon. The state park has designed a planked-walk trail with an accompanying interpretive brochure as a guide among the ruins, which were placed on the National Register of Historic Places in 1971.

At the center of the site, in Complex 4, a large open depression is all that remains of a Great Kiva, the northernmost one of its kind in Utah and unusual in that these are not common north of the San Juan River. Like other Great Kivas, this one was probably roofed and was used for inter-community ceremonies because of its large size. The flat top or plaza was no doubt used for dances and ceremonies, plus a playground for children while their mothers ground corn, prepared meals, and made pottery and baskets. Imagine the men nearby making tools, or adding on to a pueblo. One can see the living quarters and storage areas of a family. Some rooms were entered through the roof.

At Complex 6, two large depressions are either kivas or pithouses of an earlier occupation at Edge of the Cedars. One kiva has a restored roof atop the original walls. Visitors can climb down into this kiva in the same manner as the Anasazi and consider the past.

Complexes 1, 2, 3, and 5 are unit-type pueblos that were built approximately 900 to 1,000 years ago. They consisted of a row of surface rooms on the north side, and sometimes the west side, of a kiva.

To the north, the Abajo (Blue) Mountains can be seen above the landscape of the mesa. These are essential to the settlement of this area because they provide the water that flows into Westwater Creek and nourishes the plant life and the people. The prehistoric farmers were also attracted to the fertile red-brown loess soil in the area. Porphyritic gravels, originally from the knolls and ridges of the Abajo Mountains, were crushed and used as tempering materials by prehistoric inhabitants in ceramic vessel construction.

In 1978, a museum was built at Edge of the Cedars State Park. It exhibits an excellent collection of Anasazi artifacts and pottery. The human history—Anasazi, Ute, Navajo, and Euro-American settlers—is traced in other exhibits. Native American pottery can be purchased in the gift shop.

In 1993, the museum was closed while some expansion took place. At that time, an antiquities workshop was held to sort and catalogue artifacts for permanent storage at the museum. The prehistoric artifacts were originally thrown together in 100 archive boxes full of mixed tags and labels. Part of the Passports in Time program sponsored by the U.S. Forest Service, the workshop offered volunteers the opportunity to experience archaeology work first hand. Participants came from all over the country at their own expense. They found it exciting to be immersed in the entire collection and work with the various pieces of pottery. The red ware pottery, from the Pueblo 1 time period, was unique to this area and was traded to places as far away as Mesa Verde.

The artifacts were sorted and catalogued according to individual sites. This will aid in tracing the settlement and dating of each site. Museum curator Todd Prince remarked that this workshop did in one week what would have taken him two years to accomplish alone. There are, however, 400,000 to 500,000 objects still in storage that have not yet been sorted and catalogued.

Intriguing outdoor sculptures complement the exterior of the museum building. These are sticklike forms of people and animals. Corn grows behind the museum; a covered picnic area is off to one side.

This state park encompasses one of the many prehistoric ruins found in the Four Corners region, from tiny granaries to the incredible wonders of Mesa Verde. So rich in artifacts is the area that problems are encountered when people do not respect the artifacts left by the Anasazi Indians. With pots sometimes selling for five figures, greed sometimes overshadows the fact that looting ancient sites is strictly forbidden and illegal under federal law. Besides that, it shows great disrespect for this ancient culture whose burial grounds are often disturbed during such pillaging. Those who wan-

Sculpture outside museum at Edge of the Cedars State Park

der the backcountry may come upon unknown artifacts, which can provide a high point to your explorations as you realize that you have seen something seldom, or never, seen before. You can damage such finds with your oily and sweaty touch, so do not touch them. Look and walk away, enlightened and happy in this mental communication across the years.

To continue this tenuous connection with the ancient ones, travel to nearby Newspaper Rock via Utah 211 (Squaw Flats Scenic Byway), 14 miles north of Monticello. Newspaper Rock was a state park until 1993, but it is now managed by the BLM. On a vertical sandstone wall are many petroglyphs, symbols etched by humans as far back as 1,500 years.

What do these petroglyphs mean? The Hopi Indians still use some of these figures in religious ceremonies that their ancestors, called *Hisatsinom* (or Anasazi by archaeologists), etched as rock art. Some drawings are connected to astrological events, some to calendars, some to hunting magic. Archaeologists believe some rock art depicts maps that lead to water. Is it possible some rock art is prehistoric graffiti? There is still much to learn about what the ancients have said with these petroglyphs, but it is fun to do your own sleuthing.

GOOSENECKS STATE PARK

Hours/Season: Overnight; year-round

Area: 10 acres

Facilities: Picnic tables, observation shelter, 12 primitive campsites, vault toilets, *no fee, no water*, phone: (801) 678-2238

Attractions: Photography, geology, scenic view

Nearby: Natural Bridges National Monument, Monument Valley

Access: Go 3 miles northwest of Mexican Hat on US 163, then 1 mile north on Utah 261, and then west on the paved park road for 4 miles to the overlook

▲ The view of the Goosenecks of the San Juan River seen at the state park
⊥ viewpoint is a world-famous example, almost too perfect, of "incised
meanders." Millions of years ago the land here was much flatter, and then a
period of uplift occurred. Rivers were forced to follow steeper courses, and
this intensified downward erosion.

Controversy exists as to whether meanders follow the original pattern of
flow on flatter terrain or whether rivers worked their way downward into
pre-existing geological features. Recent speculation is that a combination of
both of these theories may be the best answer to the geomorphic problem.

There is no doubt, however, that erosion—caused by water, wind,
frost, and gravity—is a magnificent sculptor and that this viewpoint is
awesome. Stand at this 4,500-foot elevation and look into this chasm to see
the winding loops of the San Juan 1,000 feet below. The upper one-third of
exposed rock and the surface you stand on is Permian, while the lower
two-thirds of exposed rock is Pennsylvanian Hermosa Formation, as
shown by fossil evidence.

Erosion still goes on relentlessly. During the spring runoff, as much as 34
million tons of sand, mud, and gravel are transported downstream by the
San Juan River. This quantity of sediment does not include the cobbles,
pebbles, and huge boulders that
are unmeasurable and very energetic in causing further rear-
rangements. Intensified erosion
occurs when water is augmented
with all of this load.

Though there are only about 8
inches of rainfall here yearly,
violent thunderstorms do occur
in summer and can produce
flash floods that raise a stream 10
feet in an hour or so, and these
storms flush the San Juan River
of loose silt and sand.

Goosenecks State Park is undeveloped for the most part.
Twelve primitive campsites with
picnic tables are scattered back
from the edge of the cliff, and
vault toilets are available. If you
camp here, be prepared by bringing water, food, and other necessary gear. Enjoy the solitude then
of a wild place far from much in
the way of civilization. During
the daytime, though, it is a little
disconcerting to find Indian jewelry being sold here.

*Meander of the San Juan River at Goose-
necks State Park*

There are no trees for shade, so it is a pleasure to find a large covered picnic table that serves also as an observation shelter. Summer temperatures are often over 100 degrees Fahrenheit. Winter and spring are usually dry, though a little snow may fall. It is often below freezing in winter.

One can walk along the rim in both directions for a long distance, viewing the brown, silt-laden San Juan River and the regularity of its looping course. It meanders back and forth for more than 5 miles while traveling only 1 linear mile. One can see how debris has piled up at the points where the river pivots.

Lucky travelers will see kayaks or rafts floating down the river. With a BLM permit, one can launch at Mexican Hat for a 57-mile trip down the San Juan River to the Clay Hills Crossing. This river float requires intermediate skills and passes through Goosenecks and Slickhorn Canyon before ending a short distance into Lake Powell.

To capture light on the river and canyon walls, midday photography is better than the usual end of the day for other scenes. Otherwise, one gets only deep, dark shadows where one knows there is a river.

With these spectacular sheer canyon walls, it seems a dichotomy to find flat sagebrush desert stretching out for miles, peppered with blackbrush, saltbush, prickly pear, Russian thistle, Indian ricegrass, and sporadic wildflower blooms. Though chipmunks are frequently seen, the terrain supports only small populations of wildlife, with a few rabbits, rodents, desert reptiles, and an occasional fox, coyote, or bobcat. Migratory birds sometimes follow the river, and cliff swallows, ravens, red-tailed hawks, or golden eagles are possible sightings.

Several noteworthy attractions are nearby. It would be a shame to miss traveling 21 miles southwest on US 163 to Monument Valley, the magical natural landscape that belongs to the Navajo Indians. A gravel auto-tour loop provides good views of the buttes and mesas that rise abruptly from the valley floor, some looking like massive rock mittens sprouting from the ground.

The second good choice is Natural Bridges National Monument. There are two possible routes. The shortest one is north on Utah 261 to Utah 95, the scenic Bicentennial Highway. The other is longer: Utah 163 east, US 191 north, and then west on Utah 95. Don't make this decision lightly. When one reads the warning signs approaching a hazardous section from flat desert on Utah 261 on the shorter route, one wonders what it will be like. The road goes almost straight up the walls of a red rock canyon, like a giant stairstep in the terrain, a cliff-hanger road (*of corduroy gravel*) with sharp hairpin curves, over 2,000 feet up in 3 miles of road. There are no turn-outs or places to stop, so you are committed once you begin this stretch. (I had a flat tire a few days later and am very thankful it didn't happen there.) This stretch of road is called the Moki (the Mormon name for the Anasazi) Dugway (carved out of solid rock). It was constructed during the 1950s uranium boom, down the cliff face that drops off Cedar Mesa, so that ore could be hauled away.

Natural Bridges National Monument has a 9-mile, one-way road that passes three bridges (Kachina, Sipapu, and Owachomo) that have been carved out of sandstone by the action of desert streams. Hiking trails, of varying difficulty, lead to all three bridges. These bridges formed when great looping meanders broke through thin rock walls at curving points. Will these be formed in the future at Goosenecks?

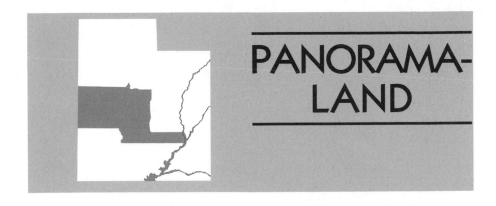

PANORAMA-LAND

Minerals in striped stone formations often impart colors of yellow, purple, red, white, and rust that sometimes occur close together and led the Indians to call this region "The Land of the Sleeping Rainbow." Equally appropriate, the Utah Travel Council has chosen to call the region Panoramaland.

From west to east, Panoramaland begins with basin and range country at the Nevada border, the gateway to Great Basin National Park. Confusion Range and Disappointment Hills hint at some of the hard times in this stark country where some found gold and precious minerals. Topaz Mountain has been set aside for rockhounds, who will also find *trilobites* and *brachiopods* in the surrounding desert. Amid this landscape lies the usually dry Sevier Lake, the southernmost extension of ancient Lake Bonneville, which did have blue water when Great Salt Lake was rising in the mid-1980s.

Yet in the midst of sagebrush, lava rock, extinct volcanoes, and junipers, just west of Topaz Mountain, a wetland oasis exists at Fish Springs National Wildlife Refuge. Those willing to take the long desert drive may see herons, egrets, swans, geese, and perhaps kit foxes, badgers, and coyote. Certainly, they will find solitude. Farther east are acres and acres of moving sand dunes in the Little Sahara Recreation Area, set aside for off-highway vehicles.

The eastern half of Panoramaland is quite different, with parts of four national forests within the region. Those seeking water sports will find four state parks with reservoirs—Yuba, Palisade, Piute, and Otter Creek—all offering a little something different, yet all capitalizing on streams originating in the high forest country.

Opposite: *Flower-edged walkway leading to Territorial Statehouse*

Morning reflections at Palisade State Park

History buffs will find recent Fremont Indian discoveries illustrated at Fremont Indian State Park. Trails will lead them to rock art. Early Mormon memorabilia are exhibited at Territorial Statehouse State Park, Utah's oldest existing government building.

Two scenic byways offer superb scenery and outdoor experiences. Nebo Loop Scenic Byway (38 miles) begins at the town of Payson and ascends into the Wasatch Range past lakes, campgrounds, hiking and horseback trails, and Devil's Kitchen Geologic Interest Site, a red-stone amphitheater complete with spires that contrasts sharply with the mountain greenery of the Uinta National Forest. Hikers who want to reach a mountain summit in one day have access to the Mount Nebo Trail. The byway is closed in winter.

The second byway is the Fish Lake Scenic Byway (23 miles), which accesses one of the gems of Panoramaland, the Fish Lake Basin high country. Whether you want to pursue hiking, horseback riding, mountain biking, camping, fishing, or just relaxing, it is all there. A log lodge and other resorts have long welcomed travelers, and winter sports are centered in Fish Lake Basin. Do take the entire loop tour when the weather is good.

From Fish Lake, it is not far to Capitol Reef National Park, a place not to be missed. As you travel toward the park on Utah 24, consider trying the homemade pickle or pinto-bean pie at the Sunglow Restaurant in Bicknell. Or have dinner at the Capitol Reef Cafe in Torrey. One writer described this place as "an incredible find in a physically beautiful but palate-starved place." Written up in books, the trout is excellent, fresh or smoked, and everything else is fresh, including corn and the special ten-vegetable salad, a delicious surprise.

Then you are soon at Capitol Reef. What were the thoughts of the Mormon pioneers who settled among the colored walls of these canyons that are radiant at sunset? Brigham Young kept sending out his people in search of new lands. At the junction of the Fremont River and Sulphur Creek, the bottomland provided good grazing and farmland and the village of Fruita was settled. Orchards were planted and residents sold peaches, cherries, apples, and apricots that thrived in the protection of the Waterpocket Fold, a reeflike ridge that juts upward with sawtooth edges. The wonder is that these orchards still thrive under the park service and visitors can pick them for a small fee. Two especially worthwhile shorter trails go to Hickman Bridge and Cohab Canyon.

Summer temperatures in Panoramaland vary from highs in the nineties in the desert to perhaps eighty degrees near the mountains. Only 2 to 4 inches of rain water the landscapes. Spring and fall have delightful temperatures, although summer is fine in the high mountains. Winter high averages are in the thirties, with a lot of snow falling in the high elevations.

PALISADE STATE PARK

Hours/Season: Overnight; year-round
Area: 64 acres
Facilities: Picnic tables, 53 campsites, group camping, group pavilion, wheelchair-accessible restrooms with showers, sewage disposal, sandy beach, boat ramp, 18-hole golf course, club house with snack bar and camping supplies, phone: (801) 835-7275 (office), (801) 835-4653 (golf course)
Attractions: Golfing, nonmotorized boating, paddling, windsurfing, fishing (ice fishing in winter), swimming, sun bathing, hiking, bird-watching, ice skating, cross-country skiing, tubing and sledding, photography
Access: From US 89, just north of the town of Sterling, go 2 miles east on signed road to park

If you've been looking for a lake without motorboats, Palisade State Park will do nicely. So put your canoe (or your sailboard) on top of your vehicle, grab your fishing pole, and head for some quiet recreation. This 75-acre reservoir, on the western slope of the Manti Range at an elevation of 5,800 feet, has a long history of attracting visitors.

It was back in the 1860s that Daniel B. Funk, an early settler of the surrounding Sanpete Valley, dreamed up a summer and weekend resort scheme that became reality with the encouragement and assistance of Brigham Young. Funk obtained a land patent from the government after bargaining with Chief Arapeen, a Sanpitch Indian, for this property.

Funk and his family then set to work building a dam on Sixmile Creek, with a canal to the present lake site, not an easy chore back then. By 1873 there was a 20-foot-deep reservoir. Next came the additions of a dance pavilion (Mormons did like to dance), rental cabins, and facilities to encourage recreational fishing, rowboating, and picnicking. Shade trees were planted. In winter, the family cut ice from the lake and stored it to make ice cream, which later sold for five cents a plate.

Soon recreation seekers were coming to Funk's Lake on horseback or by horse and buggy. A steam-powered pleasure boat furnished excursions, but this capsized in 1881, drowning eleven passengers. Mr. Funk died in 1887, after which the resort had a series of owners.

In 1894, the Sanpete Valley Railway Company constructed a branch line to within 500 yards of the lake and more visitors arrived at Funk Lake. After World War I, a second steamboat, though smaller and for only six passengers, was launched on the lake and gave rides for several years.

One of the owners changed the name of the reservoir to Palisade Lake in the 1920s, thinking that it resembled the cliffs called the Palisades that were along the Hudson River in his home country back East.

The Great Depression slowed the flow of people to this recreation area, and a fire destroyed the dance pavilion. After World War II a resurgence in visits to Palisade Lake occurred, and people came for swimming, fishing, and ice skating in winter. Sanpete County donated the property to the state park system. By this time, the water depth of the lake had been increased to about 40 feet to meet irrigation needs.

Several different camping areas edge the lake. Turn right at the entry station for individual campsites. The original Pioneer Campground is easy to recognize with its wonderful old shade trees. Continue past this for

Golfers at Palisade State Park

Arapeen Campground, which has a nice choice of spacious and varied sites near the sandy beach (which is really small gravel). Many trees provide shade throughout the park. A gateway from Arapeen Campground provides easy access to the golf course and clubhouse, which has a PGA professional and a full range of services and supplies.

For group camping at Sanpitch Campground, turn left at the entry station, where there is a group pavilion and dumping station for RVs.

Throughout the day and the seasons, the lake runs through a sequence of color changes, sometimes green or blue, other times taking on the hues of sunrise and sunset. The morning after a thunderstorm, I watched rose-colored clouds reflected over the lake's surface in the crisp coolness of dawn.

The lake is small enough for an easy hike around its perimeter. From Arapeen Campground, walk past the beach to the trail along the undeveloped side of the reservoir, a beautiful stretch just above a rocky beach. The path twists and turns among trees with lichen-colored boulders on the hillside above the trail. Watch for frequent sightings of kingfisher, great blue heron, Western tanager, flicker, or hawk. Squirrels, hares, and rock chucks are often seen on the slopes. From fall through spring, be alert for mule deer. Look for cactus and wildflowers in season.

This peaceful side continues to the dam at the other end of the lake, where there is a walkway across the dam. Though the trail ceases, it is easy to continue around the lake, going first past some wetlands, then the group campground, the ranger station, and the inlet to the lake from Sixmile Creek. Next comes another good birdwatching wetland area near the boat ramp, where canoes slide into the water. Pass Pioneer Campground and continue to Arapeen Campground. Several resident geese are seen in this area.

Anglers can fish for rainbow and cutthroat trout. Winter brings ice skaters and cross-country skiers.

Sixmile Canyon Road cuts east just before you enter Palisade State Park. This road accesses the Dan Henry Trail #122, with a connection in the process of being constructed to the Great Western Trail.

The towns of Mayfield and Manti both have roads that go east to connect with Skyline Drive atop the Wasatch Plateau. There you will find campgrounds, hiking, a fine autumn leaf display, and Nordic skiing in winter.

The annual Mormon Miracle Pageant is staged on the grounds of the impressive Mormon Temple in Manti, one of the oldest Mormon settlements, in July.

YUBA STATE PARK

Hours/Season: Overnight; year-round
Area: 629 acres
Facilities: Picnic tables, 26 campsites, group camping, group pavilion, wheelchair-accessible restrooms with showers, sewage disposal, boat

docks, and boat ramp at developed Yuba area on west side of reservoir; picnic tables, primitive camping, boat ramp, and vault toilets at Painted Rocks on east side of reservoir; phone: (801) 758-2611

Attractions: Boating, fishing (ice fishing in winter), water skiing, windsurfing, sailing, swimming, mountain biking, waterfowl hunting in season

Access: The developed area of Yuba is 30 miles south of Nephi, take park road off Interstate 15; Painted Rocks is 15 miles south of Levan off Utah 28

The history of the naming of Yuba State Park would appear to be a unique one. In California, the name Yuba is of Indian derivation, but this is not the case in Utah's park. This dam, the largest on the Sevier River, was constructed by local farmers and ranchers who had the option of losing their water rights or doing the actual building of the dam. These workers called the barrier *U.B. Dam*, and they had a song with lyrics that mentioned they were damned if they worked and damned if they didn't work. The phonetic sound was later spelled Yuba.

Now called Yuba Reservoir or Yuba Lake, the original name was Sevier Bridge Reservoir. When full, the waters cover a surface area of 10,000 acres, or 20 miles long by 2 miles wide. Built over several long years of work between 1902 and 1917, there was almost a disaster in the spring of 1907, when the amount of snowmelt was particularly high. Water poured out of the res-

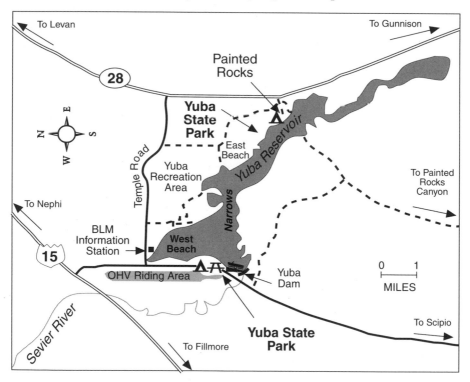

Main campground overlooking reservoir at Yuba State Park

ervoir faster than the spillway could release it, and the dam structure was threatened. As the water reached a peak in mid-June, a rider warned the large number of people assembled at the Mormon church at Deseret, 40 miles west. They responded to this alarm with heroic measures, blasting a temporary spillway to relieve the pressure on the dam.

Yuba State Park is located in the Sevier Valley, part of a narrow depression that cuts through the geographic center of Utah. The developed area is on the west side of the reservoir, just north of the dam. With waters reaching seventy degrees during the summer, visitors are frequent. Water skiers and swimmers delight in this pleasant temperature that cools them from the surrounding air. A wading area is available for children.

Anglers go out in boats or relax in chairs along the gravel banks with a fishing pole. There is year-round fishing for walleye, yellow perch, northern pike, and catfish. The recreation area is open to waterfowl hunting during the designated season.

The campsites are scattered upon a hillside overlooking the water, with picnic tables that are covered by slatted tops and backs to let the breeze through but give some shade. Some sites have double picnic tables. Quite a few trees have been planted to provide shade. A large round brick grill, under a roofed pavilion in the day-use area, is perfect for groups.

Ground squirrels are numerous in the park. Do not be surprised if you put out your lawn chair and one curls up on it for a while.

The Painted Rocks area is on the east side of Yuba Reservoir, a short boat trip or a considerable drive. A gravel road provides driving access to a

Houseboat in the Painted Rocks area of Yuba State Park

primitive camping area, with no real sites as such. A couple of picnic tables and vault toilets are available, but no shade, though a few shrubby junipers are seen. A huge paved boat ramp provides good launching. A rough spur road goes a short distance south for more isolated camping with one table.

The Painted Rocks area has nice views of cliffs across the water. Water skiers skim the water; a houseboat may be docked at water's edge. Most of the park land is on this side of the lake, named for the cluster of prehistoric petroglyphs and pictograms that can be viewed by boat just north of the boat ramp and in several places around the reservoir.

Much evidence indicates that ancient Native Americans inhabited the area. Stone tools, broken pottery, rock art, and remnants of several camps have been found around the reservoir. One also sees more recent mining and ranching evidence. Visitors are allowed to explore the area, with an eye for finding traces of these old cultures, but please do not disturb or remove any ancient artifacts. Report finds to the Utah Division of Parks and Recreation or the Bureau of Land Management.

Other primitive camping areas at North Beach are managed by the BLM. A historic marker is found in this area that commemorates the passage of Fathers Dominguez and Escalante through here in September of 1776, on a route-finding exploration from Santa Fe, New Mexico.

TERRITORIAL STATEHOUSE STATE PARK

Hours/Season: Day use; year-round, daily except Thanksgiving, Christmas, and New Year's Day
Area: 3 acres
Facilities: Picnic tables, museum, restrooms, phone: (801) 743-5316
Attractions: Historical museum
Access: In Fillmore, at 50 West Capitol Avenue

▲When you visit Territorial Statehouse State Park and walk toward the building, envision the proposed final product. This red sandstone building is just one wing of the four that were planned when in 1851 Brigham Young directed construction of the building that he hoped would be the state capitol building in the town of Fillmore. The four wings were to project outward from a central unit, which would be taller than the wings and topped with a Moorish dome. Truman O. Angell, credited with the design of the Mormon Tabernacle in Salt Lake City, was the architect. Funding permitted only the construction of the south wing.

Brigham Young had high hopes. In 1851, the town of Fillmore did not exist yet. The town was named after Millard Fillmore, president of the United States from 1850 to 1853, as thanks from Young for his appointment as governor of Utah Territory by President Fillmore. From 1847 to 1850, the territory had been called the State of Deseret. The petition for statehood, however, was denied at that time. The Utah Territory was roughly four times what became the state of Utah in 1896.

The territorial legislature did meet in this building for one full session in December 1855, so it is Utah's oldest existing governmental building. Conflicts between the Mormons and the United States government eventually led to Salt Lake City being named the seat of government in December 1858.

After that, the statehouse served as a civic center, religious meeting house, school, theater, and jail before it fell into disuse and demolition was threatened. In the mid-1920s, the Daughters of the Utah Pioneers (DUP) restored the building as a museum, and it opened in 1930 under the direction of the Utah State Park and Recreation Commission, with the DUP as custodians. It became a state park in 1957, and is now on the National Register of Historic Places. It houses a pioneer collection plus items from the late nineteenth and early twentieth centuries.

The grounds of the museum include a pleasant shady picnic area and an All American Rose Society garden. An 1867 rock schoolhouse and two restored pioneer cabins are also on the grounds.

On the main floor of the museum, one sees portraits of the original pioneers of 1851 and some of their memorabilia. Try your hand at the multiple-choice puzzle that asks you to match pioneer artifacts.

Several rooms branch off the main hallway, each with a theme. One room has a sewing machine, a rocking chair, a period dress, china from Denmark, bonnets, spectacles, and many handsome quilts—Hope Chest, Crazy Patch, and Friendship designs. A simulated bedroom is complete with fireplace, wardrobe with clothes, shoes, accessories, and a rolling-pin bed with ropes to hold the reversible mattress of straw for summer and feathers for winter. The parlor is furnished with an organ, gramophone, bibles, writing desk, stereoscope, intriguing chandelier, and the good furniture of the time.

As you travel the hall going from room to room, many items are seen along the hall walls. Here are books, encyclopedia, telephones, an old switchboard, an 1856 typewriter, music pieces, and instruments that include an accordion and a violin. Check out the pamphlet "Strange Language of Deseret," with its alphabet in which each letter had only one sound. It did not succeed, though the Mormons gave it a grand try.

The kitchen illustrates the amount of time spent here in the pioneer lifestyle. At first the floors were of dirt, and the furniture and fireplaces were crude. Here was the spinning wheel, the candlemaker, and the butter churn that kept the women busy all day. A dining room has items that came later, a pine china cabinet, and many types of china.

The upstairs is a great open meeting room with pianos and chairs. Two huge chairs with the Great Seal of the State of Utah were brought here after Utah became a state. This legislative hall contains many paintings by pioneer and contemporary Utah artists, including works by Donald Beauregard, a Fillmore native who studied in Paris.

One is sure to notice throughout the statehouse that old portraits seem to be everywhere. In fact, they number over 300. Most are charcoals, though there are a few photographs.

Legislative hall, Territorial Statehouse

In the basement, one room has Paiute Indian artifacts—arrows, bows, and arrowheads. Walk past a huge old camera and notice the old hand-made bricks that form the interior wall. The room that served as a jail looks pretty uncomfortable.

The materials of clothing and other household uses are illustrated in a room with textile fibers and information on how they were produced. Here are cotton, flax, wool, silk, the weaving loom, and the spinning wheel.

It was a rough-and-tumble life, and the room of weapons and saddles illustrates this, with its collection of firearms, swords, and ropes.

Consider the many skills needed in the pioneer life of building a town. These are summarized in the room that recalls the stone cutter, the cooper, the blacksmith, and the carpenter. Their tools and portraits make it easier to envision their lives.

Certainly, one room must be dedicated to farming equipment, the life-blood of survival. One exhibit shows the many types of barbed wires.

One comes away from this museum with a good feel for what the Mormon pioneer life encompassed, from its crude beginnings of self-sufficiency to a somewhat easier living, from vast amounts of time spent in survival activities, yet with hints at some pleasures and hobbies.

Though Fillmore didn't become Utah's capital, it is a viable city of about 2,000 residents, located at 5,100 feet just west of the Pahvant Range and Fishlake National Forest. To the west is the sharply contrasting country of the Sevier/Black Rock Desert with its numerous volcanic remains.

FREMONT INDIAN STATE PARK

Hours/Season: Overnight; year-round
Area: 889 acres
Facilities: Picnic tables, 31 campsites, group camping, visitor center with video program, gift shop, wheelchair-accessible restrooms, vault toilets, phone: (801) 527-4631
Attractions: Fremont Indian artifacts and history, rock art, paddling, fishing, wildlife viewing, 4 interpretive trails (1 wheelchair accessible), forest hiking
Access: Off exit 17 from Interstate 70, 23 miles southwest of Richfield

Although local residents had hints of the archaeological sites that existed in Clear Creek Canyon, the official discovery of the largest known Fremont Indian village occurred in November 1983, in the midst of the construction of Interstate 70. Archaeologists uncovered eighty residential structures and pithouses, and many storage granaries.

The highway construction was delayed until several tons of cultural material were carefully removed for preservation. The original excavation site was destroyed, but all of the artifacts found are housed in the visitor center of Fremont Indian State Park, which was established by the Utah Legisla-

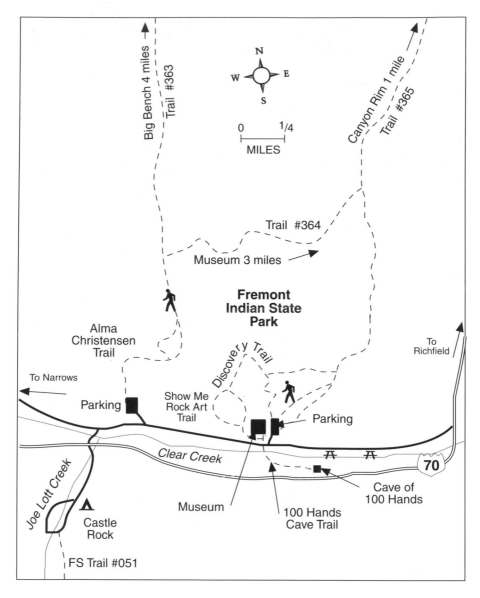

ture in 1985. The park's aim is to preserve Clear Creek Canyon's treasury of rock art and archaeological sites. The museum also provides information about present-day Indians.

Perhaps the best introduction to this park is the orientation video shown in the visitor center. It is probable that the pithouses in the village found here, Five Finger Ridge, were occupied from A.D. 1000 to 1280.

These Fremont Indians hunted for game, collected seasonal wild food in the marshes of Clear Creek, fished for trout, and farmed in the canyon bottoms. Squash, beans, and corn were no doubt their crops, with some of these stored for winter and emergencies. This food was supplemented with pinyon nuts, acorns, wild seeds, bulbs, and berries. Deer, rodents, mountain sheep, and buffalo were in the area.

The museum's many exhibits illustrate the tools and belongings of Indian life, though these are only pieces in a puzzle that represents the Fremont cultural lifestyle. Individuals do not appear to have had long lives, perhaps only about thirty-five years.

The museum asks, "What can we learn from them?" The clues are in their pottery, grinding stones, arrowheads, baskets, weaving, tools, and other findings that suggest how they lived, fit into this environment, and were buried.

The choice of location at 5,900 feet seems good. Artifacts found here show that it was along a trade route between the canyon and the Mineral Mountains, where there is obsidian. Indications are that Clear Creek Canyon had hunter-gatherer inhabitants as early as 5200 B.C. Much later, Spanish explorers may have passed this way. We know that Jedediah Smith went through the canyon in 1826. What is today's freeway route was discovered long ago.

The visitor center also has a gift shop with books, postcards, and other items. Nearby is a reconstructed pithouse.

Do hike the paved Show Me Rock Art Trail (wheelchair accessible) just outside the museum. The petroglyphs were chipped, chiseled, or etched into a tuff rock formation that weathers and slowly destroys the panels of rock art. Very fragile, these petroglyphs must be treated with respect and never touched, or marked with bullet holes—which has happened. Some of this rock art is almost 1,000 years old. Listen for canyon wrens in the slot in the canyon.

A handout correlates interesting information, even legends, to the numbered sites. A reed depicted upon a canyon wall represents the hollow structure that let the Indian people climb into the Promised Land. The twin warrior mounds were where the Spider Woman, the creator person, mixed four colors of the Earth—yellow, red, white, and black—then molded them and covered them with a white cape that was creative wisdom. After she sang the creative song, she uncovered the forms, which were now human beings.

Some petroglyphs commemorate hunting magic. One theory is that some rock art is just doodling, but another is that the Fremonts liked to brag a little, that the bighorn they killed was bigger than the one someone else captured. We can only conjecture what the artist meant with his or her rock art, but that makes it imaginative fun for everyone.

The Discovery Trail branches off from the Show Me Rock Art Trail and immediately climbs steep, uneven rocky stairsteps and passes more rock art. This trail branches to a couple of return trails south to the museum, the longer one with exhibits and good views. This latter trail branches off north to Trail #365, which reaches the canyon rim in 1 mile. Another trail (#364) goes west after hiking a short distance north on #365. Trail #364 is a connecting spur to the 4-mile trail north to Big Bench, #363. The distance from the museum to the Big Bench Trail is 3 miles. If you go south on the Big Bench Trail, you will come to the upper end of the park's Alma Christensen Trail, which can be accessed directly by driving west 0.3 mile from the visitor center to a parking area along the frontage road.

The Alma Christensen Trail is a 0.75-mile interpretive walk to the tablelands above the cliffs on the north side of the canyon. It climbs a short distance in the beginning and then is fairly level. The trail is named for an early settler whose family's cabin was at the site of the trailhead parking lot. This self-sufficient family's gardens, orchards, livestock, and alfalfa fields were located across from where the freeway is now. When a little cold cash was needed, Mrs. Christensen rented rooms to travelers and a sign outside said "Meals all hours." Several families who lived along Clear Creek got together for some fun, and Mr. Christensen had a reputation as a dancer.

Along the hike, look for mule deer tracks, which led the settlers to another meat source. Evidence of the Numa Indians, ancestors of today's Utes, Paiutes, Shoshones, and Gosiute Indians, has been found in this area. Walk around the wickiup near the trail, built of juniper branches that were covered with rabbitbrush. This could accommodate a small family. Obsidian pieces, remains from toolmaking, are seen to the west of the wickiup. There is also a metate and a mano, stone tools used to grind cattail into flour and pinyon nuts into meal. The gritty food that resulted is what wore the enamel off the Fremonts' teeth. These Indians also used the local rock, called Joe Lott tuff (from a volcanic eruption), to make large tools because it is sturdier than obsidian. One wonders whether Alma Christensen discovered artifacts of the Fremont Indians and what he thought about these findings.

The trail goes through a Colorado pinyon/Utah juniper forest that furnished firewood for the Christensens and served many uses for the Fremont Indians—houses, rope and twine, clothing, bags, fuel, medicine, and stuffing for moccasins. Edible plants and animals are part of this ecosystem.

In the right light, one can see a primitive trail that leads to the top of a mountain near the Big Bench. Hunters were successful in finding meat in those higher elevations. Look the other way, across the freeway, and you will see the Tushar Mountains. Turn right now to return on a loop trail to the main path.

The easy 0.75-mile 100 Hands Cave Trail starts at the visitor center, crosses the road and Clear Creek to a fenced-off cave with pictograph hands all over the inside walls. This is the only trail on which mountain bikes are allowed.

Several points along the road can be checked out. Two day-use picnic areas are east of the visitor center. West of the visitor center 1.5 miles is the Narrows, a place where you can see the erosive action of Clear Creek. The Rim Rock Trail, to the west, is washed out in places and should not be hiked without park permission. More trails are in the planning stage.

Clear Creek is a good intermediate run for canoes. Put in at the Pole Creek confluence west of the park for a short run (2 miles) in a narrow canyon until the canyon widens and take-out is possible.

Reconstructed pithouse at Fremont Indian State Park

Castle Rock Campground is a pleasant place to stay overnight. Register at the visitor center and then drive to exit #17 on the freeway, but don't take it. Take the overpass and proceed on the graded road to where it dead ends at the campsites (3 1 miles from the visitor center), where a delightful, quiet overnight stay is possible.

Joe Lott Creek runs through the middle of the campsites, and there are bluff-colored pinnacles that are called "Little Bryce" because they are so similar to the formations in Bryce Canyon, except their color is not as rosy-pink. The rocks catch the early morning light quite brilliantly. Once a Forest Service campground, it has been upgraded and has new restrooms. A geology exhibit is planned. Many trees provide shade, and one hears the quiet murmuring of the creek. If your timing is right, watch a full moon rise above the cliffs.

You are now in the Fishlake National Forest and FS Trail #051, accessed in the campground, goes up into the Tushar Mountains. Gentle at first, the trail gradually becomes moderate in difficulty as the rocky path changes to one of soft dirt, mostly in the shade. The trees become bigger, and red rock formations are glimpsed in the openings. Gambel oak, aspen, pine, and paintbrush are seen and the path crosses Joe Lott Creek and then follows it along a bank above the water. Look for an eagle's nest in a treetop. After a while the creek is crossed again. The trail continues, but just a sampling is quite rewarding.

The Joe Lott Formation found in Clear Creek Canyon is the result of massive volcanic explosions in the Tushar Mountains that occurred about 15 million years ago. This explosion covered the land with a thick layer of volcanic ash, which settled, cooled into layers, and fused to become the tuff material upon which petroglyphs were etched. In the lower canyon, there is columnar jointing where distinctive six-sided pillars were formed when the volcanic material cooled and cracked vertically. Other columns, pillars, buttes, and pinnacles were formed by the weathering caused by wind, freezing, thawing, and the creek itself.

Gordon Topham, the park manager, was written up as a pioneering archaeologist by Tom and Gayen Wharton in their guide book, *Utah*. He grew up in the area and collected many arrowheads and pottery pieces that he now knows are illegal to take, and he gets this message across to others. For one thing, where artifacts are found is important in understanding what they mean. On the way to this insight, he has become an authority on arrowheads and pottery pieces. Artifacts are still being found. A recent discovery was some corn cobs that were radiocarbon-dated back to 175 B.C., before corn was thought to have been cultivated in this part of the world. Topham never tires of learning about the lifestyle of the Fremont Indians, of finding more clues.

Respect Clear Creek Canyon because of its past, but also because it is religiously important to the Paiute Indians today.

Special events occur frequently at the park. In August, the annual Park's Birthday Party is held, and several art shows are featured during the year. Other events include pottery-making workshops, fun runs, Indian Pow-wows, and celebrations at summer solstice and autumn equinox.

PIUTE STATE PARK

Hours/Season: Overnight; year-round
Area: 40 acres
Facilities: Picnic tables, primitive camping, vault toilets, boat ramp, *no fee*, phone: (801) 624-3268
Attractions: Fishing (ice fishing in winter), boating, water skiing, swimming, rockhounding
Access: Off US 89, 6 miles north of Junction

Though undeveloped, Piute State Park is at the edge of a scenic reservoir, a place that attracts anglers to try for some trophy fishing. Rainbow trout, cutthroat trout, brown trout, and smallmouth bass are found here.

The Tushar Mountains rise across the highway to the west, and the water of the lake is smack against the cliffs of the Sevier Plateau. Visitors can pick their own primitive sites for camping, perhaps adjacent to one of the picnic tables that have good views. Vault toilets are available, although hard to approach in midsummer if the mayflies are thick. A few trees punctuate the arid terrain.

A weekend will find the boat ramp doing a fair business with fishermen

View of reservoir at Piute State Park

and water skiers taking off into the water. White pelicans and terns fly over-head. Picturesque coves and inlets bordered by boulders and gravel beaches offer some exploring for bipedal wanderers. If a storm blows in, you may see the water change colors from pastel green to aqua to blue to gray before it rains.

At an elevation of 5,900 feet, the Piute Reservoir dam was built on the main fork of the Sevier River in 1908 by Robert D. Young, who also built the Otter Creek dam. Both the 3,360-acre reservoir and the county are named for the Native Americans who dominated this area at one time, though the spelling is that adopted years ago by the state legislature. The Southern Paiute were a tribe of Shoshonean stock. The name has also been spelled Pahute and Pah-Ute, and obviously has Ute connections.

There is waterfowl hunting in season and the area is supposed to be good for rockhounding. OHVs are allowed near the reservoir in several areas outside the park.

If you approach the park from the north, look for Big Rock Candy Mountain 24 miles south of Richfield on US 89 at Marysvale Canyon, an unusual peak, though perhaps becoming a bit commercialized now. This chocolate-brown–yellow-colored mountain is reported to be the only formation of its kind. Burl Ives sang about it, so it is pretty well known. Part of the Tushar Mountains, these peaks are remnants of extinct volcanoes that were formed 20 to 31 million years ago and contain numerous mineral deposits.

OTTER CREEK STATE PARK

Hours/Season: Overnight; year-round
Area: 80 acres
Facilities: Picnic tables, 30 campsites, group camping, wheelchair-accessible restrooms with showers, sewage disposal, boat ramp, fish cleaning station, boat docks, phone: (801) 624-3268
Attractions: Fishing (ice fishing in winter), boating, swimming, ice skating, wildlife viewing
Nearby: Fish Lake Scenic Byway
Access: Off Utah 22, 4 miles northwest of Antimony

Otter Creek flows through a valley bounded on the west by the Sevier Plateau and on the east by the Parker Range. Because of this, Otter Creek Reservoir is a long narrow lake in the valley between peaks.

The hard-working Mormons who constructed the dam on Otter Creek never envisioned the multiple recreational uses that the reservoir now provides. One of these is trophy fishing in the 3,120-acre reservoir. In the cool waters at an elevation of 6,400 feet, rainbow trout, cutthroat trout, and some large hybrids that weigh up to twelve pounds are caught. It is easy to see many fingerlings along the edge of the water. Fly fishing is popular in the large pool below the dam. Winter brings ice fishermen and skaters.

Several camping choices are found in Otter Creek State Park. The main campground has redwood privacy windscreens with back-in spots on the beachfront sites and pull-through sites in the second row. Tent sites are behind these. Two overflow areas also have waterfront sites with tables. Several trees offer shade.

The lake is within the Pacific Migratory Bird Flyway so spring and fall offer good birdwatching with a large number of waterfowl, raptors, sandhill cranes, ducks, whistling swans, gulls, plovers, sandpipers, eagles, turkey vultures, and songbirds. But birds are not hard to spot at other times of the year. A walk east past the campsites reveals a marsh area where hyacinths grow, Canada geese are seen, and swallows catch insects on the wing.

One of the oldest dam projects in Utah, the filling of Otter Creek Reservoir is a fine example of Mormon hard work and pioneering spirit. Irrigation water for farming was an important factor in having a life in this place the Mormons had chosen.

In the mid-1890s, farmers in this area had some experience with digging canals to get irrigation water but no know-how on constructing a large-scale dam. Yet that is what they needed and decided to build, though only after many heated discussions that included selecting the site on Otter Creek, just before it flows into the East Fork of the Sevier River.

Water rights were applied for and then the group applied for a bank loan. When financial assistance was denied by the banks of Utah, six of the ten directors of the Otter Creek Reservoir Company walked out of a meeting, declaring the project hopeless. But there were still four members who wanted to go ahead with the dam construction and they appointed one of the directors, Robert Dixon Young, to be the supervisor, though he had no experience in dam building, nor was he an engineer.

Young moved into a cabin overlooking the damsite with his pregnant wife and two small children. Two state inspectors came and said that machinery costing from $25,000 to $100,000 would be needed for the project. Yet Young told them there was little money so the project would begin with volunteer labor and homemade equipment—those components so important in the Mormon settling of Utah.

When ground was broken on October 19, 1897, most of the farmers were too busy to come themselves but sent their sons. The result was a crew of one man and three boys that worked in the mud and improvised simple tools. Then in February of 1898, a loan through a New York bank finally rescued the project and other banks followed suit with money for equipment. Only near the end of the project, when success seemed likely, did Young receive any pay for his work.

When state engineers inspected the 40-foot-high, earth-filled dam they called it "one of the best and more secure earth reservoir dams in the country." The dam has held well through the years. Some recent work by the state has added improvements.

It is interesting that necessity provided Young with his niche in life. He went on to build the Piute Dam (financing was easier with this one), served as vice-president of the International Irrigation Congress at St. Louis in 1919, and traveled with a group of government engineers on a survey trip down the Colorado River looking for damsites in 1922.

While in this vicinity, plan to travel the 23-mile Fish Lake Scenic Byway, which is 38 miles northeast of this park, north on Utah 62 and then south on Utah 24. (You will cross the route of the 200-mile ATV Paiute Trail on Utah 62.) This road accesses the developed area around Fish Lake, a scenic location with a lodge, resorts, and several campgrounds set among aspen- and spruce-covered slopes, a great place to visit in the heat of Utah's summers. (Wallace Stegner enjoyed visits to Fish Lake.) Hikers will like the choice of trails. The 5-mile Pelican Canyon Trail climbs to an elevation of 11,000 feet. Easier hikes are along the lake. Do continue on your auto tour past Fish Lake, Widgeon Bay, and Johnson Valley Reservoir, where the road turns downhill soon and follows the Fremont River, with interesting views all the way to its junction with Utah 72.

The 26-mile Fish Lake Loop for mountain bikers is a full-day ride in alpine country starting 3 miles south of the rustic Fish Lake Lodge. It climbs to a ridge with views of Fish Lake and Capitol Reef and returns to the lodge via a singletrack asphalt path.

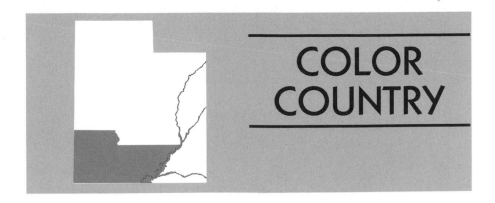

COLOR COUNTRY

Calling this region Color Country is almost an understatement. The brilliant corals, pinks, reds, and golds of sandstone canyons and cliffs are especially awesome in the wash of a sun low on the horizon, but there are also the soft greens of spring leaves along the Virgin River and the rich blues of the waters of Lake Powell—and there is so much wild, rugged scenery that it is difficult to find places to build cities.

If one starts at the northwest corner of the region, however, one begins with a harsh desert territory that is lonely yet filled with lures for rockhounders. Minersville State Park serves as a good base for anglers and for exploring this region of mineral deposits. The history of this part of the region is told at Iron Mission State Park, where a good exhibit of old vehicles and Indian artifacts supplements the pioneer history of iron mining.

The major cities in this relatively unpopulated region are Cedar City and St. George, where many people are moving to enjoy the temperate year-round climate. From St. George, good recreation is a short distance to the west at Snow Canyon State Park. Colorful slickrock, lava flows, and hidden canyons offer privacy and quiet.

Go east from St. George to Zion National Park, where the Virgin River has carved an exquisite canyon that can hardly contain its rush of visitors. For less congestion, travel 5 miles of switchbacks on the Kolob Fingers Scenic Byway to the northwest corner of Zion for splendid overlooks and hiking trailheads. One can hike to Kolob Arch, the largest freestanding arch in the world.

Travel a few miles east of Cedar City past Navajo Lake and then north to see Cedar Breaks National Monument, a miniature Bryce Canyon at a higher elevation, complete with bristlecone pine trees. Skiers and mountain bicyclists head for Brian's Head just to the north. Hundreds of miles of

Opposite: *Panorama Trail at Kodachrome Basin State Park*

backroads and world-class singletrack trails are available for bike touring in the Dixie National Forest.

Go south to the Arizona border and find that even the sand dunes are more colorful at Coral Pink Sand Dunes State Park. Take time to look for rare plants and animals among the dune formations.

Bryce Canyon National Park is in the middle of the region, a place foreign writers picked as their favorite in the United States. The trail along Wall Street, where tall conifers grow up through slots between pinnacles of rose-colored sandstone, is unbeatable and unique.

East of Bryce Canyon is one of the most scenic drives in the country, the Boulder Mountain Scenic Byway, Utah 12. Take the side road to Kodachrome Basin State Park to see the unique sand pipes, or chimneys, that rise above the desert floor. Then continue east on the byway, but leave time for stops at Escalante State Park to hike among petrified wood, where color takes on a new dimension. Nearby is the Escalante River backcountry and the trail to Calf Creek Falls.

Prehistory of the Anasazi Indians and some of their ruins await you at the town of Boulder before you head to the top of Boulder Mountain and into the Dixie National Forest. From Boulder, it is 66 miles by dependable vehicle or by mountain bike on the Burr Trail through Capitol Reef National Park.

One begins to hunt for more adjectives to describe all the wonders of Color Country. One of the last free-roaming herds of buffalo is found in the wild country of the Henry Mountains.

All along the eastern border of the region is Glen Canyon National Recreation Area, where houseboats float Lake Powell. One has to wish, though, that one could have floated this section of the Colorado River when it was still natural. Edward Abbey, along with a few others, was lucky enough to accomplish that goal.

The elevation varies from over 2,000 feet to over 11,000 feet in this one region, offering almost unlimited recreational opportunities. Choose dry-powder snow, snowshoeing, ice fishing, hiking, rafting, horseback riding, mountain biking, or year-round tennis and golf. Boaters and anglers find reservoirs at Gunlock, Minersville, and Quail Creek state parks.

Temperatures reflect the elevation. Summertime temperatures at St. George can be over one hundred degrees, but nearby Cedar Breaks will require a coat. You will benefit by referring to a topographical map when in this region.

ANASAZI INDIAN VILLAGE STATE PARK

Hours/Season: Day use; year-round
Area: 6 acres
Facilities: Picnic tables, group picnicking, restrooms, visitor center, historical exhibits, phone: (801) 335-7308

Attractions: Anasazi artifacts, Anasazi dwelling replica, excavated ruins, photography
Nearby: Clem Church Memorial Highway, Utah 12 Scenic Byway
Access: City limits of Boulder, on Utah 12

Upon entering Anasazi Indian Village State Park, one goes back in time to learn about a culture quite different from that of the present-day picturesque cattle ranching town of Boulder, though perhaps the surrounding terrain is much the same.

In the heart of the canyon country of this region, on a mesa at 6,700 feet, it is believed this site was inhabited by one of the largest Anasazi communities west of the Colorado River from A.D. 1050 to 1200. Preliminary investigation of this site was done in 1927 by the Peabody Museum. From 1958 to 1959, the University of Utah excavated the site and uncovered eighty-seven rooms. The site was then covered with plastic and dirt until 1978, when excavation and stabilization were begun. It became a state park in 1960. The village remains largely unexcavated, though excavations continue on a small scale.

The artifacts removed from the village are on display in the park's museum. Most of what you see has been found here, except for the perishable items. Exhibits inform about the Anasazi culture, pottery, and stone tools. Replicas of a petroglyph panel and a storage granary are seen. Maps help you orient the village to other prehistoric groups.

One display tells how making arrowheads was an "art, a personalized craft," which took about an hour to get good results. Hammerstones, stone axes, baskets, and pottery are exhibited. There is no evidence of the Anasazi using a potter's wheel; pots were made by rolling the clay. They were influenced by the Kayenta branch of Anasazi with fine pottery of black on white, black on red, and polychrome pots. These Anasazi exchanged goods with the Virgin, Mesa Verde, and Chaco Anasazi. An Olivella shell, a shell necklace (from the coast, buried with turquoise and a bowl), arrow shafts, and an atlatl are all finds that help explain the Anasazi culture. A chart tells about the medical contributions made by these Indians.

Based on what has been learned, a diorama that depicts life in the original village is on display to help you visualize the routine chores of pottery making, building repairs, carrying water, grinding corn, and bringing in game.

The village was near the fertile soil, available wood and stone, and streams of the Aquarius Plateau. The East Fork of Boulder Creek flows near the village and is still a good trout-fishing stream. Useful plants and animals were around, so their site had considerable resources. As part-time farmers, they raised corn, beans, and squash in plots by the village. As hunter-gatherers, the Anasazi killed small game, deer, and desert bighorn sheep and collected seeds, nuts, and berries.

Besides reconstructing Anasazi culture from the excavations, the time of occupation has been estimated from the pottery and with dendrochronology, studying the tree rings of timber used in their structures. Additional studies will help to pinpoint the exact dates that these people lived here.

Replica of Anasazi structure at Anasazi Indian Village State Park

A question often arises: Why did the Anasazi leave this village? It appears that the site was burned (by the inhabitants?) and abandoned about A.D. 1200. Possible answers include resource exhaustion, drought, pressure from other peoples, and population growth. Speculation is that these people migrated to the Kayenta region of northeastern Arizona, where they had cultural ties, and which was perhaps where they came from.

Be sure to go outside to see the six-room replica of an Anasazi dwelling. This illustrates a room-block of three habitations and three food-storage rooms. Jacal- and Kayenta-style masonry were used in the construction of such structures. These walls are irregular in thickness and size, a type of masonry that is different from the finely finished stone walls of Mesa Verde and the almost mortarless walls of Chaco. Rather, these walls seemed to require the gluing effect of mortar to continue to stand.

The population of this Anasazi Indian Village is estimated at 200, and there are about 100 or more structures—habitation structures, pithouses, storage units, and at least one ramada/shade structure—on this 3-acre site. A self-guiding trail continues past an authentic pithouse habitation, not a kiva, and then past three mealing bins that are part of an L-shaped pueblo. One can still see the evidence of fire destruction. The wood in the pithouse had to be replaced, but the original pithouse holes were used for anchorage.

To simulate more of the atmosphere of the village, corn is still planted, along with squash and beans. One sees the fertile farmland backed by red rock scenery that made this site an attractive choice.

Individual and group picnicking facilities are available under cottonwood trees. The park occasionally gives workshops or talks to education groups; requests can be made.

As you continue your travels, do complete the entire length of Utah 12 from US 89 to Utah 24 as this 122-mile scenic byway (the Clem Church Memorial Highway) connects some of Utah's best views and attractions. Entry at its northern end quickly takes you climbing up to the 9,200-foot summit pass of Boulder Mountain. Wayside viewpoints point out vegetated rangeland, Mount Ellen, Mount Pennell, Lower Bowns Reservoir, and a view of Capitol Reef's Waterpocket Fold that gives you a good overall perspective of it. The road then winds down through the forest to Boulder and Anasazi State Park. At Boulder, the Burr Trail Road (a dirt road also used by mountain bikers that is impassable for vehicles when wet) goes east to Capitol Reef and then jaunts north to follow the Waterpocket Fold.

South of Boulder, the byway offers wonderful views of red rock country on the shoulder of the Aquarius Plateau. The highway provides access to Hell's Backbone Road, Calf Creek Recreation Area, Escalante Canyons, Hole-in-the-Rock Scenic Backway, Smokey Mountain Road Scenic Backway, the petrified forest near the town of Escalante, Bryce Canyon, and finally Red Canyon. All told, these are awesome landscapes. Early explorer/geologist Clarence Dutton wrote that the Aquarius "should be described in blank verse and illustrated upon canvas."

ESCALANTE STATE PARK

Hours/Season: Overnight; year-round
Area: 1,351 acres
Facilities: Picnic tables, 22 campsites, wheelchair-accessible restrooms with showers, group camping, group pavilion, sewage disposal, boat ramp, visitor center, firewood, phone: (801) 826-4466
Attractions: Hiking, boating, fishing (ice fishing in winter), swimming, wildlife viewing, petrified wood, photography
Nearby: Calf Creek Falls Trail
Access: Go 1 mile west of the town of Escalante on Utah 12, then take signed Wide Hollow Road 1 mile north to park

One of Utah's most intriguing state parks, Escalante has Wide Hollow Reservoir to satisfy fishing, boating, and swimming enthusiasts; considerable wildlife within the park; and two hiking trails where colorful chunks of petrified wood are liberally scattered about the ground. There are even a few fossilized dinosaur bones. The park is also a great base for backcountry

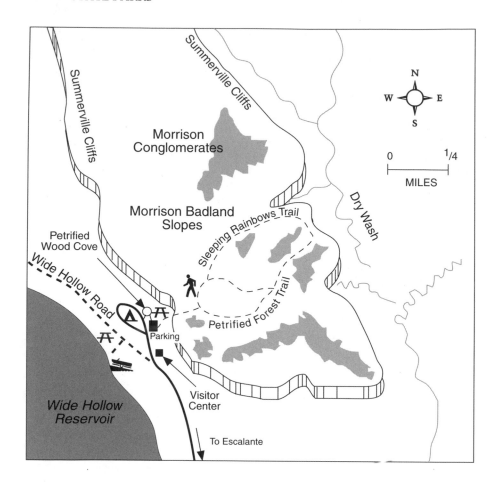

explorations, complete with the hot showers needed after a trek.

The expedition of Escalante and Dominguez did not come near this area, but a member of John Wesley Powell's survey party of 1872, Almon Harris Thompson, first explored the Escalante River and decided to name it after Escalante. Later the town, and then the state park, shared that name. The word *escalante* also means "to escalate upward, like stairsteps," which describes the plateaus surrounding the park.

Within the state park boundaries, 30-acre Wide Hollow Reservoir was constructed in 1954, at 5,800-foot elevation, to provide irrigation water for the town of Escalante. The lake is stocked with rainbow trout, and there is also bluegill. Cottonwood trees edge the lake where overflow camping and picnic tables are located adjacent to the boat ramp. Green fields across the water are backed by good views of the Aquarius Plateau and patches of red rock cliffs.

The campground loop is between the lake and the elevated land where the trails are located. Nice sites have both back-ins and pull-throughs, some have shaded tables and tall trees. Many chukars roam the campground and will eat out of your hands.

The park is listed in *Utah Wildlife Viewing Guide* as one of the few wetland birdwatching sites in southern Utah. Stroll along the waterfront. You might sight immature white-faced ibises, geese, and coots in the summer heat. A pair of boat-tailed grackles has been spotted near the campground. Other wildlife in the area includes small rodents, lizards, deer, and coyote.

Desert terrain abuts the north edge of the campsites with prickly pear, Engelmann's hedgehogs, wildflowers in season, and a huge chunk of slickrock complete with a pothole. The plants and animals are typical of the Upper Sonoran life zone, with pinyon and juniper.

A visitor center was added to the park in 1991, with a display of petrified wood, petrified dinosaur bones, ammonite fossils, and shell fossils. An exhibit explains the formation of petrified wood with colors added by iron compounds and other minerals.

Wide Hollow Road continues through the park as a dirt road for walking and mountain biking. Plans call for a mountain-bike connection to Posey Road.

The star exhibits of Escalante State Park are the two trails through natu-

View of Wide Hollow Reservoir from the Petrified Forest Trail at Escalante State Park

Rock formations and pieces of petrified wood along the Petrified Forest Trail at Escalante State Park

rally deposited petrified wood washed down from nearby badlands, or painted desert, after erosion uncovered and loosened these jeweled rocks from their buried positions. Some pieces are nearly 5 feet in width.

The 1-mile, self-guiding Petrified Forest Trail begins with a short climb past black boulders, remnants of lava flows, and precariously balanced rocks covered with colorful lichens and mosses. Some rocks have stripes or smears of desert varnish, shiny black or rusty oxidation products of iron and manganese, a coating of glaze that has taken thousands of years for sun, heat, and moisture to produce. The path then traverses through a "pygmy forest" of pinyon and Utah juniper, stunted because of limited water. Though small in size, many of these trees are hundreds of years old.

The painted desert comes into view, part of the Morrison Formation. Some 150 million years ago, this highly mineralized stratum was a shallow lakebed, streambed, or floodplain. Rich in nutrients and plant life, these floodplains were roamed by dinosaurs.

After these initial trail discoveries, pieces of petrified wood begin to appear along the trail, ranging in size from small pieces used in toolmaking, left by the Anasazi and Fremont Indians, to huge sections of trees. If you watch carefully, you can follow washes for some distance, marveling at the rosy red, amethyst, gold, purple, amber, silver, and orange hues. What makes them interesting is the weaving of the colors, the patterning of cracks, the veins of contrast, and the overlays of contrasting lichens—artworks strung along a pathway.

When volcanoes erupted, ancient conifer logs, remnants of a more tropical landscape, became buried under mud and volcanic ash. Oxygen for normal decomposition was not available. Sediments added in stratified layers of color formed badlands. As this happened, mineral-laden ground water circulated slowly through the logs. Deposits of quartz and colored minerals crystallized within the log cavities, leaving some of the cellulose still present, and often retaining the shape of the log, while producing store-houses of gemstones.

The magic becomes visible when the soft, porous clays of the badlands suck in the waters of a summer thundershower, expand, then dry and crumble at the edges. The next rain will send mineral-ized log fragments journeying down a wash. This Utah preserve contains about 5.5 million tons of exposed fossilized wood.

The optional 0.75-mile Sleeping Rainbows Trail loops off from the nature trail. Though a vast amount of petrified wood is seen on this trail, it is quite steep and requires considerable scrambling around and over rocks.

After the optional loop rejoins the nature trail, you will pass the largest single deposit of petrified wood on the trail. Envision a time when this tree was alive in a rich flood-plain nearer the equator and 5,000 feet lower in elevation than today. Though slowly, time has greatly changed this tree and the terrain. *Remember that it is unlawful to collect or deface petrified wood.*

A worthwhile side trip from Escalante State Park is the 5.5-mile round-trip Calf Creek Falls Trail, 17 miles northeast of Escalante. Park at the day-use area and walk a short piece on the campground road to the beginning of the trail, where you may pick up an interpretive brochure. An easy to mod-erate trail, the path roughly follows Calf Creek, past deer tracks, beaver ponds, cattails, and lush wetlands on a strip of bottomland between red rock cliffs. Notice the fish in the clear water and watch for rock art and gra-naries. Open at the beginning, the last part of the trail has more shade. This is an excellent example of the part wetlands played in the choosing of sites by prehistoric Indians.

The destination is a 126-foot waterfall that plunges down sandstone walls smeared with golds, browns, and greens into an inviting clear pool—

great for photography and cooling off. Back at the day-use area, this pretty creek rolls slowly over slickrock, making ripples and reflecting the soft greens of overhanging trees.

KODACHROME BASIN STATE PARK

Hours/Season: Overnight; year-round
Area: 2,241 acres
Facilities: Picnic tables, 27 campsites, group camping, wheelchair-accessible restrooms with showers, sewage disposal, firewood, concessionaire, guided horseback rides, phone: (801) 679-8562, (801) 679-8536 (Trail Head Station)
Attractions: Hiking, mountain biking, horseback riding, geology study, arch, photography
Access: From Cannonville on Utah 12, go 7 miles south on Cottonwood Canyon Road

▲ With a name like Kodachrome Basin, one expects colorful surroundings and you will not be disappointed. One guidebook writer proclaimed that this state park was probably his family's favorite place in Utah. Europeans associate this kind of scenery with Western movies and cowboys riding into the sunset.

Until a party from the National Geographic Society came through the park in 1949, the place was known as Thorley's Pasture, after a local rancher. The National Geographic Society renamed it Kodachrome Flats for obvious reasons, but a rumor circulated that Kodak was not pleased. To avoid any problems, the Bryce Lions Club, who sponsored the state park, changed the name to Chimney Rock, which was also fitting. Guess what? It turned out that Kodak liked the exposure of the other name, and it is now known officially as Kodachrome Basin State Park.

Ever since the 1930s when the Civilian Conservation Corps (CCC) built the dirt road, this area has been a favorite picnic stop. It slowly evolved into a developed state park, with all the amenities, though power and telephone required drilling through the white sandstone cliff north of the campground and 6 miles of pipe were needed to bring in spring water. Now the park even has a concessionaire, but it is still a remote place with some quiet space, except on holiday weekends.

The road to the park was paved not too long ago but is now almost worse than some of the dirt roads around. In late 1993, a petition about fixing the road was circulating. The road still presents no problem for a passenger car that goes slowly over the potholes.

Amid the spectacular rock formations are towering, monolithic spires called chimneys or sand pipes, which are unique to this area. Geologists have theorized that this region was once similar to Yellowstone National Park, with underground springs and geysers. In time, and after geological

Group campground at Kodachrome Basin State Park

changes, the spring channels dried out and filled with sediment, which so-lidified. The softer Entrada sandstone surrounding this core eroded away and left the filled-in springs, or sand pipes, standing. Sixty-seven of these rare chimneys of various sizes and shapes have been identified in the park. They range from 2 to 52 meters high, with some serving as good navigation points.

The campground loop has spacious, private sites with some juniper trees for shade. Chukars are often busy near campsites, trying to find shade and scooping out nests in the dirt under trees to cool off. These birds are not very skittish when acclimated to people. A large group site has electricity and all the amenities needed for camping.

Rock formations and coves are near the campsites with ever-changing colors ranging from gray and white to several shades of red and orange, depending on the mood and light of the time of day. Some of the slickrock is easy to explore. Many layers of geological formations are seen in the strata of the park. It is a place of extra fascination for geologists.

At 5,800 feet, in the southern desert of Utah, the best seasons for activities are early spring and late fall, when there is solitude, quiet, and unique desert beauty. It is a good place to stay overnight when the moon is full and lights up the night and the rock formations.

Conveniently located in the center of the park, Bob and MiraLoy Ott own and operate the Trail Head Station, a concession that has a good range of supplies and gives out friendly information. It is also headquarters for

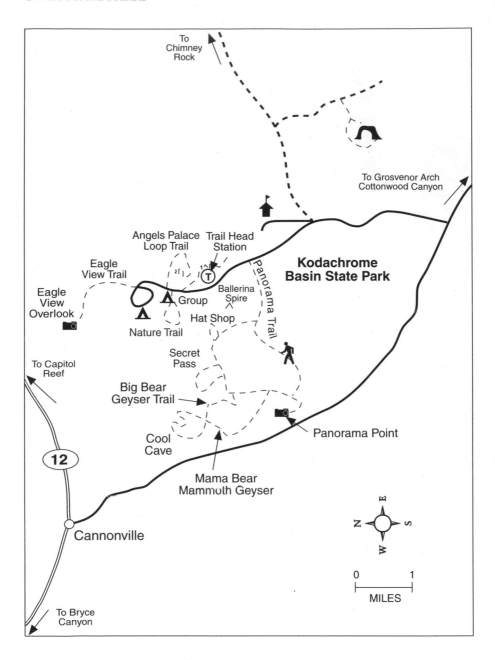

Scenic Safaris, where Bob offers guided trail rides and stagecoach trips. One-hour stagecoach rides cater to young people, the handicapped, and senior citizens. With several hiking trails in the park open to horseback riding, customers can choose trail rides of varying lengths, from one hour to a half-day. Bob helped lay out the Big Bear Geyser Trail, which is now open for hikers, though he's been taking trail riders on it for a few seasons and pointing out the highlights along the trip. A variety of one-hour trips is offered on the Grand Parade, the Panorama, or Angels Palace Loop trails.

Hikers have several options. The 0.4-mile nature trail begins near the campground. Pick up a guide at the beginning of the trail. If you don't know many of the desert plants—juniper, sagebrush, pinyon, buffalo berry, Indian rice grass, false buckwheat, four-winged saltbush, snake weed, princess plume, rabbitbrush, yucca, Mormon tea, and prickly pear cactus—now is your chance to learn to identify them and how they function, even after they die, in this ecosystem. You will also learn some of the processes of erosion and see purple soil caused by the iron-oxide content. Different rock layers are pointed out and, of course, there is a large chimney as well as a small one.

The easy Panorama Trail is longer, a 3-mile loop (mountain bikes are allowed on this trail, except for Panorama Point). From the trailhead off the park road south of the campground, the path begins along an old wagon road. The desert surroundings are colored with golds, reds, and purples of sunflowers, sagebrush, paintbrush, rabbitbrush, and other plants that have adapted to the dry climate. Behind the flat desert are varied views of the basin's rock formations.

The trail turns north off the road to access some interesting formations. The Hat Shop is reached via a 0.25-mile side trip near Ballerina Spire, a sand pipe. The next side trail is the Secret Pass, a narrow path between red rock walls after skirting slickrock and a cone-shaped rock. Supposedly, one sees a rock that resembles a large white buffalo.

Shortly after returning to the main trail, the turnoff to the optional 2-mile Big Bear Geyser Trail jogs off to the southeast. This trail loops around past Big Bear and Mama Bear, a cool cave, and Mammoth Geyser before returning to the Panorama Trail. Continue on this trail south to an obvious spur that climbs steeply to Panorama Point.

From here the return loop is a path through yellow-green stands of grasses and darker green junipers. Some microbiotic crust is seen (see Dead Horse Point State Park) along this section of the loop. There is also rose-colored finely powdered soil, an erosional product that is very soft and crumbly and forms shapes that look like slightly hardened mud sculptures.

Across from the group camping area is the 1-mile Angels Palace Loop Trail, a strenuous bit of maneuvering in pretty spectacular rocky terrain and hardened mudlike soil.

A rather new addition to the trail system is the 1-mile Grand Parade Trail, across from the Nature Trail, which leads past some of the chimneys and toward the Trail Head Station.

A very strenuous and treacherous hike leads to the top of the cliff edge north of the campground. This is the 1-mile Eagle View Trail. At first, as you approach the cliff, this is a quite pleasant uphill path. As you get close to it you see a short, brisk dirt path that soon jogs left. Before you hike this, look up the white sandstone cliff face to see the whole trail as it ascends to a break in the top rim of the cliff. There is no vegetation and there are sheer

Trail Head Station offers horseback riding and tours at Kodachrome Basin State Park

edges along the entire trail, so do be sure-footed and energetic. The amazing thing is that the trail was made originally to drive cattle down from the cliff to the basin about the turn of the century and the path was used until 1977. Boy Scouts help upgrade the trail for park use.

Another trail leads to Shakespeare Arch, which park manager Tom Shakespeare discovered fairly recently while searching for a coyote den. A couple of miles of dirt road, which can be bad, access the 0.25-mile nature trail to the arch. This gives you another chance to experience the desert, which offers so much variety and discovery for the observant hiker. Chimney Rock can be seen from the trail.

CORAL PINK SAND DUNES STATE PARK

Hours/Season: Overnight; year-round
Area: 3,730 acres
Facilities: Picnic tables, 22 campsites, restrooms with showers (available from Easter to late October), group camping, vault toilets, sewage disposal, visitor center, water in winter only at the visitor center, phone: (801) 874-2408
Attractions: Hiking, nature trail, dune formations, off-highway-vehicle area, nature study, geology study, photography

Access: 5 miles north of Kanab on US 89, then 9 miles southwest on signed
Hancock Road to park; going south from Mount Carmel Junction on US
89, turn southwest onto Sand Dunes Road in 2 miles

▲ Extensive sand dunes in all terrains have their addictive attractions, but
rose-colored hills of sand surrounded by warm-hued cliffs make Coral
Pink Sand Dunes State Park a special place to explore. The only major dune
field on the Colorado Plateau, the park is developed just enough to enhance
your visit, yet it is still enough off the beaten track to be a jaunt into wild
country.

At 6,000 feet, between the White Cliffs (which is the lighter top half of
Navajo sandstone) and the Vermillion Cliffs, the park was established in
1963 to provide "access to the dunes to the public for varying uses while
still protecting the natural resource and providing for public safety."

The entrance station to the park also serves as a visitor center and displays an interesting bottled collection of sands from around the world. Live
salamanders and scorpions—in enclosed tanks, naturally—are frequently
on exhibit, and a great illustration of a rare tiger beetle hangs on the wall.
Ranger John Huston is in the process of accumulating a file of dried and la-
beled plant species. He continues to work on this project and is quite willing
to share this file to help others with plant identification.

The day-use area, complete with picnic tables, is south of the visitor center. The nature trail and the two largest dunes are accessed from this parking area. The campground is nearby, where the park road dead-ends at a
loop of roomy pull-through sites with quite a few small trees.

The geology of these dunes is a fascinating subject. The sand is derived
from Navajo sandstone from the geologic period called Middle Jurassic, so
the same iron oxides and minerals that give us spectacular red rock country
are responsible for this landscape of coral pink sand. Fully 98 percent of
Navajo sandstone is grains of quartz crystals that were once loose sand
dunes. With time, a cement of lime, iron oxides, and clay substances
bonded these grains together into a hard material. Geologists have found
cross-bedding and other curving patterns, plus the tracks of dinosaurs, that
indicate the sands were laid down by wind in an arid time.

With more passage of time, weathering and erosion of the sandstone
again produced sediments that were carried here by winds to form sand
dunes. The high concentration of iron oxides continues to color the dune
formations that are estimated at 10,000 to 15,000 years old. The colors are
especially rich at sunrise and sunset, the best times for photography.

Some 2,000 acres of the park are dunes. To have dune formations, three
components are necessary—wind, sand, and space. Sand grains between
0.1 and 1 millimeter seem to be of the right weight to be blown into dune
formations by winds. The winds must be strong enough to move the sand.
At Coral Pink Sand Dunes State Park, the wind is funneled through a con-
stricting notch between Moquith and Moccasin mountains (south of the
park), increasing its velocity, a phenomenon known as the Venturi effect.
Once the wind reaches the open valley, the velocity decreases and sand is

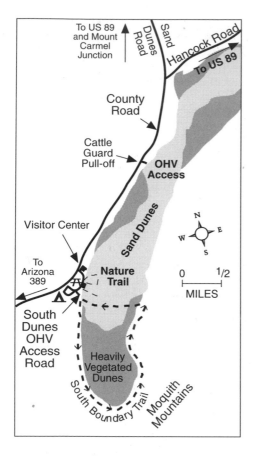

deposited in this space. Another wind blows east between Moccasin and Harris mountains and adds to the boiling effect where currents merge and drop sand.

Wind directions produce specific dune formations. Obstacles in the path of sand movement sometimes play a role. Most common here is the "barchan" formation, which is shaped like a crescent moon. As the dune grows around an obstruction, sand grains are blown around the edges, producing "horns" that point away from the wind. The windward side slopes gradually, but the slip face on the leeward side of the formation is steep where sand drops over the top of the dune.

This park also has an unusual formation, a "star" dune, caused by winds from several directions. It is huge and near the largest barchan dune. Parabolic formations are also found in the park. These are produced when blowing sand tears a hole in vegetation and piles up sand in this area. These formations can be quite large, often looking like a barchan dune in reverse.

Sand dunes are one of the most changeable of landscapes. Each day, there are subtle differences in the fluid nature of the terrain. The sand dunes themselves influence where additional action takes place and the wind rearranges them and adds contours to basic formations. Even the dunes themselves move slowly.

It is often a surprise to people that vegetation in the dunes is one of the attractions. A few pioneer plants can establish themselves on the blowing sand, putting down many rhizomes, creeping underground stems and roots, to anchor them. Notice the sometimes huge hummocks, clumps of these plants that catch sand and are stimulated to grow more to keep their tops above sand. Vegetation growth causes stabilization of dunes, preventing their movement. But violent weather can also bury the vegetation.

Two vegetation and wildlife zones are found within the park. At the lower elevation, the pinyon-juniper zone contains many plants—yucca, mule ears, sunflowers, and other wildflowers—and the most prevalent animals are mule deer, coyote, jackrabbit, and other small animals. The second life zone is that of the ponderosa pine, at elevations of 6,900 feet and above. Small pools of water attract animals in these upper dunes.

A fascination of dunes is the wind-driven ripples in the sand and the written evidence of animal life that is often nocturnal but leaves patterns upon the sand. Bird tracks, the uniform footprints of the camel cricket, beetles scurrying, and the night struggles of predator and prey are all fun to try to interpret. Spadefoot toad, tiger salamander, raven, bobcat, kit fox, kangaroo rat, hummingbird, eagle, and rattlesnake are more of the animal species found in the area.

Although one can orient oneself across these sand dunes in many places, there are three designated hikes. The first is a newly constructed nature trail, roughly 0.5 mile, which begins at the day-use area and has numbered exhibit signs along the passage over sand. You will learn about the distinct species of mule ears, *Wyethis scabra*, that covers huge areas with yellow flowers from May to July—along with the blossoming of other species—called the "Botanical motif of Coral Pink Sand Dunes." Information about the fertilization of Kanab yucca by the yucca moth, a view of the largest grove of ponderosa pine, and an introduction to several other plant species, some quite rare, are included on this self-guiding trail. You will also learn that sand acts as a huge sponge that soaks up water. As the wind scoops out sand and exposes water, ponds called deflation plains are seen at certain times of year. Melting snow also forms ponds, and it is these waters that nourish toads, salamanders, aquatic insects, and other life.

A second hiking destination lies across the sand from the day-use area,

Mule ear hummocks at Coral Pink Sand Dunes State Park

where you may climb either, or both, the barchan or star dune, a short though energetic ascent. These highest dunes are around 200 feet. The round trip is about 1.5 miles and strenuous.

The park map also shows a third hike that takes off from the day-use area and curves around the edge of the dunes to finally cut straight across the sand on the return. About 5.5 miles in length, this route is not something to attempt lightly as it is in soft sand all the way. Get a copy of the hiking handout from the visitor center.

Along Sand Dunes Road north of the visitor center, several pull-off spots access different areas of the dunes. It is in one of these areas that a threatened species of milkweed can be found, near a ponderosa pine stand. It grows right on the sand and drops its huge seed pods onto the sand, where they can sprout.

Explorers should be cautious when orienteering across dunes, noting landmarks for navigation, carrying water, and being prepared for emergencies or getting lost.

The park ranger also mentioned that Harris Mountain, on the west side of the road, can be climbed by experienced hikers who can find routes up it, though there is no official trail. Check with the ranger.

Many arrive at this park to ride off-highway vehicles in the dunes. Since the sand is so fine-grained here, vehicles are mostly dune buggies, but four-wheel-drive vehicles with superwide flotation tires are adequate.

Hikers descending "barchan" sand dune at Coral Pink Sand Dunes State Park

Besides obeying the state rules for OHVs, some special rules apply at this park. Vehicles must stay 10 feet away from any vegetation and 100 feet away from pedestrians. All vehicles using the dunes are required to have an 8-foot-from-the-ground whip with flag. No vehicles are allowed in the fenced natural area located northeast of the picnic area along the campground access road. All vehicles must remain on the pavement at all times while in the campground. Access to the dunes is via the Dunes Access Road (divided sand road) just outside the campground. Quiet hours are from 10:00 P.M. until 9:00 A.M., with no vehicles, generators, or disturbances allowed at those times. Dune running time is from 9:00 A.M. until 10:00 P.M. No vehicles are allowed on the dunes at other times.

The park reminds OHV drivers that it is a privilege to ride in the dunes. To continue to do so requires that rules must be obeyed, and caution and courtesy must be foremost at all times. The park personnel have a reputation for seeing that drivers follow the rules and respect the hours of operating OHVs.

QUAIL CREEK STATE PARK

Hours/Season: Overnight; year-round
Area: Leased
Facilities: Picnic tables, beach, 23 campsites, wheelchair-accessible restrooms, group camping, group pavilion, boat ramp, fish-cleaning station, phone: (801) 879-2378
Attractions: Boating, water skiing, fishing (ice fishing in winter), swimming
Nearby: Zion National Park
Access: From exit 16 off Interstate 15, 3 miles east off Utah 9

The location of Quail Creek State Park in the southwest corner of Utah, at an elevation of 3,300 feet, makes it the lowest of Utah's state parks. The subsequent warmer climate promises year-round recreation and water sports. In fact, attendance records for the year 1992 rank it fifth among the state parks. It is downright hot in summer, but then most of the visitors are in the water during the hottest part of the day. Boaters and water skiers zoom through the water in front of the striated gold, gray, and orange shades of the rimming cliffs.

Quail Creek Reservoir was constructed in 1988, with the namesake creek originating on the lower slopes of the Pine Valley Mountains and entering the lake at its northernmost edge. At one time the habitat around the creek was home to large numbers of quail, but most of these have since been shot by hunters.

The basin that was filled by the reservoir contained Indian petroglyphs on some of the boulders. To preserve these valuable prehistoric records, the boulders were moved to higher ground.

Although water from Quail Creek helps to fill the reservoir, most of the water is from the nearby Virgin River. The 202-foot-high diversion dam is concrete with a hydroelectric power plant (2,340 kilowatts) located above the dam.

The campground is on a hillside overlooking the water, with shaded picnic tables and large pull-through sites. There are a few small trees but no real shade against the scorching summer heat. The day-use area has large covered picnic shelters, a fish-cleaning area, and a beach for water access.

The 600-acre reservoir has a maximum depth of 120 feet, so it is cold enough to sustain the rainbow trout (which are stocked), bullhead catfish, and crappie, while the largemouth bass (also stocked) and bluegill thrive in the warmer, upper layers of water.

The waters of the reservoir inundated one of two sites of the Harrisburg farming community that existed from 1860 to 1890. The first site was abandoned in 1862 because of flash floods on Quail Creek, and the community was relocated upstream. (Flash floods caused great havoc in the irrigation attempts of the early Mormon settlers.)

The village of Harrisburg was an agricultural center that produced cotton, corn, and sorghum. The miners at the nearby Silver Reef mines, where production began in 1875 west of Leeds, relied on this community for many essentials. Problems at the mine, severe droughts, and a plague of grasshoppers led to Harrisburg's decline. Ruins of some of the town's old stone houses and stone walls can be seen near the western entrance to the park, on an unmarked road south of Leeds and east of Interstate 15.

It is of interest that one of the founders of Harrisburg was Moses Harris, a mountain man in his younger days. He was one of those who responded to the famous advertisement placed in the St. Louis *Missouri Gazette* by William Henry Ashley (the well-known fur trader) on February 13, 1822. This ad called for "100 enterprising young men" to ascend the Missouri River to its source, "there to be employed for one, two or three years," with the finding of beaver and other furs to be their main objective. It was certain that adventure would be involved since the area was mostly unknown to the Euro-Americans.

Quail Creek State Park can serve as a camping base, especially for travelers participating in water activities, and for those who want to visit nearby Zion National Park, which has become so popular that it is quite crowded.

The park name "Zion" came from a Mormon, Isaac Behunin, who is credited with saying, "These great mountains are natural temples of God. We can worship here as well as in the man-made temples in Zion, the biblical 'Heavenly City of God.' Let us call it Little Zion." Consider that Mormon pioneers actually farmed and lumbered in and around the canyons of Zion National Park.

The Virgin River has carved the spectacular canyon of Zion, its green waters contrasting with the rich, reddish colors of rocky formations and peaks that are mostly Navajo sandstone. Today, some visitors to Zion drive the scenic road to the Temple of Sinawava, stopping along the way at viewpoints. Others come to backpack long trails, while some take day hikes. Get acquainted with the gorgeous scenery by taking the 2.2-mile round-trip hike to the Lower and Upper Emerald pools. Another introductory hike is the easy, 2-mile round-trip stroll that starts at the Temple of Sinawava (wheelchair accessible with assistance) and has views of hanging gardens and the beginning part of the Virgin River Narrows. Or hike 0.25 mile up the trail to see the Weeping Rock and views of Great White Throne and Zion Canyon. It is sometimes difficult to find parking near popular trailheads unless you arrive early in the day.

Campground overlooking reservoir at Quail Creek State Park

SNOW CANYON STATE PARK

Hours/Season: Overnight; year-round

Area: 6,500 acres

Facilities: Picnic tables, 36 campsites, group camping, group pavilion, wheelchair-accessible restrooms with showers, vault toilets, sewage disposal, electrical hookups, firewood, concessionaire, phone: (801) 628-2255

Attractions: Hiking, horseback riding, wildlife viewing, photography, geology, rock climbing, sand dunes, arch, lava caves, red rock formations to climb, nature trail

Access: 11 miles north of St. George off Utah 18, or enter park from the south by going through St. George, then west through Santa Clara, and follow signs north to park for a total of 7 miles from St. George

Snow is not what attracts over half a million visitors annually to the warm, sunny marvels of Snow Canyon State Park, the third most popular of Utah's state parks. Discovered by early cowboys checking for lost cattle, the park was named after Lorenzo and Erastus Snow, early pioneer leaders.

189

The geological wonders, in various shapes and colors, are enough to charm visitors—and moviemakers—to come to Snow Canyon, which covers an area of 6,500 acres with elevations ranging from 2,600 feet on the canyon floor to the 3,500-foot-high volcanic cinder cones at the northern end of the park. Enough exploration possibilities for many a day invite you to stay a while at the campground.

At the lowest elevation in Utah, and farthest south, summers are long and hot, winters are mild, and fall and early spring are good times to visit, but even in summer the Shivwits Campground is often full. Until a century ago, the Shivwits Indian Tribe hunted in Snow Canyon.

As one pulls into the developed area of the park, it is somewhat surprising to see a circle of lush green lawn that is watered frequently and rimmed with tall trees, a cool retreat where a couple of domestic chickens roam free. This is the picnic area. Cottontail rabbits also come here for meals.

Across the road are the campsites with hookups, fourteen pull-through sites with roofed, sheltered picnic tables. Although the other campsites are not always shaded, they are scenic and varied. Along the road to the north, the sites are among red rock formations, some quite private. One site is even near petroglyphs, which are fun to discover without directions.

A camping loop where more single sites and group camping are available swings south from the entry station. This camping area is quite appealing, with interesting desert terrain, a few trees, and good views of the scenic canyon. The group campsite has horseshoes and a cement court that works for volleyball or basketball, and is lighted at night. Besides large picnic tables, there is a two-tiered concrete affair that looks like it would serve nicely as a small stage. Pampas grass lines the walk to the restrooms.

The campground is a good spot to relax and watch wildlife. In summer, the crickets in the vegetation in certain spots perform a chattering nighttime song. You may see Gambel's quail, easy to identify with the black spot on the unscaled belly of the males. They are often busy gathering acorns on the ground under the Gambel oak trees, which seems appropriate. Squirrels also find acorns and rush around with full mouths.

The park has put up a nice natural-history identification exhibit, complete with photos, near the picnic area to acquaint visitors with the flora and fauna of Snow Canyon. The endangered desert tortoise inhabits the area, feeds on grasses, and digs long tunnels. The habitat of the primarily nocturnal sidewinder rattlesnake just reaches into the southwestern corner of Utah. The endangered Gila monster, with its persistent gripping jaw, is the only poison lizard in the park, but it only eats three to four meals a year. It stores fat in its tail. Some of the other animals in the area are the Great Basin rattler, chuckwalla lizard, white-tailed antelope squirrel, banded gecko, desert cottontail, scrub jay, butterflies, black-chinned hummer, hawks, and ravens.

Flower species to look for include Indian paintbrush, sacred datura, brittlebush, Mojave aster, Eaton's penstemon, narrow-leaf and other yucca, prickly pear, long-leaved phlox, desert marigold, and western peppergrass. It would be good to take a flower identification book along on your hikes as some of the desert terrain is quite varied.

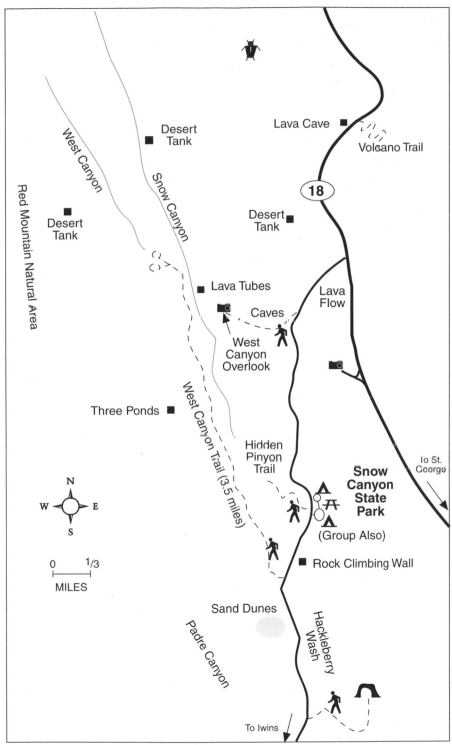

Desert
Tank

West Canyon

Snow Canyon

Lava Cave

Volcano Trail

18

Red Mountain Natural Area

Desert
Tank

Desert
Tank

Lava Tubes

Caves

Lava
Flow

West
Canyon
Overlook

Three Ponds

West Canyon Trail (3.5 miles)

Hidden
Pinyon
Trail

Snow
Canyon
State
Park

To St.
George

N

W   E

S

(Group Also)

0   1/3

MILES

Rock Climbing Wall

Sand Dunes

Padre Canyon

Hackleberry Wash

To Iwins

Campground for recreational vehicles at Snow Canyon State Park

Massive steps of slickrock towers surround the campground and entice visitors to explore them. Some can be climbed to hidden places, with some caution. One explorer found a small meadowlike area and potholes on top. Some of the rock formations strongly resemble swirled sand dune formations.

Approximately 130 million years ago, most of southern Utah was covered with sand dunes that the winds shifted and layered until time compressed them into rock. Today, we can see cross-sections of these layers, sometimes as horizontal lines, sometimes as diagonal lines, where they have been exposed by erosion.

The geology of Snow Canyon is much influenced by lava flows laid down at different times in the past. Two distinct flows are seen in the park. The flow along the ridge above the campground is about 1 million years old, while the lava on the desert floor is only 10,000 years old. Jagged black lava chunks are scattered among the desert vegetation and in crevices of the red Navajo sandstone formations. Some sandstone is topped with an extrusion of lava cylinders. Cinder cones rise above the land, and lava caves dip down into it.

Green vegetation of the desert floor adds color balance to the orange- and buff-colored sandstone canyon walls that are often jointed and seamed at old fault lines. Some large sandstone rock formations are full of indentations, creases, and ridges, with plants pushing through in a myriad of places. A thin patina of blackish desert varnish makes stripes against the rusty colors of rocks that are permeated with iron oxides.

One needs to experience the terrain by going out into it, and several trails lead to different discoveries. You might want to start with the 1.5-mile self-guiding Hidden Pinyon Trail, which starts across the road from the campground. Pick up a brochure from the entry station.

Hidden Pinyon Trail first crosses open desert strewn with lava rocks, then leads into a canyon over slickrock openings and out again. It then enters another small canyon where the entrance is between huge slabs of sandstone and then into more open but rocky areas with good mountain, canyon, and geology views. Lichens and microbiotic soil are seen on lava stones along the path, which is well marked with bordering rocks. When the path comes out onto open desert, and another trail connects to natural rainwater ponds, you can take a return east to the campground along an old road or go back through the first small canyon and return the way you came.

The Hidden Pinyon Trail is a good introduction to many desert plants. The handout points out cliffrose—that favorite of Edward Abbey that Indians have found so useful—desert almond, Englemann prickly pear, hackberry, banana yucca, and purple torch cactus, among other species. One is somewhat awed to find that some creosote bushes are older than the giant redwoods or the bristlecone pines, with some stands between 11,000 and 12,000 years old. Genetic clones just continue to grow outward from the central core.

Another popular trail leads to Johnson Arch, which begins at trailhead parking a short distance south of the campground. En route you will pass a vertical section of rock wall on the east side of the road that is frequented by rock climbers with ropes (a moratorium was recently instituted on placing additional bolting in the rocks of the park, since management feels there are adequate bolted routes). Then, on the west side of the road, is a patch of low sand dunes that is a small playground for barefoot children where the wind has found space to deposit colored sand because further movement is blocked by red sandstone boulders.

The 0.75-mile hike to the arch is easy. It starts on open desert sand, then traverses a road with lava rock and onto a sandy ledge that leads into a pretty, small canyon. This pleasant, cool destination is by a wash bordered with huge boulders and red rock walls. The arch is high up on the rock cliffs, not easy to reach, though some experienced people do make the climb. It is easily viewed, however, from below. To photograph it, afternoon light is best.

Along the road north of the campground is a 0.5-mile trail to lava caves that continues another 0.25 mile to the West Canyon Overlook. The fairly easy trail begins on open desert with a few ups and downs over a chipped lava path that is most comfortable with good hiking boots to cushion the feet. You can easily miss a deep cave, with an opening of about 10 feet, on the hike out. Children should be watched so they do not fall into it, as it looks like a sheer drop of some distance. Another cave is to the left of the trail. So much lava is around that it is easy to miss the caves.

The view from the end of the trail at the West Canyon Overlook should not be missed, a marvelous place to inspect varied geology and to see down

Climber exploring slickrock at Snow Canyon State Park

into the floor of West Canyon, where an old road exists. At this point, one can easily climb around stairstep ridges of slickrock and see lava hills, and a variety of curved, striated sandstone formations that really cannot be adequately described. It is a place to pull out a macro lens and shoot closeups of patterns in the rocks.

A longer 3.5-mile trail for hikers and horseback riders goes up West Canyon. If you want a short, steep trail, drive north and turn left on Utah 18; it is not far to two cinder cones. The first one has a steep trail that zigzags up its loose sides.

With all the good hiking trails, it seems a little incongruous that one frequently sees people walking the road for long stretches. They come from the health and fitness spas in the town of Ivins, to the south.

During the year, several special events are scheduled. These challenge physical fitness and feature different age groups from children to seniors. Some years, hot-air balloons are launched on a special day.

GUNLOCK STATE PARK

Hours/Season: Overnight; year-round
Area: 549 acres
Facilities: Primitive camping, vault toilets, boat ramp, fishing pier, *no fee*, phone: (801) 628-2255

Attractions: Boating, fishing (ice fishing in winter), water skiing, paddling, swimming
Nearby: Pine Valley Mountains
Access: 15 miles northwest of St. George via Utah 8, past Santa Clara and then Shivwits, and north on signed county road to park

A scenic drive on winding paved roads laced with colorful canyons and ranches is the route to Gunlock State Park, where weekends are apt to be full of fun activities. Considered an undeveloped park, it does have the essential basics: a huge parking lot, a boat ramp, and vault toilets—and it is free. Expect hot summer temperatures at this 3,600-foot elevation in Utah's Dixieland, but that only makes floating on rafts, swimming, and water skiing all the more enticing. Even toddlers enjoy the water using the slow slope of the boat ramp for wading while holding mother's hand. A lunch break sitting at the edge of the water under shade trees is a pleasant affair, watching the more energetic movements on the water. Fishermen come for the quality year-round boating and fishing that includes channel catfish, crappie, and largemouth bass. A pier is next to the boat ramp.

On the opposite side of the reservoir, a picturesque tent-camping spot awaits those who either boat across or walk along the dam top (a small parking area is adjacent) to reach this area. Canoeists find this a quiet place for setting up camp, with calm waters for paddling away from the busier shore. Canyons and mountains border the reservoir, and ducks swim about.

Gunlock Reservoir has provided recreation since the 117-foot-high, earth-filled dam was completed in 1970. Built for irrigation water and flood control, the reservoir is approximately 2 miles by 0.5 mile.

The name Gunlock is the same as the small farming community a mile to the north. A Mormon pioneer born in Ohio, William Haynes Hamblin (nicknamed Will or Bill) settled in the present area of the lake in 1857. Gunlock Will was a good hunter and sharpshooter, and was skillful in repairing gunlocks, which are the firing mechanisms of muzzleloaders. He became an elder in the Mormon Church, married twice (to sisters), and fathered seventeen children.

Gunlock Will's brother, Jacob Hamblin, was actually the more well-known of the two. He was a Mormon settler and a missionary to the Indians of southern Utah and northern Arizona, in particular the Shivwits tribe of the Paiute Indians, who still live in this area.

The county road to the park is the Old Spanish Trail that was used by horsemen and raiders from Santa Fe, New Mexico, to Los Angeles from the 1820s until the gold fields became the destination after 1849 and a shorter route was taken instead.

When the weather gets hot and you want to head for some quiet, cool mountain time, continue north on the road past Gunlock as it follows the Santa Clara River to its source. Pass extinct volcanoes and Baker Reservoir, and then take the road east of Central to the town of Pine Valley and continue on to the Pine Valley Recreation Area in the Pine Valley Mountains and Dixie National Forest.

A sparkling blue lake is rimmed with ponderosa pines, and a string of campgrounds follows the beginnings of the river to road's end. Several trails lead off past alpine meadows and thick pine forests into the heart of the mountains, including a 15-mile loop hike that enters the Pine Valley Mountain Wilderness. Mule deer are seen in the Pine Valley area from spring through fall. Pine Valley is also a major winter sports area.

IRON MISSION STATE PARK

Hours/Season: Day use; year-round except Thanksgiving, Christmas, and New Year's Day, winter hours are 9:00 A.M. to 5:00 P.M., summer hours are 9:00 A.M. to 7:00 P.M.
Area: 10.9 acres
Facilities: Picnic tables, museum, wheelchair-accessible restrooms, phone: (801) 586-9290
Attractions: History exhibits, horse-drawn vehicle collection, Indian and pioneer artifacts, pioneer cabins, covered wagon
Nearby: Cedar Breaks National Monument
Access: 585 North Main, in Cedar City

Iron Mission State Park tells the story of the development of Iron County. The pioneer Mormons who began settling Utah in 1847 were strong on self-sufficiency, but they lacked the availability of iron products and this was a serious concern. Wagon wheels needed iron rims, and nails, and-irons, even sleigh runners required iron to produce them. In 1849, the discovery of iron deposits in southern Utah prompted Brigham Young to send volunteer missionaries to set up an iron industry, and a colony to operate it.

In December of 1850, 119 men, 31 women, and 18 children set out with 129 wagons to settle at a "work mission." In typical Mormon fashion, they brought essential tools, saddles, seeds, window glass, farming equipment, and a variety of animals. They wintered in what is now the town of Parawan, the county seat, and planted needed crops there in the spring.

After that task was accomplished the miners and iron workers of the group went a short distance southwest and selected a site near Coal Creek. Besides carrying the all-important water, this creek passed over coal deposits that they hoped would be useful in their iron works. By the fall of 1852, the Deseret Iron Company completed construction of a small blast furnace and began operation of the first iron foundry west of the Mississippi. Fuel and lime were added to the surface iron ore found nearby and put into the furnace until molten. This was poured into molds to form iron "pigs" and then refined.

Many problems faced the miners and settlers—floods, grasshoppers, winter weather, and water-power problems. Perhaps the worst problem was related to the iron production. The enterprise included skilled workers but not the chemical research facilities necessary to develop good pigs of iron. The only usable iron products they were able to manufacture were crude implements, nails, and a few kitchen utensils. Just across the border in Nevada the Mormons incurred similar problems in making lead products. The lead contained too much silver, and many an animal was shot with a silver bullet.

As a consequence of these difficulties, the foundry closed down in late 1858. Though many settlers left, some stayed to farm and raise stock in what is now Cedar City (again a misnomer for the juniper trees that were thought to be cedars).

The museum at Iron Mission State Park has a diorama based on descriptions of the original foundry. A look at a detailed map of the area just west of Cedar City reveals the considerable influences of iron. Iron Springs Creek, Iron Mountain, and Old Irontown are clustered together with several designated mines.

The state park museum has a good collection of horse-drawn vehicles that reflects the pioneer life of Utah farms and towns from 1870 to 1930. The late Gronway Parry started the collection and restoration of these vehicles that were later sold to Cedar City. When the state park was opened in 1973, the city gave the collection to the Utah Division of Parks and Recreation.

Popular exhibits include the re-creation of a Wells Fargo stagecoach and an authentic overland stage supposedly riddled with bullets by Butch Cassidy's gang in the Four Corners area. It is possible today to have an exact stagecoach replica made in Boston for about $100,000. An exhibit informs about stagecoach etiquette. An old milk wagon, hauling wagons, horse-drawn farm machinery, mail carts, a "one-horse open sleigh," and a hearse are also displayed. A white hearse was used for children, black for adults.

An ad for grave diggers lists qualifications such as no allergies to dampness or mold, no abnormal fear of depth or night crawlers. Another ad reads, "Why walk around half dead when we can bury you for only $22?" Industrial vehicles include a dumpbelly and freight wagons, a low-wheeled dray, and a water-sprinkling wagon.

Then there is the romantic surrey with the fringe on top, which was a type of carriage first used in New York City in 1872 and then in the West by 1900, at a cost of $50 to $100 each. Check out a carriage with red velvet upholstery, another with a carriage lamp, a

Covered wagon on museum grounds at Iron Mission State Park

Spalding carriage, piano box buggies, and a Clarence carriage for a large family (an upper-class, Rolls Royce–type carriage cost about $2,000). A roof-seat brake was used to break in horses. The mountain wagon was durable and practical in rural areas. Indications of the future are seen in the Stanhope Phaeton—a forerunner of today's compact car—and an original Studebaker White Top Wagon—the forerunner of today's station wagon—complete with brakes.

Indian relics are not neglected in this museum. Some 200 items make up the William R. Palmer Collection. Palmer was formally adopted by the Southern Paiutes in 1926 because of his understanding and sympathetic research of the Paiute culture. Included among the Indian items are a ceremonial dress, a beaded papoose, purses, gloves, various pottery, moccasins, arrowheads, jewelry, corn grinding stones, a polychrome bowl, oose root (cactus, used as soap), a small animal-skull ladle, and a double-spouted wedding jar. There are baskets used for water jars, cleaning, clothes, winnowing, and the gathering of grains and pine cones. Feathers, drums, and bows and arrows are vital examples of Indian life.

Many of the exhibit items are those of early pioneer life; some are necessities and others are pieces that added decoration and beauty—rag rugs, looms, milk cans, old sewing machines, baby clothes, phonographs, handiwork, tools, guns, and a barbed-wire collection. A glance at reading material includes the *New England Primer* and the *Breeder's Gazette*.

Outdoors there is a pioneer cabin, the oldest log cabin in southern Utah, built in Parowan in 1851. Many people lived in this building and a total of twenty-four children were born in it. A huge collection of old wheels, farm equipment, and a covered wagon are also seen on the lawn surrounding the museum.

With all the wealth of these collections, there is yet more to come. So many artifacts for display have been acquired that there are plans for more buildings.

A picnic area and grill are available outdoors. In July, an Artist in Residence Series is held from Thursday through Saturday.

From the 5,800-foot elevation of the Iron Mission, it takes only about thirty minutes to be at an elevation of 10,500 feet on the edge of the Markagunt Plateau at Cedar Breaks National Monument. This can bring a quick change in temperature.

A 5-mile scenic drive in the high country of this park accesses four viewpoints that highlight the rock amphitheater that is more than 2,000 feet deep and over 3 miles in diameter. Colors vary in the prevailing light, but the iron and manganese minerals paint the rocks red, yellow, and purple.

Three trails can be hiked. The 2-mile Alpine Pond Loop passes many interesting natural items that include rhyolitic tuff, a sinkhole, wildflowers, a view of Brian Head, and a pond that is a focal point for wildlife. The Ramparts Trail goes along the rim of the amphitheater and passes an ancient bristlecone pine. Only experienced hikers should take the hazardous Rattlesnake Creek Trail with its steep terrain and possibility of flash floods, and only after talking to a ranger.

MINERSVILLE STATE PARK

Hours/Season: Overnight; April to November
Area: 207 acres
Facilities: Picnic tables, 29 campsites, overflow camping area, group camping, electric hookups, boat docks, boat ramp, restrooms with showers, sewage disposal, fish-cleaning stations, phone: (801) 438-5472
Attractions: Boating, fishing (ice fishing in winter), swimming, bird-watching, water skiing, windsurfing, waterfowl hunting in season
Nearby: Rockhounding
Access: 12 miles southwest of Beaver off Utah 21

Minersville State Park is noted for being a prime fishery, but only in certain years. The word gets out quickly to avid anglers when the fishery is at its best. (See later discussion on factors involved.) This 1,130-acre reservoir, at 5,500 feet, is located on a finger of the Escalante Desert between the Mineral and Tushar mountains in southwest Utah, at the edge of the Great Basin.

The ore deposits in the Mineral Mountains brought a group of settlers to the area on May 17, 1959, and they chose a site on Beaver Creek to the west of this reservoir. Since they came to mine silver and lead, the name of their town appropriately became known as Minersville. Several dams built up-

Campsite near reservoir at Minersville State Park

199

stream to store irrigation water washed away, and the existing dam was completed in 1914.

The layout of camping at the state park is somewhat questionable. Those wanting electrical hookups at their sites will be delighted. These sites have covered picnic tables with an overhead light and cupboards on one wall for storing utensils and other gear. To camp in these sites, one must pay the extra fee for available hookups whether you use them or not. Another camping area is behind this, a huge parking lot with no individual sites, grills, or other such amenities. On the far side, some distance from the restrooms, are three scattered picnic tables, with no shade anywhere. To park here one pays the same price as at other campgrounds where one has good sites but no hookups. An overflow camping lot is also available, with even fewer conveniences.

During the day, water skiers, windsurfers, and silent boats move across the water. Few trees offer shelter against the summer heat, which is often in the mid-nineties. Rather, this is an arid landscape more occupied by sagebrush and wild grasses. A few cottonwood, willow, and Russian olive trees are in moister areas. One can see juniper and pinyon in the foothills of the mountains.

It is not unusual to see several immature white-faced ibises feeding on small fish, crustaceans, and insects at water's edge. In summer, white pelicans are not difficult to spot, nor are Caspian terns, great blue herons, boat-tailed grackles, killdeer, and sandpipers. Many birds stop here during migration—double-crested cormorants, western grebes, common loons, mergansers, and a number of others. At night, owls can be heard in the campground.

Although numerous other wildlife species reside in the area, these are more difficult to observe. Jackrabbit, mule deer, skunk, rock squirrel, cougar, and coyote are around. Reptiles are easier to see, and rattlesnakes find habitat to their satisfaction.

The fishing situation here is complicated, and special regulations are in effect. The reservoir is stocked with rainbow trout and smallmouth bass, and there is a fishery for the wild cutthroat. Fishing is prohibited in this park from January 1 through May 28 (at the time of writing), and only artificial flies and lures can be used. Possession of any bait is unlawful here. The trout limit is one fish for all anglers, with a minimum size of 20 inches. (Few were expected to be of this size in 1993.) Six smallmouth bass may be caught by a licensed fisherman. These rules may change annually so check with the Wildlife Board for Fish and Crayfish. Those fishing are strongly urged to catch and release, and to exercise caution to put the fish back alive.

The fishery problems are threefold—the Utah chub population (a native minnow that competes for nutrients with trout), trout predation by birds (a study revealed that the cormorants and loons catch more than the anglers), and overharvesting by anglers. To attempt to eliminate the nongame fish, Minersville Reservoir has been treated, at a cost of more than $20,000 per treatment, more times than any other water in Utah. Following such chemical treatment, fishing is good for one or two years, with limit catches of one- to two-pound trout, followed by a few years of poor fishing.

A new plan evolved in 1991. Stocking with smallmouth bass and aiming for bigger trout helps check the chub population following treatment. Stocking with fish when bird migrations are lowest and stocking with larger trout are part of the strategy. Restrictive measures for anglers will help ensure a better fishery. Fishermen can catch as many fish as in the past *if* they use catch and release for the most part. Concerns should be addressed to the Utah Division of Wildlife Resources, Box 606, Cedar City, Utah 84720.

Another water-related activity at Minersville is the Utah Summer Games, with triathalon, sculling, and Hobie Cat events featured.

The countryside surrounding Minersville is good rockhounding terrain. Obsidian found in Beaver County's Mineral Mountains was a valuable resource for Native Americans. These mountains were the major source of implement-grade obsidian between eastern California and northern New Mexico. Besides the county's old mine dumps and ghost towns that provide exploration, what may be the largest deposit of opalized material in the country has been opened for rockhounding a few miles north of Milford.

North of Minersville State Park, accessed via Pass Road (and other more primitive roads), garnet, gold, idocrase, aquamarine, smoky quartz crystals, and blue beryl can be found. The Creole Mine (stay off private property or seek permission), 5 miles northeast of the town of Minersville, has many excavations in the area where it is possible to find garnet, amethyst, bornite, fluorite, epidote, hematite, opal, tourmaline, and chrysacolla.

About 10 miles north of Beaver, there is gold panning in Indian Creek. A few miles southeast of Beaver, on South Creek Road, low ridges on both sides of the road offer hunting for agate—blue, white, yellow, and mossy chalcedony. Between Minersville State Park and west to Nevada are more distant rockhounding spots.

Several words of *caution* are needed before going rockhounding. For one thing, the terrain is rugged, isolated, and requires the physical ability to negotiate it successfully. Carry emergency gear, water, food, blankets, maps, and the necessary tools for digging rocks and minerals. Directions to areas do not constitute permission to enter. Be extremely alert for open mine shafts and rattlesnakes. Check with local authorities regarding regulations for taking rocks and camping possibilities. Beaver County puts out a brochure with directions to several rockhounding areas, but the county is not responsible for trespass, liability, or damages because of information received therein. Good sources for more detailed information are the rock shops in the area.

APPENDIX

ADDRESSES AND TELEPHONE NUMBERS

Utah Division of Parks and Recreation

Administrative Office, 1636 West North Temple, Suite 116, Salt Lake City, UT 84116–3156; (801) 538-7220

Northeast Region Office, P.O. Box 309, Heber City, UT 84032–0309; (801) 645-8036

Northwest Region Office, 1084 North Redwood Road, Salt Lake City, UT 84116–1555, (801) 533-5127

Southeast Region Office, Suite 7, 1165 South Highway 191, Moab, UT 84532; (801) 259-3750

Southwest Region Office, 585 North Main Street, P.O. Box 1079, Cedar City, UT 84720–1079, (801) 586-4497

Reservations: (800) 322-3770; 8:00 A.M. to 5:00 P.M. (Mountain Standard Time), Monday through Friday

Anasazi Indian Village State Park, P.O. Box 1329, Boulder, UT 84716–1329; (801) 335-7308

Antelope Island State Park, 4528 West 1700 South, Syracuse, UT 84075–6861; (801) 773-2941

Bear Lake State Park, P.O. Box 184, Garden City, UT 84028–0184; (801) 946-3343

Camp Floyd/Stagecoach Inn State Park, P.O. Box 446, Riverton, UT 84065–0446; (801) 768-8932 (April to November), (801) 254-9036 (office)

Coral Pink Sand Dunes State Park, P.O. Box 95, Kanab, UT 84741–0095; (801) 874-2408

Dead Horse Point State Park, P.O. Box 609, Moab, UT 84532–0609; (801) 259-2614

Deer Creek State Park, P.O. Box 257, Midway, UT 84049–0257; (801) 654-0171

East Canyon State Park, 5535 South Highway 66, Morgan, UT 84050–9694; (801) 829-6866

Edge of the Cedars State Park, P.O. Box 788, 660 West 400 North, Blanding, UT 84511–0788; (801) 678-2238

Escalante State Park, P.O. Box 350, Escalante, UT 84726–0350; (801) 826-4466

Fort Buenaventura State Park, 2450 A Avenue, Ogden, UT 84401–2203; (801) 621-4808

Fremont Indian State Park, 11550 West Clear Creek Canyon Road, Sevier, UT 84766–9999; (801) 527-4631

Goblin Valley State Park, P.O. Box 637, Green River, UT 84525–0637; (801) 564-3633

Goosenecks State Park, P.O. Box 788, Blanding, UT 84511–0788; (801) 678-2238

Great Salt Lake State Park, P.O. Box 323, Magna, UT 84044–0323; (801) 250-1898

Green River State Park, P.O. Box 637, Green River, UT 84525–0637; (801) 564-3633

Gunlock State Park, P.O. Box 140, Santa Clara, UT 84765–0140; (801) 628-2255

Historic Union Pacific Rail Trail State Park, P.O. Box 309, Heber City, UT 84032–0309; (801) 645-8036

Huntington State Park, P.O. Box 1343, Huntington, UT 84528–1343; (801) 687-2491

Hyrum State Park, 405 West 300 South, Hyrum, UT 84319–1547; (801) 245-6866

Iron Mission State Park, P.O. Box 1079, 585 North Main, Cedar City, UT 84720–1079; (801) 586-9290

Jordan River State Park, 1084 North Redwood Road, Salt Lake City, UT 84116–1555; (801) 533-4496 (office), (801) 533-4527 (golf course)

Jordanelle State Park, P.O. Box 309, Heber City, UT 84032–0309; (801) 645-8036

Kodachrome Basin State Park, P.O. Box 238, Cannonville, UT 84718–0238; (801) 679-8562

Lost Creek State Park, 5535 South Highway 66, Morgan, UT 84050–9694; (801) 829-6866

Millsite State Park, P.O. Box 1343, Huntington, UT 84528–1343; (801) 687-2491

Minersville State Park, P.O. Box 1531, Beaver, UT 84713–1531; (801) 438-5472

Otter Creek State Park, P.O. Box 43, Antimony, UT 84712; (801) 624-3268

Palisade State Park, P.O. Box H, Manti, UT 84642–0076; (801) 835-7275 (office), (801) 835-4653 (golf course)

Piute State Park, P.O. Box 43, Antimony, UT 84712–0043; (801) 624-3268

Quail Creek State Park, P.O. Box 1943, St. George, UT 84770–1943; (801) 879-2378

Red Fleet State Park, 4335 North Highway 191, Vernal, UT 84078–7800; (801) 789-4432

Rockport State Park, 9040 North State Highway 302, Peoa, UT 84061–9702; (801) 336-2241

Scofield State Park, P.O. Box 166, Price, UT 84501–0166; (801) 448-9449 (summer), (801) 637-8497 (winter)

Snow Canyon State Park, P.O. Box 140, Santa Clara, UT 84765–0140; (801) 628-2255

Starvation State Park, P.O. Box 584, Duchesne, UT 84021–0584; (801) 738-2326

Steinaker State Park, 4335 North Highway 191, Vernal, UT 84078–7800; (801) 789-4432

Territorial Statehouse State Park, 50 West Capitol, P.O. Box 657, Fillmore, UT 84631–0657; (801) 743-5316

This Is The Place State Park, 2601 Sunnyside Avenue, Salt Lake City, UT 84108–1453; (801) 584-8391

Utah Field House of Natural History State Park, 235 East Main Street, Vernal, UT 84078–2605; (801) 789-3799

Utah Lake State Park, 4400 West Center Street, Provo, UT 84601–9715; (801) 375-0731

Veterans Memorial State Park, 17111 Camp Williams Road, P.O. Box 446, Riverton, Utah 84065–0446; (801) 254-9036

Wasatch Mountain State Park, P.O. Box 10, Midway, UT 84049–0010; (801) 654-1791 (visitor center), (801) 654-0532 (golf course)

Willard Bay State Park, 650 North 900 West #A, Willard, UT 84340–9999; (801) 734-9494

Yuba State Park, P.O. Box 159, Levan, UT 84639–0159; (801) 758-2611

OTHER UTAH INFORMATION

National Park Service, P.O. Box 25287, Denver, CO 80225–0287; (303) 969-2000

State Paleontologist, Utah Division of State History, 300 Rio Grande, Salt Lake City, UT 84101; (free booklet: *Visitor Information Guide to Fossils in Utah*)

U.S. Bureau of Land Management, 324 South State Street, Suite 301, P.O. Box 45155, Salt Lake City, UT 84145–0155; (801) 539-4001

U.S. Forest Service, Regional Office, 2501 Wall Avenue, Ogden, UT 84401–2394; (801) 625-5306

Utah Division of Wildlife Resources, 1596 West North Temple, Salt Lake City, UT 84116–3195; (801) 538-4700

Utah Tourism and Recreation Information Center, Utah Travel Council, Council Hall, Capitol Hill, Salt Lake City, UT 84114–1369; (801) 538-1467

INDEX

About the Author

Jan Bannan grew up among the flat cornfields of southern Illinois, but she felt she had come home when she moved West. Though she loved biochemical research (but not windowless labs), exploring the outdoors persuaded her to become a writer/photographer. Now living in Newport, Oregon, Jan has wandered alone with her camera through Baja, gone on safari in Kenya, and explored all over the West. She has spent considerable time over the last few years in Utah, taking roads less traveled and hiking many miles into beloved mountains and canyons to make her own discoveries.

Her credits include *The New York Times, Wildlife Conservation, Wilderness Magazine, Trailer Life, The Seattle Times,* and *The Oregonian.* She has also published a children's book, *Sand Dunes.* Jan is currently working on a recreational guide book to unique western landscapes and another on weekend getaways in Oregon and Washington.

THE MOUNTAINEERS, founded in 1906, is a nonprofit outdoor activity and conservation club, whose mission is "to explore, study, preserve, and enjoy the natural beauty of the outdoors...." Based in Seattle, Washington, the club is now the third-largest such organization in the United States, with 14,000 members and four branches throughout Washington State.

The Mountaineers sponsors both classes and year-round outdoor activities in the Pacific Northwest, which include hiking, mountain climbing, ski-touring, snowshoeing, bicycling, camping, kayaking and canoeing, nature study, sailing, and adventure travel. The club's conservation division supports environmental causes through educational activities, sponsoring legislation, and presenting informational programs. All club activities are led by skilled, experienced volunteers, who are dedicated to promoting safe and responsible enjoyment and preservation of the outdoors.

The Mountaineers Books, an active, nonprofit publishing program of the club, produces guidebooks, instructional texts, historical works, natural history guides, and works on environmental conservation. All books produced by The Mountaineers are aimed at fulfilling the club's mission.

If you would like to participate in these organized outdoor activities or the club's programs, consider a membership in The Mountaineers. For information and an application, write or call The Mountaineers, Club Headquarters, 300 Third Avenue West, Seattle, Washington 98119; (206) 284-6310.

Send or call for our catalog of more than 300 outdoor titles:
The Mountaineers Books
1011 SW Klickitat Way, Suite 107
Seattle, WA 98134
1-800-553-4453